"A WORK OF EXTRAORDINARY (...
SION . . . This brilliantly conceived and (...
pathbreaking study that adds flesh to H(...
ingenious art behind her complex life."

—MICHAEL ERIC DYSON
Author of *Holler If You Hear Me:*
Searching for Tupac Shakur

"Farah Griffin has written a deeply-personal meditation on the mysteries of Lady Day. At the same time, she has produced a rich reading of the narrative of that life that our collective imagination has been writing for these many years. She is fascinating, evocative, and rewarding. Nobody—bet on it—will ever write about Billie Holiday the same way again."

—JOHN F. SZWED
Author of *Jazz 101*

"What a lovely book! Farah Jasmine Griffin's clear-eyed but affectionate study reveals the many versions of the jazz singer Billie Holiday. Acknowledging the power of the tragic, mythic Holiday, Griffin prefers to take her place beside the marvelous Abbey Lincoln and to celebrate Holiday's artistic genius."

—NELL IRVIN PAINTER
Author of *Sojourner Truth:*
A Life, A Symbol

"Beautifully written . . . Using an exciting array of sources, and rereading ones we thought we already knew, Griffin explores Holiday as national and international icon and as highly personal heroic presence."

—ROBERT G. O'MEALLY
Author of *Lady Day:*
The Many Faces of Billie Holiday

"Griffin engages readers throughout with her consistently intriguing observations."

—*Publishers Weekly*

In Search of Billie Holiday

If You Can't Be Free, Be a Mystery

Farah Jasmine Griffin

Ballantine Books   New York

For

Emerson Maxwell Griffin

(1926–1972)

Thank you for sharing your love for
The Prettiest One
(Mena, Muzzy, Mommy)

Our People

Our Music

Freedom

For

Wilhelmena Griffin

(1927–)

Who gave me life and then gave me the world

I adore you

And,

for

Black American Artists

Fact is, the invention of women under siege
has been to sharpen love in the service of myth.

If you can't be free, be a mystery.

From "Canary," RITA DOVE

"The bird that would soar above the level plain of tradition
and prejudice must have strong wings. It is a sad spectacle to
see the weaklings bruised, exhausted,
fluttering back to earth."

Mademoiselle Reisz
The Awakening, KATE CHOPIN

"Who do you love among us, Sassafrass? Ma Rainey,
Mamie Smith, Big Mama Thornton, Freddie Washington,
Josephine, Carmen Miranda? Don't ya know we is all sad
ladies because we got the blues, and joyful women because we
got our songs? Make you a song, Sassafrass, and bring it out
so high all us spirits can hold it and be in your tune.
We need you, Sassafrass; we need you to sing
best as you can; that's our nourishment,
that's how we live."

Billie Holiday to Sassafrass,
in *Sassafrass, Cypress and Indigo*,
NTOZAKE SHANGE

Contents

Preface

*T*HIS IS NOT A biography of Billie Holiday. Nor is it a musicological study. I am neither musicologist nor musician. I am, however, a fan, not quite fanatical but certainly devoted. I am also an intellectual, a writer and a black American woman deeply fearful of the implications of some of the Holiday myths for other black women and girls.

For this reason I am interested in the myths that surround Holiday. I think they continue to hold a great deal of interest and importance because of what they reveal about their creators and the audiences who consume them. For years now, I have been a collector and student of artifacts that claim to "represent" or "portray" Holiday.[1] In the pages that follow I attempt to explore dominant myths about Billie Holiday and to demonstrate the danger these myths pose for those of us who might get written into them or, worse yet, who might write ourselves into the corners they create.[2]

Along the way, I cannot escape from positing an alternative fictional Holiday. There is no getting back to the genuine, "real" or "authentic" woman. I hope that this book will contribute to an understanding of the icon that will work in the interest of those people who share the most with the historical Holiday. In doing so I hope to suggest to other women, particularly unconventional, multidimensional black women, and especially young black women, that Holiday's fate as we have come to know it was not a fait accompli. To be talented, black, sensual and complex does not have to lead to addiction, a life of unhealthy relationships and an early, tragic death.

Though women such as Hettie Jones, Leslie Gourse, Linda Dahl, Angela Davis and Alexis De Veaux, to name a few, have written chapters, a children's book, essays and poems about Holiday, to my knowledge, this is the first adult book about Holiday by a woman. Linda Kuel died before she was able to produce her much-awaited biography, though Robert O'Meally and Donald Clarke relied extensively on her research. Unfortunately, Kuel's archive was unavailable to me because I could not afford the extravagant access fee required by its owner. I trust that this lack of access has not negatively influenced the story I want to tell.

Inspired by the mystical number seven, as in Seven Wonders of the World, the seven continents, the Seven Heavens, the Seven African powers, the Seven Sisters of sleep, and the Seventh Son born with a veil, the chapters of this book number seven as well. In honor of the music that inspires it, the book opens with an overture and closes with a coda. The Overture, "A Mourning Song," is a personal history of my relationship with Holiday's music. Part One is divided into four chapters exploring versions of Holiday that emerged during her lifetime or in response to representations of her life. Chapter One explains the contemporary rendering of Holiday as talented and tragic victim. Chapter Two focuses on three of the most influential means—mainstream media coverage of her arrests, her own autobiography, *Lady Sings the Blues,* and Diana Ross's film *Lady Sings the Blues*—of creating a myth of Holiday as the drug-addicted, physically abused woman who only sings a sad, sad blues. Chapter Three uses an *Ebony* cover story about Holiday and a tape of one of her rehearsals to reveal the way her complexity challenges notions of respectability and divisions of class within the black community. Chapter Four details the role of European intellectuals both in appreciating Holiday's gifts as well as in contributing to stereotypes of black American artists. In this chapter, I also consider some of the many white men who controlled Holiday's career throughout her life.

Part Two looks at alternative portrayals of Holiday, most of which emerged following her death in 1959. Chapter Five is concerned with black intellectuals' interpretation of Billie Holiday and the political and cultural implications of her life and music. I devote Chapter Six to the kinds of desire Lady inspires and the manipulation of that desire by members of two seemingly unrelated groups, corporate advertisers and American poets. In Chapter Seven, I focus on the way that the great jazz vocalist Abbey Lincoln has built upon the legacy of Billie Holiday as a means of positing what I believe to be the most significant legacy Holiday left us. Finally, the Coda, "A Morning Song," is a meditation, prayer and praise song for Lady Day inspired by her television appearance in 1956.

Scholars and other interested readers in search of more in-depth theoretical implications of my argument should refer to the extensive endnotes.

Portrait of a Lady: A Note on the Photographs

FEW JAZZ ARTISTS have been photographed as much as Billie Holiday. There are the shots of her in performance—on stage or in rehearsal. There are newspaper photographs that capture the forlorn woman, incarcerated yet again. And then there are the Portraits of the Lady: formal photographs of Lady Day that transmit the beauty, despair, joy and mystery that she has come to represent. I have placed six iconic photographs at the opening of the following chapters: A Mourning Song, Lady of the Day, Lady-like, Ebony Lady, Lady's Men and a Woman's Day, and Longing for Lady. The seventh photopraph, with which I close the book, is reproduced here for the first time. Each of these formal portraits, powerful in its silence and apparent ubiquity, has been reproduced numerous times on posters, book covers, T-shirts, albums and CD covers. Each seeks to present a unique version of Lady Day. Together, they form a visual narrative of the life and legacy of Lady Day.

Refusing us complete access, Lady Day dons a mask of mysterious glamour (circa 1935).

OVERTURE: A MOURNING SONG

> That's what my dead father was to me—on a reel
> for my comfort, better than life.
>
> —BETSY SHOLL, "DON'T EXPLAIN"

> We learned by her example, the good and the bad.
> She was an incredible talent, a great songwriter,
> a shrewd businesswoman, and a very nice Lady.
> . . . We also looked at her story and vowed not
> to let that be our story. We knew how brilliant
> and multitalented she was, but she had problems.
>
> —GLORIA LYNNE

MY MOTHER named me Farah Jasmine; my father nick-named me Jazzy. While my mother's choice was inspired by Moslem royalty, Empress Farah Diba and Princess Yasmin Khan, my father's was as much a tribute to the music he loved as a diminutive of Jasmine. Farah Jasmine was the name into which I would grow. Jazzy is the name by which I was called throughout my early life. At first, only those who knew me in an "official" capacity—teachers, doctors, classmates—called me Farah. "Jazzy" is home, South Philly, double-dutch, glamorous aunts, hip uncles and Daddy.

My father's pantheon of jazz geniuses included Charlie Parker,

Miles Davis, Frank Morgan, John Coltrane and Billie Holiday. Of these, I claimed Miles and Billie as my own. Though it seems I have known about her my entire life, my fascination with her surfaced following my father's death in 1972, when I was nine years old. Along with his closets full of paperbacks, notebooks and albums, I inherited his lower lip, his political sensibilities and his passion for "the" music, "our" music—jazz.

Eventually, my curiosity about Billie Holiday mirrored my curiosity about him, about the things he loved. My inquisitiveness about him, my desire to share something with him, to emulate him, and my fear of inheriting the demons that I suspected haunted him, led me to explore that which he seemed to have found compelling. I wanted to possess the things he valued; I also wanted to learn about the mysteries his death left unsolved for me. Among other things, Billie Holiday became for me a tangible symbol of paternal longing. She was not the first vocalist I remember hearing; that was Gloria Lynne, after whom I named my first cat. Nor was hers the voice that reigned supreme in my home during my teen years; my mother and my aunts found solace and understanding in the voices of Aretha and Gladys. However, after my father's death, when I began to listen to the albums he left behind, Lady came to occupy a very special place in my psyche, in my life. Her "They Can't Take That Away from Me" seemed to express my own feelings about losing my father. I remember her voice, almost a whisper: so plaintive, so pretty.

My mother gave in to my request for materials by and about Billie Holiday in spite of her initial reluctance to do so. They were not hard to find because my father died the same year that Motown released the film *Lady Sings the Blues*. I discovered that there was an autobiography and numerous magazine covers, articles, reissued recordings and biographies of her. My collection of all things related to Holiday began then. Billie Holiday's biography (not her lived life, but the stories told to explain that life) frightened and fascinated me. With a few major exceptions, we were born into similar worlds: Both of us were born in Philadelphia General Hospital into a world populated by the black working poor and aristocrats of urban street life. We both entered our teen years looking older than we were. We had extremely close relationships with our mothers. Out of longing for our music-obsessed fathers, each of us pursued that which fascinated them. (In her case, it was the jazz life and artistry; in mine, jazz and books.) Our gifts were recognized early on and became the means by which we distinguished ourselves.

But here the similarities end. I was born in the 1960s to married adult parents, and I came of age during a time that followed the height of the civil rights, Black Power and feminist movements. Before entering high school, I had access to books by Toni Morrison and Ntozake Shange. Also, unlike Holiday, I was nurtured in a protected space created by parents, an older sister, aunts, uncles and smooth-talking, street-smart nieces, nephews and boy cousins. This was a kinship that marked and protected me as I walked through streets filled with danger for a girl developed too soon. In some places I wore an aura that said "Don't fuck with her; she belongs to us." Only this, the political and social conditions of our times, the adoration and protection of a family who loved me and all the consequences that followed, separate my early life from Billie Holiday's. These important differences stood between the sexual abuse, early sexual activity, drugs and prison that awaited the woman-child who would become Lady Day and me.

By the time I was thirteen I claimed the nickname Lady. No one called me this, preferring the pet name, Jazzy. Knowing of my self-designation, my aunts gave me barrettes adorned with fake flowers for my hair. Much to my dismay, I could not sing, but I could certainly act the part. Around that time, I discovered an early version of "Them There Eyes" and wanted to become everything implied in that flirtatious, youthful voice. Billie Holiday's music created a land of fantasy, a retreat from my world of unmerciful teasing about my dark skin and too-fast-developing body. Sometimes I wondered if she, like so many of my peers, held dark-skinned women in contempt. (Today, though, I'd rather not know. Having recently found out that two of my childhood idols, Martin Luther King and Miles Davis, found dark women unattractive immediately gave me a feeling reminiscent of my early adolescence. Though I still love both of them, I will never think about them in the same way. Malcolm, however, maintains his revered status.)

For my sixteenth birthday, my mother gave me my own gardenia plant. Billie Holiday along with Sylvia Plath escorted me through my melodramatic adolescence. In college, Holiday's most famous songs and her voice helped define key moments in my life in an overly sentimentalized way. I barely pass a math class, because I am out with my boyfriend all night before a 9 A.M. exam, "Ain't Nobody's Business If I Do." Everybody knows "You Don't Know What Love Is Until You've Seen the Dawn with Sleepless Eyes." My mother and I have a tiff over my grades and my late hours, "God Bless the Child." Said boyfriend has been seen with another woman, "Don't Explain."

Finally, a graduate school apartment decorated with poster-size images of Holiday at every stage and phase of her career documented her physical transformation from breathtaking beauty to tired, frail, sad, well-worn woman. This gallery offered evidence for me of the fate that awaited a black woman who dared to live her life in an unconventional manner, who abused drugs and alcohol, and who followed her creative vision against all odds.

Unfortunately, as I came to know Holiday through visual and written materials, I came to know her as a victim and consequently came to define my father in that way too. They were sacrificial geniuses to sexism, racism, and poverty. This notion of their victimization, of course, influenced the way I saw my father's life and death and influenced the way I heard her recordings.

Although I always considered myself a fan of her music, I did not begin to engage it until I went to graduate school. Then I started to understand and appreciate her extraordinary artistic gift. I replaced all albums with CDs and purchased ones I never had. In the last two decades the quantity and quality of Holiday recordings has exploded, as has my collection of them.

During this period, as I was trying to carve out my own intellectual identity, it became of the utmost importance for me to search for a

Holiday who was more than a victim. As I aspired to create a body of work that would be taken seriously, I became aware of the dangers in defining her only by the tragic moments in her life without any attention whatsoever to her artistic legacy. I needed a Lady who was not always, and certainly not only, a victim. Through her work, I began to see a woman who made choices—some good, some detrimental. A woman who loved being part of a community that appreciated and recognized the beauty in the music she loved. A woman who insisted on living her life in her own way, who liked to have a good time, and attempted to be as free as possible in a world that sought to deny her even a modicum of freedom. In 1991 I read Robert O'Meally's *Lady Day: The Many Faces of Billie Holiday* and discovered, for the first time, evidence of her artistic training and devotion to her craft. At this time, songs such as "Now Baby or Never" replaced "My Man" in the soundtrack of her life—and mine—that played continuously through my head.

During these years, Holiday became a different kind of model for me, one more like the figure Bruce Crowther describes:

> A musician may play with dazzling virtuosity—that tells you he knows his instrument. But he need play only a simple phrase to melt every heart in the room—if he has the talent to choose the right phrase. Billie Holiday had that talent. (Crowther, 81)

It was this element of Holiday's talent that intrigued me the most and that gave me a sense of my own potential. In most rigorous Ph.D. programs you are forced to come face-to-face with all of your insecurities and limitations. I attended graduate school at a time and in a place—Yale—where many people seemed to have "dazzling" intellectual "virtuosity." Fluency in the languages of poststructuralism and postmodernism—not necessarily their meanings, but the ability to talk that talk, to use the vocabulary—seemed to be as valued as other conventional evidence of intelligence, talent, possibility.

As I listened to Holiday, and learned about the subtlety of her art and talent, I learned that such subtlety, such apparent simplicity, did not undermine the enormity of her contribution. Listening to her pare down a lyric and melody to the barest minimum free of pretension, making it impossible not to confront its meaning, became a model for me of a way of doing intellectual work. This, along with the affirmation of peers and mentors, gave me a sense of security in my own understanding and articulation of my ideas.

As a young professor I returned to Billie Holiday as a means to regain a sense of purpose in my own work. On March 21, 1994, shortly after completing my first book and three days shy of the twenty-second anniversary of my father's death, I wrote the following in my journal:

> If I could write on anything I wanted, I would write a book about Lady Day. Linking my work to professional advancement alone gives me neither a sense of purpose nor pleasure. So I want to do something that does both. I have been obsessed with Billie Holiday since I was a child.

This book is the result of my desire to write honestly and in a different voice about something that is as meaningful to me spiritually and emotionally as it is intellectually: Honesty, Spirit, Emotion, Intellect. These are the words that come to mind when I think about Billie Holiday after listening closely to her body of work.

In many ways, this transformation in my understanding of Billie Holiday is what led me to devote the critical tools I have gained through my practice as a cultural critic, my intellectual skills as a critical thinker, and my passion for jazz and for Billie Holiday to this book: an exploration of the way her image circulates in our culture and a consideration of the contest over the meaning and currency of that image.

Because of my own investment in many versions of Holiday's icon over the years, I am willing to admit that I do not escape positing my own version of Lady Day. Nor do I want to escape doing so. Mine is not the first, nor will it be the last. It is just one of many, evolving as the need for them arises. I hope to suggest that Holiday offers a model of a kind of woman who is simply too complex to be contained by the tragic victim narrative that has predominated in even some of the most sophisticated representations of her life. Sometimes she was a victim, sometimes she was not. Always she was a woman committed to her craft. Her greatest legacy to everyone, but particularly to black women, is her warning to us of the pitfalls that await us and a vision of possibility in spite of the obstacles that seek to limit and in some cases destroy us.

Part One

Founding Myths

"She was not the woman on the stool holding the glass of gin and looking downcast and pained. Or she was not only that figure, even at the last."
—Robert O'Meally *(Milt Hinton, 1959)*

1

Lady of the Day

M Y STUDENTS LOVE Mary J. Blige. I purchase her CDs, dance to the songs from the first one. I like her sass, appreciate her beauty, am charmed by her ghetto girl shyness, but I do not share their adoration of her. Two former students, Nikki and Malik, are especially passionate about her. Nikki cherishes what she sees as the honesty of her lyrics. "She's our Billie Holiday," Malik states emphatically. "Oh, please!" I think but do not say. Another, Salamishah, explains: "She captures all those moments in your life, like when you break up with someone. You feel her pain. You think 'Thank God; my pain isn't as bad as hers.' Each album is closer to what she wants to be, closer to what you want for her, closer to where you want to be too."

I love my students partly because they never stop believing in my capacity for growth. I have come to think when they speak about Mary

J. Blige as their Billie Holiday, even more than the music, they mean the life; more than the voice, they refer to Holiday's life as they know it. And in this sense she may very well be their Billie Holiday. "She is one of ours, we want her to be happy, she sings for us, through us, to us." Does this comparison come out of any real sense of Holiday's life and the enormity of her talent or is it one that is constantly made for them in most media coverage of Blige's struggles?

Hip-hop journalist dream hampton has written of both Mary J. Blige and another contemporary black female vocalist, Erykah Badu, as artists with the potential to be modern-day Billie Holidays. Of Badu she writes, "Once you feel the vibration from the timbre of Erykah Badu's voice, you will understand immediately [the comparison] is no marketing ploy. In fact, a comparison to Billie could bear weight that no new singer would want to inherit. The expectations soar. The tragic life that was Lady Day's haunts."[3] Here, Billie Holiday is a revered ancestor; however, the weight of being named her heir is doubly heavy: first because of the expectations of artistic achievement, and second because of the fear of the dire circumstances of her life and death.[4]

In the case of Blige, hampton asserts, "practically everyone I poll says that Mary reminds them of Billie Holiday." Blige, however, is quick to distinguish herself from Holiday. When hampton asks her what word immediately comes to mind when she mentions Holiday, Blige responds: "Dead. Like Phyllis Hyman. Dead." She goes on:

> I know that's hard. But the reason Phyllis and Billie are dead is 'cause they thought they could turn to a man or a drug for the love they needed. I'm not trying to preach, but that love, the love that makes you able to look in the mirror and be happy, that love comes from God.[5]

It seems the more Blige tries to distance herself from Holiday, the more the media insists on making the comparison. At the end of the last century *Notorious,* the magazine published by Sean "Puffy" Combs, asked young contemporary artists to comment upon major celebrities of the twentieth century. Asked to comment on Holiday, Blige writes:

> Our voices are similar in terms of style and the truth and the sadness in our music. But I refuse to be compared to Billie Holiday. Please compare me to the living. Don't compare me to the dead . . . I've seen the Diana Ross movie about her life and I have a collection of her music.

Death. Pain. Sadness. This is what Holiday signifies for this young artist, and she is terrified of the comparison. Her understanding of Holiday's life and legacy is formed by her interactions with the Diana Ross film and the dominant portrayals of her, so that Blige has every reason to be fearful. Elements of Holiday's life have been used to create a story that defines other black women artists such as Abbey Lincoln, Chaka Khan and Phyllis Hyman.

The one-dimensional Holiday with which Blige is familiar is a dangerous one. When an article on Chaka Khan opens by telling us that she sits beneath a poster of Billie Holiday, it is with the expectation that readers will conjure images of enormous talent, voracious appetites for drugs and self-destruction, even if these images are false ones. When a poet writes a tribute to Phyllis Hyman, who committed suicide, with allusions to Billie Holiday, we are asked to make similar connections.

How sad for us that this is all we believe we've inherited from Lady Day. The means by which these interpretations of her life are transmitted—movies, anecdotes, books—are all so powerful as to make this particular version seem ubiquitous.

Who was Billie Holiday? Why do we think of her only in terms of tragedy and failure? Are alternative interpretations of her life possible?

i.

The real musician is not the man who can knock your eyeballs out with fast, difficult runs. He's a real musician if he can make the simple songs vibrate and sparkle with the life that is within them.

—JULIUS LESTER

For all the praise that Billie Holiday gets as a vocal stylist, she's seldom acknowledged as a musical genius. She was the first to prove that you could make soft sounds and still have a powerful emotional impact. She was understanding jazz long before Miles ever stuck a mute in his horn; she was the true "birth of cool."

—CASSANDRA WILSON

A people do not throw their geniuses away.

—ALICE WALKER

BILLIE HOLIDAY was a musical genius. Until the recent celebrations of Nobel Prize Laureate Toni Morrison, few were willing to grant black women the title genius.[6] Since the earliest days of our nation, black women were thought to be incapable of possessing genius; their achievements were considered the very opposite of intellectual accomplishment. All persons of African descent were thought to be unfit for advanced intellectual endeavor. Black women in particular were body, feeling, emotion and sexuality. This holds true even in comparison to white women; if white women's abilities were questioned and debated, their humanity was not.

Witness the case of Phillis Wheatley, the young slave girl born in West Africa. Reared by a master and mistress who taught her to read and write, she began writing poetry as a young teen and published her first book of verse, *Poems on Various Subjects, Religious and Moral by*

Phillis Wheatley, Negro Servant to Mr. John Wheatley, of Boston, in New England in 1773. It was the first book published by an African American. Wheatley demonstrated intellectual precociousness shortly after she was purchased at the age of seven. She quickly learned to read English and Latin, and she studied history and geography. Within four years of learning to speak English, she began to write poetry. Her book was introduced by a preface written by white sponsors, offering documents to authenticate her and to legitimize her poetry. Despite international acclaim, Wheatley's abilities were challenged by many, including Thomas Jefferson, who thought blacks capable only of passion, the basest of emotions, and at best, mimicry.

Billie Holiday was a poet of a different sort. If music is a language, then Holiday's careful juxtaposition of chosen notes structured into phrases that give both beauty and meaning, makes her a poet. Unlike Wheatley, however, Holiday wasn't doing something that black women just didn't do. She didn't enter into an arena where her right and ability to sing would be questioned. No, for many Americans it would have been no surprise that a colored girl could sing; couldn't they all? And unlike Wheatley, blacks did not try to play catch-up in the musical world Holiday inhabited; they set the standards. Still, the word "genius" applied to a black woman? For years jazz was not considered a "serious" art form. Once its seriousness was granted, only male musicians were considered geniuses. Few today would deny the "genius" of Charlie Parker or Miles Davis. After Holiday's death a small group of white male jazz critics began to discuss her talent in similar terms. For them, her genius was undisciplined, and sacrificed for her insatiable appetites; furthermore, these writers all suggest that Holiday herself had no understanding of her own gifts. Following the Holiday of these portraits there emerged a Holiday who was semiliterate, read only comic books, and was barely capable of understanding the meaning of the song "Strange Fruit."

I want to qualify my use of the word "genius." At times I exchange it with the word "brilliance," which seems to be a less loaded term. But I am not using genius in the romantic sense of that tormented yet inspired individual who stands above the rest of humanity. By genius I mean the special quality of mind and aptitudes that some individuals have innately for specific tasks or kinds of work. I also want to emphasize the intellectual nature of Holiday's talent, and the word "genius" helps me to do that. Contrary to what some observers would have you believe, she was not an idiot savant, capable of profound work in one artistic area but otherwise an intellectual imbecile. It is impossible for a gifted jazz musician to lack intelligence. Artistic success in this form requires talent, intelligence and discipline.

In spite of differing opinions regarding her intellectual capacities, most informed commentators agree that Holiday's musicianship was superb. Nonetheless, people less familiar with jazz often question her status as a "great" singer. Lady Day did not have the "pure," "pretty" voice of Ella or the incredible vocal range of Sarah. (While considered better singers, the genius of even these singers has gone unrecognized. Similarly, Aretha Franklin, who was a piano prodigy at the age of two, is rarely referred to as a genius.) She didn't scat, so it's harder for people to understand what it means when one says "Holiday sang like a horn" or that she was the "consummate jazz singer." Sassy's fans might say "Listen to Sarah trading fours with Clifford Brown, Paul Quinichette, Herbie Mann and others on 'Lullaby of Birdland' if you want to know what the voice as horn sounds like." Yes, I agree. I will not make claims about who was best; I like all three. However, I am partial to Lady for reasons I've explained. All three were queens, founding mothers of modern jazz singing. Each set a standard that has yet to be surpassed. But no one has to explain why Ella is so good, why Sarah is so good. It doesn't take much to recognize the sheer enormity of their talent, nor do you have to "understand" jazz to fully appreciate their art. It is a little harder for folks to get Lady Day.

All three women were extraordinary, but Lady was first, and her art and genius were so subtle and the choices she made so fine, so minute, that they often go unrecognized. Lady's singing style says "I'm going to take my time, be cool, laid back, ease on through, and I will still get there on time without sweating." She subtly redefined and re-composed as she worked, passing her songs first through her brain, then through her heart, and finally through her mouth as a gift for all of us to hear. Billie Holiday's sound was unique; while she modeled herself after Louis Armstrong and Bessie Smith, she did not sound like them. Though she shared the clarity and diction of Ethel Waters, she doesn't sound like her either. So, while Holiday lacked Sarah Vaughan's range, Ella Fitzgerald's virtuosity and Bessie Smith's power, among them she had a unique sensitivity, timing, subtlety and fragility. Technically, she possessed the ability to bend notes exquisitely and she had an impeccable rhythmic sense: here she pushes the tempo, there she delays the entrance of a phrase. And she does so without ever losing momentum. After Louis Armstrong, Billie Holiday was the next "major innovator" of jazz singing.[7]

In addition, Billie Holiday sang lyrics with impeccable diction and clarity. Musical historian Eileen Southern notes early travelers' obser-vations of black American women who mesmerized white children and adults with their story-telling. Holiday was a twentieth-century version of these women. She painted pictures and told stories through the songs she sang, spellbinding her audiences. In performance her charisma made each member of her audience feel as though she were singing directly to them, expressing exactly what they were feeling. Even during the final years of her life, when her voice was practically gone, Holiday was still capable of rendering a lyric with profound meaning and drama. Shirley Horn says, "Billie Holiday helped to show me that lyrics have got to mean something, have got to paint a picture, tell a story."[8] There is a reason why we play her later recordings when we are feeling sad and lonely. Her voice seems to be in touch with our deepest emotions.

It is especially revealing to listen to the words of musicians who worked with Holiday, and to writers who have written about her craft. They best express how she created the music and they do so without technical jargon. They help explain what it is that makes her so unique, so important. These are the very reasons why we came to know her anyway.

Throughout her career, Billie Holiday worked with major jazz musicians, all of whom praised her musicianship and her artistry. They were among those who most appreciated the subtlety of her musical achievement. In many ways, she was a jazz musician's vocalist. Her early recordings in the thirties were with Teddy Wilson, a highly respected, classically trained jazz musician. Since Holiday, at the time, was a relative unknown outside of Harlem, these were released under Wilson's name. Even at this stage of her professional career, Wilson made note of her gifts. His description of their rehearsals suggests that, contrary to popular belief, Holiday did not just sit in front of a microphone and sing what she "felt":

> I would get together with Billie first, and we would take a stack of music, maybe thirty, forty songs, and go through them, and pick out the ones that would appeal to her—the lyric, the melody. And after we picked them, we'd concentrate on the ones we were going to record. And we rehearsed them until she had a very good idea of them in her mind, in her ear. . . . Her ear was phenomenal, but she had to get a song into her ear so she could do her own style on it. She would invent different little phrases that would be different melody notes from the ones that were written.[9]

In this description, Wilson reveals several important aspects of Holiday's artistry. Like the best instrumentalists, Holiday patiently rehearsed songs as they were written so that she could have them in her head and her ear. She was later able to improvise on the melody because she knew the song so well. Holiday would remember all of the songs they rehearsed—not an easy feat. In addition to her talent, the passage reveals her sense of discipline and practice.

Count Basie elaborates on rehearsals with Holiday. But by the time she sings with the Basie band in 1937, she is more self-assured as an artist:

> When she rehearsed with the band, it was really just a matter of getting her tunes like she wanted them. Because she knew how she wanted to sound, and you couldn't tell her what to do. You wouldn't know what to tell her. She had her own style, and it was to remain that way. Sometimes she would bring in new things and she would dictate the way she'd like them done. That's how she got her book with us. She never left her own style. Nobody sounded like her.[10]

As with Miles Davis and Louis Armstrong, we recognize her from the very first note. In spite of assertions to the contrary, Basie notes Holiday knew, "understood," what she was doing artistically.

Just what was it that she was doing? After getting the "straight" melody of the song in her ear, Holiday would then begin the process of recomposing it. In his discussion of Holiday's recording of "I'll Get By" with Johnny Hodges on May 11, 1937, British critic Humphrey Lyttelton explains Holiday's improvisation:

> As written, the song, in F major, begins on the lower F and ascends, in its two opening phrases, to an upper limit of A above the octave. Billie Holiday starts her chorus on that upper A, and indeed hinges her whole variation on it, with the result that, instead of soaring aloft, all the phrases droop downwards like the boughs of a weeping willow. Furthermore, apart from two descents to a low G in which her voice falls away to vanishing point, she restricts her range to a mere 6 notes.[11]

It would have been a more obvious choice to start on F. Billie Holiday did not choose the obvious.

Because she was such an accomplished improviser, Holiday garnered the respect of most of the jazz musicians of her day. One of her favorite pianists, Bobby Tucker, explained the difference between Holiday and other vocalists:

> One thing about Lady, she was the easiest singer I ever played for. You know, with most singers you have to guide 'em and carry 'em along—they're either laying back or else runnin' away from you. But not Billie Holiday. Man, it was a thrill to play for her. She had the greatest conception of a beat I ever heard. It just didn't matter what kind of song she was singing. She'd sing the fastest tune in the world or else something that was like a dirge, but you could take a metronome and she'd be right there. Hell! With Lady you could relax while you were playin' for her. You could damn near forget the tune.[12]

The most accomplished jazz musicians expressed the kind of admiration for Holiday that suggests their deference to her seniority and accomplishment. The great Ella Fitzgerald said of Holiday: "I idolized Billie and her songs. . . . She was the first really modern singer to my way of thinking. We all wanted to be like her" (Crowther, 69). Miles Davis was a young trumpeter when he played with Lady: "Whenever I'd go to see her, I always asked Billie to sing 'I Loves You, Porgy,' because when she sang 'don't let him touch me with his hot hands,' you could almost feel that shit she was feeling. It was beautiful and sad the way she sang that. Everybody loved Billie. . . . I loved playing with Coleman Hawkins and behind Billie when I got a chance. They were both great musicians, really creative and shit."[13] Given Davis's ability to recognize and appreciate the genius of artists as diverse as John Coltrane and Prince, it is especially significant that he refers to Holiday in the same sentence as Coleman Hawkins and that he refers to her as a "great musician." Billie Holiday had a tremendous impact on American culture. She not only influenced vocalists as diverse as

Frank Sinatra, Sam Cooke, Marvin Gaye and Joni Mitchell, but she also influenced the phrasing of instrumentalists such as Miles Davis and Mal Waldron and poets like Amiri Baraka. Even the novelist Leon Forrest claims she shaped his own storytelling craft.

During her lifetime, Billie Holiday never achieved the popular acclaim of Ella Fitzgerald. Now her music sells more than does that of any of her contemporaries. How is it, then, that she is now so popular, so well known by a public that knows so little about her?

Portrait of Lady Day as Harlem royalty.
*(Schomburg Center for Research in Black
Culture; Morgan and Marvin Smith, 1942)*

> Mom and Pop were just a couple of kids when they got married.
> He was eighteen, she was sixteen and I was three. . . .
> Mom was thirteen that Wednesday, April 7, 1915,
> in Baltimore when I was born.

So OPENS one of our most famous jazz autobiographies, *Lady Sings the Blues* (1956) by Billie Holiday with William Dufty. Well, actually the book is the result of Dufty's conversations with Holiday and his imaginative engagement with her previously published interviews. She wasn't born in Baltimore, but in Philadelphia. Eleanora Fagan (her birth name) was born to Sadie Fagan, an eighteen-year-old domestic servant, and Clarence Holiday, a seventeen-year-old guitarist who would acquire a strong reputation with the Fletcher Henderson orchestra. Fagan returned to her hometown, Baltimore, while Holiday was still an infant.

Attentive as I am to the risk of telling another version of Holiday's story, I want to provide an overview of her life and career as I have learned it from her biographers, particularly the best of them, Robert O'Meally and Stuart Nicholson. Below are the facts on which they seem to agree.

At a young age, Holiday adopted the name Billie from her favorite movie star, Billie Dove. She says her father named her Billie because she was a tomboy. (Later, friends would call her William to identify her bisexuality.) She began to use the name Holiday in order to identify herself with her father.

During her youth, truancy caused her to be in and out of institutions for wayward girls; the most influential of these institutions was the Catholic House of the Good Shepherd. At the age of eleven Holiday was sent there because the courts decided her mother was unfit to care for her. Ironically, Sadie's parenting came to the attention of the authorities when she reported that her daughter had been raped by Wilbert Rich, a forty-year-old neighbor. Upon her release, Holiday began working in a brothel, running errands, doing chores, changing towels and putting out soap. As with many victims of sexual abuse, she became sexually active at a very young age. Biographers agree that the well-developed, beautiful girl worked as a young prostitute as well. In the brothels where she worked she also began to listen to the Victrola and fell in love with the music of Bessie Smith and Louis Armstrong.

Holiday rejoined her mother in Harlem during the winter of 1929, the year of the stock market crash. She continued to work as a prostitute, and in May of that year when the Harlem brothel was raided, the teenager was sentenced to 100 days in a workhouse located on Blackwell's Island on the East River. By the age of fourteen, Billie Holiday had been physically and sexually abused, worked as a prostitute in two cities, and was already familiar with the criminal justice system. She also discovered her love of and talent for singing jazz. After her release from Blackwell's Island, Holiday decided to "stop turning tricks"; she also decided she "didn't want to be nobody's damn maid."[14] In the thirties, that didn't leave many options for an uneducated young black woman. It was during this time that she began a serious jazz apprenticeship at after-hours joints and jam sessions.

In 1933, jazz producer and critic John Hammond heard her singing at Monette's Supper Club, a Harlem after-hours spot. He wrote about her for the British magazine *Melody Maker* and immediately arranged to record her seventy-two hours after he produced Bessie Smith's final recording. During this session, Holiday recorded "Your Mother's Son-in-Law" and "Riffin' the Scotch," accompanied by Benny Goodman, Shirley Clay, Buck Washington, Jack Teagarden and Gene Krupa.[15]

Throughout 1937 and 1938, Holiday worked with the Count Basie Band. Upon leaving Basie she became one of the first black performers to integrate an all-white band when she signed on with Artie Shaw. After encountering numerous degrading instances of racism in both the North and the South, Holiday quit the band. At the age of 24, in

1939, she opened Barney Josephson's Café Society. Josephson founded the club with the goal of offering good entertainment in a socially conscious atmosphere that would attract an integrated audience. While headlining at Café Society, Holiday's reputation grew, and she became famous for her dramatic performances, sensuality, beauty and for the song "Strange Fruit," a song about lynching written by Lewis Allen (Able Meeropol). Holiday's recording company, Columbia, refused to record the song because of its controversial lyrics. Instead, she took it to Milt Gabler, who arranged for her to record it with his label, Commodore Records. Most students of Holiday mark the recording of "Strange Fruit" as an important turning point in her career. They are in disagreement, however, over the consequences of her choosing to record the controversial song. Some follow John Hammond's lead and insist that it was the beginning of her downfall because she became a singer of tragic ballads instead of the upbeat songs she originally popularized. For Hammond, recording "Strange Fruit" "artistically was the worst thing" for Holiday because she became too studied, too concerned about becoming an *artiste,* a darling of leftist intellectuals. For others, the song signaled a new development in her stage persona, distinguishing her as an actress as well as a vocalist. (Personally, I am deeply grateful for her courage in recording a song that has since become a classic in the tradition of "Lift Every Voice and Sing" and anticipating "Mississippi Goddam.")

Stuart Nicholson notes that as Holiday became associated with the song, she came to the attention of the FBI. By 1940 she started to sing "The Yanks Aren't Coming," by Harold Rome. According to Nicholson, "FBI agents leaned on club owner Ralph Watkins to stop Billie singing what was considered 'unpatriotic' material."[16] The FBI decided to open a file on her at that time, several years before she began to use heroin. The song was never recorded. Holiday also sang at benefits for the Communist Congressman from Harlem, Benjamin Davis.

From 1944 to 1950, under the guidance of Milt Gabler, Holiday recorded with Decca and Commodore. This marks the second stage of her career. During that time she recorded some of her best-known songs, including her own compositions "Don't Explain" and "God Bless the Child," as well as "Lover Man" and "Good Morning, Heartache."

Holiday was first arrested for possession of heroin at the height of her stardom. In 1947 she was sent to the Federal Reformatory for Women at Alderson, West Virginia, and she served nine and a half months. While there, she never sang one note. As was the case with many jazz artists who had been incarcerated, her cabaret card was revoked upon her release; consequently, she could not sing in New York clubs selling liquor and thereby lost a large portion of her earnings potential. She did appear at Carnegie Hall on March 27, 1948, to a wildly enthusiastic standing-room-only crowd.

In 1952, Holiday signed with Verve, thus beginning the third stage of her career. Produced by Norman Granz and featuring major jazz musicians, her recordings during the Verve years initiated her return to the small band, jam-session atmosphere in which she recorded her first sides for Columbia. For these sides, Granz used Oscar Peterson, Ray Brown, Ben Webster, Harry Edison, Jimmy Rowles, Benny Carter and Barney Kessel—among the finest musicians of the day. Although the voice is more coarse and the already limited range even further reduced, Holiday emerges from these cuts as a mature artist at the peak of her interpretive abilities. Her choices are thoughtful, original, often impeccable. I listen to these recordings as I do a Miles Davis solo of the same period. One listens as much for the spaces between the notes as one does for the choice of note. Doing so lends to a greater appreciation of her musicianship.

Billie Holiday recorded *Lady in Satin* in 1958. Critics disagree in their appraisals of Holiday's work during her last years and of this album. Some argue that her voice is weakened and that she had become a parody of her earlier self; others suggest that while her voice is not as strong, the emotional maturity and drama of her singing are more reflective of her complexity during the later years of her life. Shirley Horn recalls listening to *Lady in Satin* with Carmen McRae. According to Horn, McRae said "When you put it on, it's instant theater," to which Horn replied, "There's so much emotion there."[17] In 1959, Holiday recorded her last album under the direction of Ray Ellis. She wanted to work with Ellis because she admired the work he'd done with Frank Sinatra on *Only the Lonely*. She was terribly ill during this recording; at times, her companion/nurse, Alice Vrbsky, held her as she sat on the stool. Listening to her recordings from the earliest Columbia sides, through the Verve and Decca years to this last recording, gives the best biography of this woman who literally sang until the end of her life.

Billie Holiday died in New York on July 17, 1959, at the age of 44, from heart, kidney and liver ailments as well as lung blockage. As she lay on her deathbed, she was fingerprinted, photographed and arrested for possession and use of heroin. A nurse claimed to have found a packet of heroin on the dresser and bits of a white powder under her nose. Those who visited her said she was too weak to sniff the drug, let alone walk across the room to where the packet lay on the dresser. Subsequent autopsies showed no evidence of heroin or any narcotic. After her death, a nurse found a tightly rolled cylinder of bills amounting to the $750 she had received as an advance from *Confidential* magazine. Reports vary as to whether the money was found taped to her thigh or inserted in a more discreet location. It was all the money she had. She had been married twice, to Jimmy Monroe and Louis McKay. She had no children. She left behind an American songbook of over 300 recorded songs. She set the standard for jazz singing; she also paved the way for sepia chanteuses of the cabaret set—Lena Horne, Dorothy Dandridge and Diahann Carroll to name a few. After Billie Holiday, American popular singing would never be the same.

Holiday's life as I just described it shares much with the lives of many contemporary young women, ranging from those born to poverty to superstars such as Whitney Houston and Mary J. Blige. Given what Holiday was able to accomplish by the sheer force of her talent and her insistence on maintaining her integrity, she provides an extraordinary example of possibility for such young women, for anyone confronted with insurmountable obstacles. The problems of her life also provide a map that can help to deter others from similar pitfalls. Were this all we could learn from her, it would be more than enough. But Holiday was not only someone who rose above the conditions of her birth. She was also a brilliant artist during a time when few believed black women capable of brilliance. And yet, even today, this is not the Billie Holiday most people know. Why?

Philosopher Lewis Gordon notes that brothels, narcotics, music and tragedy all contribute to aesthetic production in the work of thinkers as different as Plato and Nietzsche. He goes on to note that tragedy's "foundations are in festivals linked to rituals of cathartic release." Hence, understandings of the tragic nature of Holiday's life and art fit into long-standing Western conceptions of art. Furthermore, Holiday's performances allow her listeners to experience the cathartic release of their own personal sense of sorrow and tragedy. We think of her in tragic terms because there are elements of her life that reinforce our own sense of tragedy and that allow us to confront and explore our own despair without losing ourselves in it.[18]

iii.

[Myth] transforms history into nature.

—ROLAND BARTHES, "MYTH TODAY"

THERE ARE IMAGES and myths that seem to swallow up individuals who are too complex to be explained by them, yet cannot escape their powerful hold. This is especially so when these myths are undergirded by social, political and economic forces. Billie Holiday emerged at a time when the dominant cultural stereotypes of black women were Mammy and the Tragic Mulatto. Black women rarely appeared in films in roles other than that of maid. It was a time when the most popular black women entertainers were Josephine Baker abroad and Bessie Smith and Ethel Waters at home. Those who wrote about Holiday tried to fit her into these available images. Writing for *Melody Maker* in 1933, John Hammond stated:

> This month, there has been a real find in the person of a singer called Billie Holiday. . . . though only eighteen she weighs over 200 pounds, is incredibly beautiful and sing as well as anybody I ever heard.[19]

This representation of Holiday sounds a great deal like similar descriptions of the young Bessie Smith. In fact, when she was filmed for the Duke Ellington short *Symphony in Black* (1935), Holiday was placed in a story much like the one in which Smith appeared in an earlier Ellington short, *Black and Tan Fantasy* (1927). The abused and dismissed member of a love triangle, Holiday is knocked to the ground, from where she sings "Big City Blues," also known as "The Saddest Tale," a song about having been wronged in love. She was packaged in a familiar story for an audience that would instantly recognize her "type."

During her lifetime, and some might argue even today, there were no images or narratives to explain a black woman who possessed all of Holiday's qualities and habits. Of course, there always have been multidimensional, complex and brilliant black women, but the dominant images did not portray them as such. Among white Americans, some black women were asexual mammies, loyal and devoted to their white employers and charges. Others were deemed "oversexed." In addition to being "oversexed," the biracial black woman—the mulatto—was "over-ambitious" and tragic as well. (Of course, any woman who was "oversexed" and "over-ambitious" had to be portrayed as tragic, regardless of her race.) Released around the time when Billie Holiday first gained public notice, the 1934 version of *Imitation of Life* (starring Louise Beavers and Claudette Colbert) helped to ensure the survival of the "Mammy" image for years to come. The film also reproduced the stereotype of the oversexed, over-ambitious, "tragic mulatto"—Peola, played by the beautiful African-American actress Fredi Washington. *Gone With the Wind,* with the simpleminded Prissy and the devoted but sassy Mammy, appeared in 1939. In an attempt to counter these images, black Americans created the image of the Negro (or Colored) Lady, a middle-class race woman, who was perhaps beautiful, but never sexual. ("Race woman" was the term used to describe those women who devoted themselves to racial uplift.) One could find her in the black press and in black literature. She might have even been a clubwoman or a church lady.[20] She was usually educated and very, very light-skinned—sometimes light enough to pass for white. Though not fair, the self-possessed, bourgeois opera singer Marian Anderson epitomized the Lady. Her famous concert on the steps of the Lincoln Memorial took place in 1939, the same year Holiday recorded "Strange Fruit."

Holiday exploded beyond the limits of all of these categories. She sought pleasure, drank and used profanity, was a very sensual bisexual. Holiday had many lovers, black and white, male and female, and she did not hide it. Not only did she like sex, she seems to have enjoyed talking about it as well. She smoked marijuana and opium, and of course, she shot heroin. Though her music is blues based, she rarely sang the formal twelve-bar blues. Throughout her career she recorded a very small number of formal blues tunes; she wrote three of these— "Billie's Blues," "Now Baby or Never" and "Fine and Mellow." By blues based, I mean the way that Holiday used phrasings, approached notes, sang "blue-notes" and other stylistic variations in order to "blue" a lyric.[21] Listen to the very last verse of "My Sweet Hunk O' Trash," her duet with Louis Armstrong, for one of many perfect examples of this.

She did not shout because she didn't have a big voice. (In fact, the refinement of microphone technology might have been as responsible for her emergence as a star as anything else.) She did not learn to sing in the Baptist church choir; she was raised a Catholic and remained so until her death. Consequently, she seems to have been more influenced by the Gregorian chants that she would have heard at mass than she was by the big-voiced sounds of those trained in the black church tradition, such as Gloria Lynne, Aretha Franklin, Marian Anderson or Whitney Houston.

She was not a maid, mammy or mother. She was not light enough to pass for white nor was she very dark. She was not petite, nor was she extremely overweight. She fist-fought men and she was beaten by them. She is alleged to have beaten her female lovers as well. She did not tolerate racist remarks, often responding with her sailor's tongue accompanied by a knockout punch. A friend recalls how she punched a drunken soldier to the ground and then stepped over him clad in full-length mink and heels only to tell a police officer, "He attacked me."[22]

At times, she was militantly pro-black, often referring to herself as a "race woman." She was elegant, feminine and loved fine clothing. She could also shoot craps on the floor of the tour bus. In many ways she could have been the model for the song "The Lady Is a Tramp." She loved to cook and feed swarms of friends and fellow musicians. Finally, and most important, along with Louis Armstrong, Billie Holiday helped to create the genre of modern jazz singing.

Eventually the stories of her arrests and drug addiction joined with her stage persona of the torch singer to create a new image, that of the tragic, ever-suffering black woman singer who simply stands center stage and naturally sings of her woes. Unlike the tragic mulatto, this image is not of someone torn between two racial worlds. Unlike the middle-class lady, she is "soiled," "ruint." Furthermore, as Robert O'Meally explains, this figure is a natural; she has no personal or artistic history, she has no musical skills.[23] She feels but does not think. She has insatiable appetites for food, sex, alcohol and drugs.

When Holiday needed money, she fit herself neatly into this and its accompanying story and made it available for sale. As such, the sensation of her life began to define her for people who did not know her. Newspapers covered every detail of her arrests and trials, but failed to pay as much attention to her performances and records. The most explicit example of her selling the story that people wanted is her autobiography. It became the source upon which subsequent narratives relied. Holiday hoped to sell the movie rights to the book, and Hollywood seemed very excited at first. There were rumors that the beautiful black sex symbol Dorothy Dandridge would play Holiday. Later there was talk of casting Ava Gardner. Then Lana Turner's name was touted as the possible star of the film. Interestingly, Dandridge would find herself captured by the previously mentioned stereotype of the tragic mulatto; she committed suicide in 1965. In the late sixties, Abbey Lincoln was considered for the role. When the film was finally made in 1972, starring Diana Ross, it reinvented Holiday's life story for a generation that knew little of her music. While the film kept her a victim, it turned her last husband, Louis McKay, into the knight in shining armor who sought to rescue Holiday from herself. The film shot Diana Ross into superstardom, sparked interest in Holiday and raised the price of the Holiday commodity. It also spawned two decades' worth of articles, essays and books claiming to reveal the "real Holiday."

SINCE HER DEATH, there clearly has been a contest over the meaning of the Holiday icon. While biographers who have tried to guarantee her legacy primarily reflect her tremendous talent, they have had to engage in a constant tug-of-war with a variety of other forces. Holiday has been variously claimed by black cultural nationalist Larry Neale, black Marxist/Leninist Amiri Baraka, black feminist Angela Davis and black cultural integrationists Albert Murray, Leon Forrest and Stanley Crouch. American corporate interests have claimed her as well. She appears as a character in at least three novels (Elizabeth Hardwick's *Sleepless Nights,* Alice Adams's *Listening to Billie* and Ntozake Shange's *Sassafrass, Cypress and Indigo*), and two films; in addition, she makes cameo appearances in the autobiographies of Malcolm X, Maya Angelou, Miles Davis and numerous others. She has provided inspiration for endless poems. As with the Mexican painter Frida Kahlo and the French singer Edith Piaf, Holiday is often portrayed as a tragic, talented woman who is a self-destructive victim. On the other hand, she lives on the edge, she transgresses, she wins recognition and respect within the male realm of jazz.

As with all American icons, Holiday is also a salable commodity. In a capitalist society, is it possible for icons to escape commodification? She was a salable commodity in her life, but now her voice circulates disembodied from its producer: the faceless voice-over in a commercial for wine or movie scene,[24] the nameless face staring from endless posters, photographs, catalogues and videos.[25]

Images of Holiday that insist upon her tragedy, sexuality and appetites sustain and reproduce ideologies of black womanhood and of jazz music. She is not only a woman who paid the price for living on the edge, not only a tragic victim who had to die, but also a black woman who suffered the fate of the jazz genius in a racist American society—substance abuse and underappreciation. In this respect, she joins other jazz icons, particularly Lester Young and Charlie Parker.

The Holiday icon presents a danger to women like Mary J. Blige because it demands that black women who refuse the limited options society designates for them be tragic figures. At its most pernicious, this interpretation of Holiday's life insists upon her victim status. Holiday as tragic victim helps to contain and control black women who are multidimensional, talented and ambitious. I am not suggesting an overarching silent conspiracy, but I want to call our attention to the way that one-dimensional images become naturalized so that we accept their inevitability. If we think of Holiday as a woman who was victimized instead of as a woman who was a perpetual victim, our perspectives of her, her achievement, and ultimately of our own possibility, change profoundly. In one song Holiday sang "I cried last night. Cried all night the night before. Woke up this morning, and I ain't gonna cry no more."[26] These lines suggest there are moments in all of our lives that bring tears, tragedy and loss. These moments need not define our lives. We can choose to find a way out of them, through them. The path away from the dark times is as varied as the way leading to them. These lyrics provide a version of Holiday I want to reveal under the layers of myths that have formed like a callus around her, or perhaps it is a version I want to create out of all of the alternative interpretations of her life and music. How do we know what we think we know about Billie Holiday? Is it possible to interpret her life, legacy and icon in a way that empowers us to realize our own potential? These are the questions with which this book is obsessed.

This Van Vechten portrait recalls Roland Barthes's notion that there is a "terrible thing in every photograph: the return of the dead." The photographer remembers photographing her for two hours, and while she was initially despondent, she returned from a brief sojourn "on a different plane, all energy, sympathy, cooperation and interest."
(Carl Van Vechten, 1949)

2

Lady-like: How We Know What We Think We Know About Billie Holiday

BILLIE HOLIDAY'S name evokes sighs and knowing glances followed by a whispered "poor thing." And then, of course, "She lived everything she sang, you know." People who watch clips of her will ask, "Is she high right there?" When viewing photographs, they immediately look to her arms, "Are there track marks there?" Knowing nods of the head suggest an intimacy, a shared secret. There is a sense of hushed curiosity that one rarely hears when one mentions Chet Baker or Charlie Parker. And yet, the number of tellers of this tale suggests it is not a secret at all. Everybody knows something. There is a remarkable diversity in the people who share this response. In my experience, there are few things about which people agree so uniformly across lines of race, gender, class and sexuality. Without even saying it, these phrases hint at tales of drugs, abusive men and racism. What is at the core of this voyeuristic and titillating curiosity about beautiful women and drugs? How do we know what we think we know about Billie Holiday? Why do we reveal what we know in low whispered tones characterized by the silent "between you and me"?

Of course, Holiday's performances in person and on vinyl lend themselves to this sense of familiarity. Her torch singing has an underlying promise: "Here I am—open, emotional, unprotected." All who saw her in person report that she had the kind of charisma that made each member of the audience believe she was singing directly to them and therefore engaging them in an intimate conversation.

Holiday's performances, or someone's memories of these performances, are joined by three major forms of representation that contribute to the dominant myths about her. The first of these is the story told by the publicity surrounding her arrests for possession and use of narcotics. The second source is the "autobiography" *Lady Sings the Blues,* penned by journalist William Dufty and published in 1956. I place autobiography in quotation marks here because Holiday's contemporaries and subsequent biographers have affirmed its fictional nature. All autobiographies are fictions to some extent, albeit some more so than others. The third and final source of myths about Billie Holiday is the 1972 motion picture starring Diana Ross, *Lady Sings the Blues,* which is very loosely based on the somewhat fictional autobiography. All three reinforce each other. Together they have built a multilayered version of Holiday's life: the talented woman who abuses her instrument, the beautiful woman decimated by age, alcohol and domestic violence, the weak-willed child-woman led astray by pimplike bad men.

While the autobiography purports to lift the veil, promising to tell the "truth" in the face of all the sensationalized stories about her, the voyeuristic dimension is most evident in the newspaper stories, the magazine layouts and the Hollywood film. Film is, after all, a voyeuristic medium. It lets us in without implicating us in the action we witness. The taboo lure of women and drugs invokes curiosity and fear;

through Holiday the curious can see but not risk participating in the act. It is almost pornographic.

Narcotics historian Stephen Kandall has written, "The connection between drugs and female sexuality has existed for thousands of years." Prints and photographs of the late nineteenth and early twentieth centuries depict privileged white women lying sensuously on brocade pillows in drug-induced states of serene ecstasy. Sometimes a sleeve falls down, revealing a downy white shoulder or the top of full, creamy breasts. In many such images, if the drug is opium, the women are joined by shady-looking, stereotypical Chinese men, thus making the connection between drugs and interracial sex.[27] In others, fully clothed men sit in anticipation of the drug's full effect on their companions. Consequently, those who sought to tell the story of Billie Holiday's life, her drug addiction, and her romantic relationships found ready and available centuries-old images of women, drugs and sex.

White Lady

FOR YEARS, one could find no birth certificate or baptismal record for Billie Holiday, so her entrance on the public ledgers appears in the records of her arrests, first as a wayward girl in Baltimore, then as a young prostitute in Harlem and finally as a heroin addict.[28] Billie Holiday was arrested for possession and use of narcotics four times: May 1947 in the city of her birth, Philadelphia; January 1949 in San Francisco; February 1956, again in Philadelphia; and in New York on her deathbed in 1959. It seems they always arrested her while she was on the road, away from home, in a hotel or in the hospital—all transient places, emphasizing a lack of stability, dispossession and homelessness. (Throughout much of her life, Holiday did not own a home.)

Articles about Holiday's arrests are always accompanied by photographs of a haggard Holiday with men. On May 27, 1947, she was

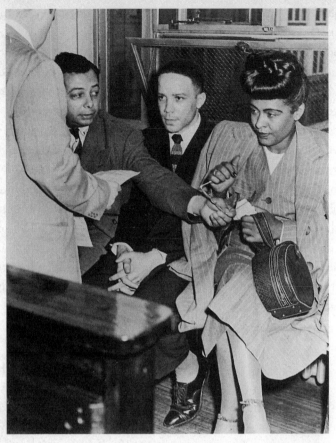

Jimmy Ascendio, pianist Bobby Tucker, and Billie Holiday in district court, Philadelphia, May 27, 1947. *(Urban Archives, Temple University)*

busted with her lover Joe Guy, but the photograph shows a youthful Holiday, dark circles under her eyes, a look of shame on her face, seated beside the dealer, Jimmy Ascendio, and the frustrated innocent, her accompanist, Bobby Tucker. In January 1949 the photographs show Holiday bedecked in full-length mink and dark glasses, every inch the star. Her "boyfriend," John Levy, stands next to her. In these photographs Lady looks like the star she is, her head held high. We can't read her expression, as her eyes are covered, yet there is the appearance of confidence. Perhaps this is because she is certain of her innocence; she does beat the rap later on. In the photographs that accompany the February 1956 arrest she is an old pro. The look on her face seems to say: "Here we go again." In one photograph from the same arrest, she is walking out of jail, holding her dog on a leash. In another she appears at the arraignment with her husband, Louis McKay; again her face is not the forlorn, embarrassed look of the earlier photographs. In fact, there is almost a look of resignation. Gone is the glamour. Her skin has the texture of a long-term addict. She holds her fur coat over her arm, and her dog, clad in his own coat, sits on top of the fur, safely ensconced in her arms. Interestingly, she holds the dog in an intimate fashion. She and McKay stand apart, much farther apart than she and Levy in the earlier photograph.

Billie Holiday and John Levy in San Francisco Courthouse, January 24, 1949. *(Urban Archives, Temple University)*

DURING THE WEEK of May 12, 1946, Lady Day played the Earle Theater on Philadelphia's South Street. The Earle was one of the nation's most prominent theaters for black entertainers and artists. Holiday stayed four blocks away at the Attucks Hotel at 801 South 15th, near 15th and Catherine streets. This area, in the heart of historic black Philadelphia, is the site of W. E. B. Du Bois's classic *The Philadelphia Negro*. The Philadelphia Black Musicians Union (called the Clef Club) met regularly at a location nearby (13th and Fitzwater). Today, this area is known as the Avenue of the Arts, and the Philadelphia Clef Club—The House that Jazz Built—is the only remainder of the area's past as a bastion of black nightlife.

At the end of her show's run, Holiday went back to her hotel, plan-

Billie Holiday charged with possession of opium in San Francisco, January 22, 1949. (*AP/Wide World photos*)

Billie Holiday and Louis McKay charged with use and possession of heroin in Philadelphia, February 23, 1956.
(*Urban Archives, Temple University*)

ning to pack and return to New York. Police arrived, claimed they found drugs and needles in her room and arrested her. Even before the reign of Frank Rizzo, Philadelphia police were notorious for harassing African Americans, and the narcotics agents who hounded Billie Holiday were well known in Philadelphia's black communities. On May 27, 1947, Holiday, facing charges of use and possession of narcotics, appeared in the District Court for the Eastern District in Philadelphia. Under the counsel of her manager, Joe Glaser, Holiday pled guilty, waived her right to an attorney and asked for treatment.

The transcripts of that trial initially convey a sense of optimism. Even the United States attorney requested she be given treatment for her addiction. Joseph G. Hildenberger described Holiday's situation as follows: "She has given these agents a full and complete statement and came in here last week with the booking agent and expressed a desire to be cured of this addiction. Very unfortunately, she has had following her the worst type of parasites and leeches you can think of. It is our opinion that the best thing that can be done for her would be to put her in a hospital where she will be properly treated and cured of the addiction" (*United States v. Billie Holiday*, #14234, May 27, 1947).

The judge acknowledges her addiction as an illness and recognizes that she had been exploited by drug dealers who overcharged her for drugs: "They kept her under opiates, largely as a matter of persuasion and coercion and failing to exercise reasonable judgement of her own." He then promises her she will receive treatment. So it comes as a surprise when, at the end of the trial, she is harshly reprimanded and sentenced to prison. "You stand here as a criminal defendant, and while your plight is rather pitiful . . . you appreciate what is right. . . . You will get treatment but . . . you stand as a wrongdoer." He then sentences her to one year and a day in the federal penitentiary.

In these transcripts, Holiday emerges as a woman between two camps of men: exploitive black pimps/drug dealers/managers/"sweethearts" and white government authorities. The black men claim to protect her from herself by securing drugs for her and doling them out to her as she needs them; they claim she would take all of the drugs at once. The white men claim to protect her from the black ones.[29]

Holiday served her sentence at the Federal Reformatory for Women at Alderson in West Virginia. She did not receive medical treatment and was instead forced to quit cold turkey. By all accounts, she was a model prisoner—so much so, in fact, that she was released seventy-two days early for good behavior. She did not sing one note during her incarceration, and when she was released, her license to sing in establishments serving liquor had been revoked. In a life full of mistakes, perhaps one of the biggest was taking the advice of her manager, Joe Glaser, to waive her right to adequate counsel. Legal experts who review the records today note that had she been properly represented, it is highly unlikely she would have done one day behind bars.

• • •

BY THE TIME OF her first drug related arrest in 1947, Holiday was a well-known vocalist. She had a strong following in New York, but tours with the Count Basie and Artie Shaw orchestras had given her national exposure as well. She reportedly earned between $50,000 and $60,000 a year. She'd released many well-received records under her own name, and she was the Queen of Swing Street. She noted: "I spent the rest of the war on 52nd Street and a few other streets. I had the white gowns and the white shoes. And every night they'd bring me the white gardenias and the white junk" (LSB, 116). All of this is to say Lady Day was a star, so her arrest was news. The June 9, 1947, issue of *Time* magazine reported, "Top-ranking blues singer Billie ('Strange Fruit') Holiday was really singing the blues. She got a year and a day in a reformatory on a narcotics charge" (42). (She was not a blues singer, and it is interesting that the song they cite is "Strange Fruit" and not "My Man" or some other tune.) An article titled "Billie Holiday Seized in Drug Case" begins:

> Billie Holiday, called by critics the greatest of contemporary blues singers, and Joseph Luke Guy, unemployed orchestra leader who either is or isn't her husband, were arrested here yesterday by federal agents on charges of illegally possessing heroin.[30]

Right away we find out about her arrest and also her questionable marital status. Furthermore, the "husband" is "unemployed." The end of the story: "In an interview printed in *PM*, Sept. 2, 1945, Miss Holiday was quoted as saying she was Guy's wife. Yesterday Glaser said emphatically that the two were not and never had been married." What does her marital status have to do with her arrest for narcotics? Very little indeed, except that it is used to indict her as an immoral woman—one who lives with a man who is not her husband and with whom she uses drugs, in a hotel room no less.

Actually, there was a more complicated path leading to Holiday's addiction. She started experimenting with illegal substances as a

young girl—as did many of her peers, she regularly smoked marijuana—primarily for pleasure, sort of like the bourgeois habit of having
an evening cocktail or glasses of wine with dinner. This was something
you did in the circles in which she traveled. In all likelihood, she ex-
perimented recreationally with other drugs as well. Her biographers
speculate that she indulged in opium, the drug of choice among the
street aristocrats as well as the wealthy socialites with whom she associated. Later, it might have been a little something to help her get
through the day, something to fight off depression (not the blues, but
the illness that today we finally recognize as a chemical deficiency;
who knows what might have become of Holiday had she had access to
Prozac, Zoloft, Paxil, Wellbutrin or any number of commonly used
modern antidepressants). At some point in the early to mid forties,
Lady Day, like the many of us who are genetically predisposed, became addicted to heroin. The life of the addict is no glamorous thing;
it is a life characterized by daily desperation, and after a while the drug
isn't so much to get you high, but to get you up and through the day.
She surrounded herself with men who would acquire the drug for her
and then charge her ten times the street price for it.

During the forties, the profile of the female drug addict changed
from the bored upper-middle-class white woman to "poorer, marginalized segments of society" (Kandall, 117). After World War II one half
of all female addicts lived in New York (Ibid., 120). Not coincidentally,
addiction became criminalized during the period between the two
world wars, and the nation's policy for dealing with addicts moved
from treatment to law enforcement and prison.

Holiday was a high-profile drug addict caught up in these larger
social forces. The media and law enforcement seemed to revel in a
voyeuristic fascination with her and an abusive harassment of her.
Each stalked her every move, and together they created a portrait
of an overindulgent, highly sexualized but emotionally immature
woman. The transcripts of her first federal trial demonstrate the Feds'
use of her as an example, hoping she would lead them to big dealers.
The pages of this document as well as the pages of her FBI file paint

her as a woman who is not too bright, childlike and led astray by men. In an effort to protect her, her friend Tallulah Bankhead used the same language in a letter to J. Edgar Hoover dated February 8, 1949:

> I have met Billie Holiday but twice in my life but admire her immensely as an artist and feel the most profound compassion for her. . . . Although my intention is not to condone her weaknesses, I certainly understand the eccentricities of her behavior because she is essentially a child at heart whose troubles have made her psychologically unable to cope with the world in which she finds herself.

While Bankhead claims to have met Holiday only twice, Holiday's biographers argue that the two had an affair.

With the power of the state and the media behind all the stories of her arrests, relationships and addiction, is it any wonder that people think they know Billie Holiday's story so well?

But even more significant than the power of the state and the media is Holiday's apparent consent. With the publication of her autobiography she seems to have capitulated to much of this view. In fact, she accepted the structure of the narrative and tried to offer a more complicated understanding of her life within its confines. If this tale sold newspapers, she suspected it would sell a tell-all book as well. And it seems Lady could always use a little extra change. I doubt she knew just how little power she ultimately would have over it.

Lady Day on Holiday: The Autobiography

STUART NICHOLSON notes that Billie Holiday created a stage persona of the beautiful woman unlucky in love who told her stories through slow-burning torch songs. The male counterpart to her character might be Frank Sinatra of the "Set 'Em Up Joe" scenario. One might think of the book *Lady Sings the Blues* as the autobiography of the stage persona.

While the autobiography did help to establish some myths of Holiday, it also sought to address, challenge and provide correctives to stories put forth by the mainstream press, which only focused on her addiction.

Until the publication of Robert O'Meally's *Lady Day: The Many Faces of Billie Holiday* in 1991, the Holiday biographers, including John Chilton and John White, based their own biographies uncritically on *Lady Sings the Blues*. Donald Clarke (1995) and Stuart Nicholson (1995) each published substantial biographies following the publication of O'Meally's book, titled *Wishing on the Moon* and *Billie Holiday* respectively. Both referred to the fictional nature of *Lady Sings the Blues*. All three—O'Meally, Clarke and Nicholson—seem to agree that the passages devoted to music-making ring most true, and even some of those are embellished for effect. They also agree that Holiday saw the book as an opportunity to make a quick buck.

Doubleday published *Lady Sings the Blues* in 1956. It sold for $3.75 and was reviewed by major newspapers and publications. The book sold 12,000 copies in the first year of publication. It has been consistently in print since then. Holiday publicized the book in radio and television interviews with Tex McCrary and Mike Wallace, and with the release of the album *Lady Sings the Blues*. Each song on the album was a chapter heading in her book; each chapter of her book was named for a song that had come to be associated with her.

Both Holiday and Dufty are listed as authors, though reviewers, critics and scholars seem to agree that Dufty wrote the book and Holiday contributed little. According to these sources, Dufty culled material from previous interviews and articles on the singer, instead of interviewing her himself. (A statement Holiday made claiming to have never read the book supports these views.) A few things are striking when you consider the various stories that circulate around the writing of the autobiography. First, almost everyone attributes the book to

Dufty and at the same time they accuse Holiday of lying within its pages. Even though he is charged with never having interviewed Holiday, Dufty escapes the charge of dishonesty. And while Holiday is accused of having lied about the details of her life among other things (i.e., claiming songs she did not write), few question the veracity of her statement that she did not read the book.

When reviewers praised the book, they focused on Dufty's skill and talent. In a review for the *Chicago Sunday Tribune,* R. G. Peck wrote:

> The book gives every indication of telling the sincere and unpretty truth about what it's like to grow up in a Negro slum. Dufty deserves praise for preventing the story from becoming artificial, contrived, or overslick in its telling.[31]

Note the concern with authenticity. It is not the story of an individual life, but one that tells "the truth of Negro life." Similarly, in *Library Journal,* C. K. Miller wrote: "A hard, bitter and unsentimental book written with brutal honesty and having much to say not only about Billie Holiday the person but what it means to be poor and black."[32] Even the prestigious *New York Times* followed suit:

> William Dufty, assistant to the editor of the *New York Post,* has displayed a remarkable virtuosity in so effacing himself as to make Miss Holiday emerge whole—colloquial, bitter, generous, loving, foolish and tragic.[33]

While the reviews cited above were favorable in their assessment of the white man's ability to give voice to the black woman, the one that follows focuses on Holiday. Ralph J. Gleason found the book

> A definite disappointment, if not a complete failure. There is none of the dignity and humanity that made Ethel Waters' moving biography, *His Eye Is on the Sparrow,* such a

powerful book. . . . Miss Holiday does not level with you and if there was to be a contribution made by a book of this sort, it would have been in the telling of the whole truth and not in a story packed with self-pity and biased by Miss Holiday's own angry view that she was blameless in everything that happened to her and she was the unending victim of prejudice.[34]

This is no song of praise, but instead an indictment. One wonders if Gleason read the book by the woman who went out of her way to consistently assert in a *Down Beat* interview in 1949: "Don't forget, though. I just want to be straight with people, not have their sympathy." The book was also reviewed in the African-American newspaper, the Baltimore *Afro-American* by the distinguished literary critic J. Saunders Redding. Exemplifying black middle-class concerns with respectability, Redding wrote, "This reviewer is no squeamish prude, but Billie Holiday and William Dufty use language so raw with so little warrant that there were times when this reviewer got real sick."[35] The legendary *Pittsburgh Courier* only mentioned Holiday's promise to name names in a prepublication item that ran on the society pages.

Two reviews did depart from the formula described above. Critic Whitney Balliett was disappointed that the book "in spite of its high decibels, . . . explains almost nothing about her art."[36] The review in *Time* magazine was one of the only ones to strike a balance between the two positions cited above: "*Lady Sings the Blues* has the tone of truth. Whether it is singer Holiday's own style or journalist-friend William Dufty's professional hand, the book's deadpan manner is a little chilling. No matter how it is told, hers is a chilling story. Billy [*sic*] sings a sad, sad song."[37] This review is even more accurate than it intends to be. The autobiography is not a song, but a series of them; it is a carefully constructed performance of a life. A realist (not realistic) portrait of the "jazz artist."

On November 10, 1956, Billie Holiday appeared at Carnegie Hall.

Her songs were interspersed with readings from the autobiography by Gilbert Millstein. The readings are rendered in the driest, dull monotone. Holiday followed with songs that seemed appropriate to the selections from the book. All in all, the concert reinforced the story of a woman unlucky in life and in love. Nicholson writes:

> The lyric content of the songs she sang were essentially passive, sorrowful, bitter or fatalistic and dealt with a narrow emotional range, a world in which everything was painted, if not black, then certainly dark blue. As was usual with her repertoire, she used "I" songs but changed the "I" from positive to negative. . . . Persona and person were now interchangeable, and now, more than ever, she had become dominated by her own legend. (*Billie Holiday,* 207)

Not all of the songs are passive, sorrowful and bitter. In addition to classics like "Don't Explain," "Yesterdays" and "My Man," Holiday also sang "Billie's Blues," "Please Don't Talk About Me When I'm Gone," "Ain't Nobody's Business If I Do," and "Fine and Mellow"—all upbeat, swinging tunes. The "I" of these songs is an assertive, take no shit, hip chick. So, contrary to Nicholson's assessment, the concert at Carnegie and the album that followed presented a far more well-rounded version of the stage persona than that of the down-and-out woman.

At least, the Carnegie Hall concert gave audiences a sense of her artistry. When the autobiography was excerpted in *Ebony* in 1956 (seven years after the 1949 cover story), a staged photographic narrative accompanied it. Within this, Holiday poses, looking over the waterfront ("I Cover the Waterfront") and standing outside of the 52nd Street clubs where she once reigned. But most unbelievable is the reenactment of her arrest: there is a photograph of her and McKay in bed, Holiday pulling the sheet around her as the police burst into her room.

And yet, in many ways, *Lady Sings the Blues* is as staged as the photographs accompanying the *Ebony* story. It should not be evaluated as a book that does not live up to its claims of "Truthfulness," but instead as another performance of the Holiday persona. Because the chapter headings are all taken from Holiday tunes, and because there are allusions to lyrics from her songs throughout the text, the content is structured and informed by the songs with which she had become associated. Chapter 22, titled "I Must Have That Man," opens with "A man can leave home one morning and come home that night whistling and singing to find there ain't nobody there but him. I left two men like that." The title echoes one of her songs, and the opening line is a reference to "Fine and Mellow": "Love is like a faucet, it turns off and on, Love is like a faucet, it turns off and on./Some time when you think it's on, baby, it has turned off and gone." The last chapter, "God Bless the Child," closes with a direct quotation from "My Man": "But all that I soon forgot, with my man. . . . Who can tell what detours are ahead? . . . Tired, you bet. But all that I'll soon forget with my man. . . ."[38]

The book gets its title from another Holiday song, "Lady Sings the Blues," a title that suggests the performative nature of the text. Readers who had seen Lady in concert received a prose version of those live, dramatic performances. In many ways, this is not the life story of Eleanora Fagan, or maybe not even the story of Billie Holiday, but it is the story of Lady Day. And that story is filled with subtle allusions to the life stories of the other two. Just as her improvisations were subtle, so too are the glimpses of truth that peep through the gaps, silences and allusions.[39] If one reads *Lady Sings the Blues* in this way, one finds new dimensions of "truth-telling." Where subsequent biographers claim embellishment or falsity, in fact, the book provides us a way of reading it that reveals something much closer to the "truth."

Interestingly, although she wrote the lyrics to the song "Lady Sings the Blues," Billie Holiday did not like it as a title for her book. She preferred "Bitter Crop," the last two words of the song "Strange Fruit." But her publishers insisted upon "Lady Sings the Blues." The implications are enormous. By calling her life story "Bitter Crop," she linked it to centuries of dispossession, oppression and terrorism experienced by black Americans. She made her story part of that larger historical narrative. As such, readers might have approached the book with a very different set of expectations. "Lady Sings the Blues" is a song that identifies her with the blues, not as a joyful music but as the music of the torch singer. When blues is defined in this way, it loses its sense of hope. Furthermore, the title singles her out as an individual with no connection to a history or a people and makes no commentary on the life she as a black woman was forced to live here.

The question that remains about the autobiography is whether or not Dufty knew the truth and chose to conceal it or hide it within the narrative, or did Holiday tell him and earlier reporters the story of her life? In some instances the latter appears to be the case. So much of the autobiography repeats information appearing in interviews given years before its publication. In other words, it was a story she had been telling for some time. This suggests she had some role in constructing the way her story would be told.

Holiday's portrait of her mother is one of the many misleading aspects of the autobiography. *Lady Sings the Blues* opens with the lines: "Mom and Pop were just a couple of kids when they got married. He was eighteen, she was sixteen and I was three. . . . Mom was thirteen that Wednesday, April 7, 1915, in Baltimore when I was born." Robert O'Meally confirms Holiday was born on April 7, 1915, in the Philadelphia General Hospital. In *LSB* her mother was sixteen when she married her eighteen-year-old father and Holiday was three, making her mother thirteen when Billie was born. In fact, Sadie Fagan never married Clarence Holiday, nor is Holiday listed on the birth certificate as the father. Sadie Fagan was nineteen when she gave birth to her daughter. Clarence Holiday would have been seventeen. Lady makes her mother a teen who is younger than her father, pregnant six years younger than her true age upon her daughter's conception. Why? O'Meally says the book "reveal[s] the person Holiday saw herself to be." How she wanted to be. I would add to this that she also sought to protect her mother. Writing in a context where black women were deemed promiscuous mothers of "illegitimate" children for whom they were unfit to care, Holiday changes all facts that might lend themselves to stereotypical renderings of her mother. Instead, she makes Ms. Fagan a teen pregnant with an older man's child. Furthermore, she makes her parents committed and dedicated enough to marry. Had she not, Sadie would have emerged as the sexually aggressive older woman.

This desire to protect her mother is evident throughout the autobiography. Sadie Fagan comes forth as a religious, somewhat naive, generous and loving woman. Holiday claims her mother boarded her out to a Harlem madam without knowing the woman's occupation. She claims she began turning tricks while there, a fact of which her mother remained ignorant. However, not only was Holiday a prostitute in New York, she had been one in Baltimore, where she was a "pretty baby"—the youngest of the working girls in the house. O'Meally quotes Pony Kane, who knew Holiday in Baltimore: "She was the youngest of all the girls. She used to wear satin slips and panties. Her being young, different fellas would like her" (85). Furthermore, Stuart Nicholson located arrest records showing that when Holiday was arrested as a teenager during a raid on the brothel, her mother, who also turned tricks there, was arrested as well.[40]

While *Lady Sings the Blues* doesn't discuss Holiday's work as a child prostitute in Baltimore, and certainly doesn't identify Sadie Fagan as having been a lady of the night, there is a provocative instance where a close reading reveals this to have been the case. It is worth quoting at length.

> All the big-time whores wore big red velvet hats then with bird-of-paradise feathers on them. These lids were the thing. You couldn't touch one for less than twenty-five dollars—a lot of money in the twenties. I always wanted Mom to have one, and when she finally made it I loved it so I'd throw a fit unless she wore it from the time she got up in the morning until she

went to bed at night. If she left the house without it, I'd carry on. She looked so pretty in it, and I thought she should look pretty all the time. She was no more than five feet tall and she weighed less than eighty pounds. In her red velvet bird-of-paradise hat she looked like a living doll. When she went out in this fancy outfit she'd always talk about getting a rich husband so both of us working girls could retire. (14–15)

Now, if big red velvet hats were recognized as the favorite hats of the big-time whores, why would Holiday want her mother to have one? Better still, why would Sadie, saint that she was, want to wear anything associated with prostitutes? If we refuse to get the connection, there is yet another clue in the second paragraph where Holiday refers to herself and her mother as "both us working girls." "Working girls" is often a euphemism for prostitute.

There are such instances throughout the text that refer to issues of sexuality. O'Meally, Nicholson and Clarke have all written that Holiday was bisexual. Though she does not explicitly say this in the text itself, she does imply it. She notes fighting off advances from lesbians during one of her prison stints, but when she acknowledges accepting the favors of another, she doesn't admit or deny involvement. Later in the book she relates the story of a wealthy socialite who is a lesbian and with whom she spent a great deal of time. Again she claims she rebuffed the obsessive advances of the woman, but she goes on to describe what seems to have been a closeted relationship.

There we were, a rich white heiress from Fifth Avenue and a Negro girl from uptown. . . . I could hang around on Fifth Avenue with Brenda and nobody so much as batted an eye—not the uniformed doorman, neighbors, servants, nobody, not even her mother. For all anybody cared, we could have been a couple of college girls out on a field trip studying race relations or some other damn kind of conditions. . . .

> A black chick and a white chick can be married and carrying
> on and everything's cool as far as the what-will-people-think
> people are concerned. (87)

Other historians and critics have confirmed that Holiday befriended respected, wealthy white women, many of whom are known to have been lesbians.

When Holiday talks about her experiences with drugs and the subsequent dealings with the law, she blames no one for her addiction but she does portray herself as someone hunted like an animal by the state. As noted earlier, subsequent readings of Holiday's FBI file show that she was tailed throughout most of her career. While agents knew she was not a big dealer, they thought she might lead them to one, and they felt arresting a high-profile singer would also be good publicity for their efforts to battle illegal drugs.

If Holiday's descriptions of the music making are among the greatest contributions of the text, so too is the picture she paints of the practices of the police and the narcotics bureau. Long before investigations of police corruption and the illegal ways officers deal with black suspects, Holiday tells her readers of police kickbacks, the agreement between police and club owners to wait until the end of the run of her shows before arresting her so that the club owners wouldn't lose a week's revenues. "If they're going to bust you, they always try to wait and do it after you've closed. If somebody is pinched in the middle of the week, club owners and theater managers have a fit; they complain the publicity gives their place a bad name and stuff like that. And the cops are usually very considerate of their feelings. But as soon as your last show is over you're on the street and all bets are off" (123). She is perfectly aware of the relationship of the state to securing the interests of white businessmen.

Holiday also tells of the sexual exploitation of women addicts and prisoners by their captors: "I wasn't too much of a drug addict for some of these federal men not to make passes at me. They might not speak to me in the street, but they'd gladly sleep with me in the Federal Building" (126).

Black men are villains in the court records. In the autobiography white men harass her and the narrative's rescuing hero is a black man, her last husband, Louis McKay. Finally, Holiday closes the narrative by focusing on her marriage to McKay and by asserting that she is now on the right path because of his love. Ironically, this device appears in earlier interviews with Holiday, though the men alternate from Jimmy Monroe to John Levy. In the end, none of these men proved to be the savior she sought.

It is highly likely that Holiday knew this at the time. And yet, the "happily ever after" narrative is so appealing, she continued to pronounce it even as she failed to live it. In this instance Mary J. Blige is right: Holiday did look for her personal salvation outside of herself in relationships with men. In her music, the lyrics she wrote, she gives a less rosy view of her life than that portrayed in her autobiography. The last song Holiday wrote (but did not perform or record) is "Left Alone":

Maybe fate has let him pass me by
Or perhaps we'll meet before I die.
Hearts will open, but until then,
I'm left alone, all alone.

The autobiography isn't about truth telling. Not really. It is about providing an alternative to the one-dimensional Billie Holiday of the popular press. While it does reinforce some of the media myths, it attempts to situate her life in context but nonetheless relies on many of the narrative devices and clichés of the one it seeks to counter. Relying on her songs for a vocabulary to narrate her life limits her within the confines of mainstream conceptions of the world. Consequently, the context she provides differs only in that it shares more about the music and the effect of racism than it does about the men and the drugs.

Lady Di

LADY SINGS THE BLUES, the film, premiered on October 18, 1972, at Loew's State Theater in Manhattan. The *New York Times* article that appeared in the society section the following day described a premiere party that raised $144,000 for the NAACP. A photograph of Roy Wilkins chatting with Gordon Parks accompanied the story. Both gentlemen were in formal attire. Roy Wilkins was the director of an organization deemed out-of-date by the younger Black Power generation. Parks was a well-known photographer for *Life,* a novelist and a filmmaker. Along with Melvin Van Peebles's *Sweet Sweetback,* Parks's most recent film, *Shaft* (1971), opened the way for the genre that has come to be known as "blaxploitation."

Charlotte Curtis, the article's author, characterizes the audience as gate-crashers in the New York society set. Curtis doesn't hesitate to comment upon the price and quality of thrift shop and homemade dresses worn by the women in attendance. This gives us a sense of the times in which the film was released. Hollywood was beginning to recognize the market potential of films with black casts, and an observer of the social elite feels free to write about black people with condescension without fear of reprimand. Both suggest that in spite of gains in civil rights, representations of black people were still stereotypical and not far removed from minstrelsy.

As I indicated earlier, since its publication in 1956, there had been talk of turning Holiday's autobiography, *Lady Sings the Blues,* into a film. Lester Cowan, producer of films, purchased the rights to the autobiography. He planned to shoot it in Puerto Rico. While Holiday was to record the songs for the movie, she was not to be in the film itself. The Baltimore *Afro-American* reported that Holiday might be portrayed by a white actress and quoted Cowan as saying: "My principal concern as producer is to find for the role an actress who can do justice to it." When asked if he had discussed casting with Holiday, he claims she said, "I am not prejudiced."[41] Of course, with a white actress in the role, the story would not have to portray the brutal racism that hounded Holiday throughout her life. While Dorothy Dandridge and her manager made arrangements for her to do the film, eventually there was talk of putting Ava Gardner, who played the mulatta Julie in the film adaptation of *Show Boat,* in the leading role. Later, Lana Turner was considered for the role as well. As absurd as it seems, this would not have been uncommon. The protagonist of the film *Paris Blues* was to have been black, but Paul Newman played the role. In part it is a reflection of Hollywood's inability to imagine black actors in substantive roles. I imagine the Holiday film would have been part of a genre that includes Frank Sinatra's *The Man with the Golden Arm,* and Susan Hayward's *I'll Cry Tomorrow.* On the record, Holiday didn't object to a white actress starring in the film based on her life. However, she is reported to have said, "Even if they get a white actress, the character she plays will still be colored. If they change that, there's no story."[42] White actresses portrayed black women characters in the 1959 version of *Imitation of Life* and the film *Pinky.*

By the militant 1960s, casting Gardner or Turner in the role would have been impossible, so the film was optioned for Abbey Lincoln, and later there was even talk of having Diahann Carroll play the part. There couldn't have been two more different actresses for the role. Lincoln had been a nightclub cabaret singer in the fifties. After she moved to Harlem and married Max Roach, she began to study jazz and change her image and her vocation. Early on, she identified Holiday as a major inspiration and influence. Lincoln made two films, the independent *Nothing but a Man* in 1965 and *For Love of Ivy* (1969). She was considered a new type of black actress-singer: one who was militantly pro-black, who wore her hair natural, and who took her art seriously and chose to be an artist rather than an entertainer. Along with Cicely Tyson and Nina Simone, Abbey Lincoln helped black Americans to create a strikingly different sense of beauty and black womanhood.

At the opposite end of the spectrum of sixties black female stars was Diahann Carroll. In the 1950s Carroll played ingenue roles in such films as *Porgy and Bess* (1959) and *Carmen Jones* (1954), where she portrayed the sweet, cute, girl next door in contrast to the sultry sexuality of Dorothy Dandridge, who starred in both films. Interestingly, during this era Carroll also appeared on Broadway as the epitome of glamour: first in *House of Flowers* (1954) and then in *No Strings,* which Richard Rodgers created for her in 1962. (She won a Tony for the latter.) Throughout the sixties she starred in films like *Paris Blues* (1961), *Hurry Sundown* (1967) and *The Split* (1968). As an actress and vocalist widely accepted by white audiences, she was rejected by younger blacks who believed her to be accommodationist, and hence socially and artistically irrelevant. Carroll was often referred to as a white black woman. She appeared glamorous, wealthy, often romantically linked with white men, and she was a constant on best-dressed lists. She was a star of stage and film whose singing voice was not recognizably "black." She was also the first black woman to have her own national television show, *Julia.* Had she been chosen to perform the role of Billie Holiday, there probably would have been even more protests than those that greeted Diana Ross.

During the same period that Lincoln and Carroll emerged as black film stars, a singing group consisting of three young black women, The Supremes, exploded onto the world stage as the most successful girl group of any race and any era. As pop icons who reached both white and black audiences, the group broke new ground for black women entertainers. Youthful, energetic and glamorous, they were the center of Motown founder Berry Gordy's vision for his record empire. And the focus of his personal and professional attention was a skinny gamine with a small, nasal voice named Diana Ross. So much was she his focus, after their initial success he changed the group's name to Diana Ross and the Supremes. Because Ross fit few of the stereotypes or characteristics associated with black women entertainers, Gordy knew she could cross over musically as well as in performance venue and medium. Ross came to represent a sixties pop glamour, first identified with the danceable tunes of Motown. Her singing voice lacked the power and depth of Aretha Franklin's and later, the bell-like clarity of Roberta Flack.

Not the best singer of the three (that was Florence Ballard), nor the prettiest (that was Mary Wilson), nor the sexiest (Florence again), Ross was ambitious, indefatigable, and she had the ability to make the audience focus on her. On January 14, 1970, Ross performed with the Supremes for the last time, and under the direction of Berry Gordy, launched her solo career. Albums, articles and television specials featuring her as a singer, dancer, comedienne and actress followed.

Berry Gordy felt the film *Lady Sings the Blues* could be the vehicle to help Ross make the transition from pop singer to international superstar. In his autobiography Berry wrote "I told Gil [Askey] to pull her back a notch from Billie Holiday and leave a little Diana Ross in there because her future's got to extend far beyond this picture" (Gordy, 315).

When it was announced that Ross would play Holiday, there was enormous resistance from the public. Understandably, critics doubted her ability as an actress. Holiday fans questioned her ability to render the songs Holiday made her own. Black audiences believed she had not suffered enough to have the emotional depth to render Holiday. Jazz innovator Rahsaan Roland Kirk wrote: "She was fine when she was in the Supremes, but why'd she have to go and ruin my Lady Day dreams?" Furthermore, according to most reports excluding her own, Ross had never even listened to Holiday's recordings.

However, in addition to performing the part of Holiday in the film, Ross recorded eighteen of Holiday's classics and released them on an album titled *Lady Sings the Blues*. While Ross is no jazz vocalist, on this album it is clear that she had indeed studied Holiday's phrasing. The album demonstrates Ross's ability to sing songs other than show tunes or those churned out by the highly successful Motown hit machine.

Though most reviews panned the film, they uniformly praised Ross's performance. Writing in the *New York Times*, Vincent Canby questioned: "How is it possible for a movie that is otherwise so dreadful to contain such a singularly attractive performance in the title role?" (October 19, 1972, p. 56). He described Ross as "an actress of exceptional beauty and wit." Another review in the New York *Daily News* (October 19, 1972, p. 116) reported "Only Diana Ross's performance gives it any real substance. Miss Ross has obviously done her homework, digging down into the lonely depths of the character. . . . She is both comically tough and childishly appealing but she is not, as the ads proclaim, Billie Holiday."

Lady Sings the Blues is not a movie about Holiday. It is a post–Black Power fantasy of a beautiful, talented, but weak and childish woman who is rescued time and again by a strong, supportive, wealthy, handsome black man. When Ross as Holiday is kicking her habit cold turkey in a padded cell, Billy Dee Williams's McKay comes in with a doctor who injects her with something to make the going a little easier, and then her black knight slips an engagement ring on her finger. This is just the incentive she needs to pull through the nightmare. He pays for her time at a sanitarium, he arranges for her to debut at a downtown club, he keeps her supplied with gardenias and he rescues her time and again. None of this ever happened. It is not surprising to learn that McKay—glamorized in the film by the figure of Williams—served as a consultant on the film.

While Holiday variously claimed to have been introduced to the drug by one of two black men, Jimmy Monroe or Joe Guy, in this fantasy, a slimy white pianist is always sneaking around, grinning and trying to get her to try the stuff. Eventually he succeeds in turning Ross's character on to heroin. Black Man good, White Man bad; Black Woman weak and simply in need of the good black man. (The film also includes Richard Pryor, who plays a weak-willed, effeminate, clowning black man, incapable of protecting Holiday.) The Billie Holiday of this film is almost always a victim: raped as a teenager ("not yet fifteen"), arriving as a country bumpkin in Harlem, reluctantly turning to prostitution. In this way it shares much with the conventions of the twentieth-century African-American migration narratives. She is a woman who never makes choices. She is tricked, manipulated and handled.

We get no sense of her as a mature, complex woman. Ross's Holiday just likes to sing. There is nothing about the music making or her relationship to other musicians as collaborator and leader, nothing about her artistic choices, none of her hipness, none of her joy or humor. We get no sense that we are watching the life story of one of the century's most important artists who gained international acclaim.

Surely it would have been impossible for any actress to satisfy those looking for Billie Holiday, but Ross is so very far from her in style, in looks, in temperament, that she immediately crushes those expectations. Consequently, once the comparisons cease, Ross succeeds in rendering a moving performance.

When the film was released it entered a market of more black films than had ever been produced in any one year.[43] Most were blaxploitation films focusing on hustling men, buxom women, drugs and Black Power rhetoric. This was the era that produced Pam Grier, who appeared in scores of films. Scenes of heroin being cut, bought, sold and shot up abound in many of the black exploitation films—so much so that they become clichés. By the time a black viewing audience saw *Lady Sings the Blues,* it was familiar with the visual vocabulary of hypodermic needles, tourniquets and the other accoutrements of heroin use.

Significantly, *Lady Sings the Blues* was also released at the same time as serious films featuring talented, complex black actresses: Rosalind Cash (who would have been extraordinary as Billie Holiday) and Vonetta McGee in *Melinda,* Diana Sands in Maya Angelou's *Georgia, Georgia* and, most significantly, another "new black actress," Cicely Tyson, in *Sounder.* When the Academy Award nominations were announced, both Ross and Tyson were nominated for Best Actress, the first black actresses nominated since Dorothy Dandridge for *Carmen Jones* in 1955. They competed with Liv Ullmann (*The Emigrants*), Maggie Smith (*Travels with My Aunt*) and the winner, Liza Minnelli (*Cabaret*). *Lady Sings the Blues* acquired four other nominations: art direction, set design, musical score, costume design and writing. It won none of these awards (*The Godfather* walked away with the most), but it was an impressive showing for a black film, even by today's standards.

While most viewers have taken seriously the film's portrayal of Lady's tragic life, thereby unnerving those who knew and worked with Holiday as well as most die-hard Holiday fans, I believe the film made an important contribution to Lady's legacy. *Lady Sings the Blues* is significant because it serves as a transition in one lesser-known direction of the trajectory that Holiday helped to initiate.

Billie Holiday was a serious artist who was also a crossover performer with a popular audience. In addition, she not only initiated the trajectory of modern jazz singing, she also opened doors for a cadre of beautiful young black women who sang in nightclubs in front of predominantly white audiences. Consequently, while Carmen McRae, Dinah Washington, Abbey Lincoln, Shirley Horn and Cassandra Wilson are daughters of Holiday's artistic legacy, so too are Lena Horne, Dorothy Dandridge, Leslie Uggams, Diahann Carroll and Diana Ross. When Holiday opened Café Society in 1939, she became the first black woman to do so in a downtown club. There, she appeared nightly, glamorous and "all stillness and quiet fire."[44] Hazel Scott and Lena Horne, both of whom epitomized upper-middle-class, ladylike black entertainers, followed her. Here we see the emergence of a different kind of black woman entertainer. There was the classic blues singer, then the jazz vocalist, epitomized by Holiday, Fitzgerald and Vaughan, and then there were the glamorous, beautiful song stylists whose looks, gowns and stage presence were more important than their voices (Nancy Wilson was the exception) or their ability to improvise. They were usually described as sepia, tan, café au lait, beige, honey or at their darkest a deep caramel. Visually pleasing to a white or racially mixed audience, distant, smoldering but tasteful: Lena Horne in the forties, Dorothy Dandridge, Eartha Kitt in the fifties, Diahann Carroll, Barbara McNair in the sixties and Diana Ross in the seventies.

Ross inherits this legacy, adds to it the flamboyant international spectacle introduced by Josephine Baker, to emerge as the first post–civil rights black female superstar. In fact, the film project most coveted by Ross was the Josephine Baker story (later a star-making vehicle for Lynn Whitfield). Had Ross made this film, her film history would have included roles that brought together both of the legacies of which she is an heir. Even without the second film, just as Holiday was the first of her kind, with the help of *Lady Sings the Blues,* Ross initiated another stylistic direction for black women artists and entertainers.

The film also made a second important contribution to Holiday's legacy. Ironically, resistance to the film inspired a decades-long search for "the Real Billie Holiday" in the form of articles, albums, revisionist biographies and documentaries. In so doing, it unleashed hundreds of new versions of Holiday, making it next to impossible to get back to any "real" or authentic version. At first, Holiday's contemporaries began to issue the call for a corrective to the film. In the Sunday *New York Times,* jazz critic Nat Hentoff wrote: "Very little of [Billie], the one to whom music mattered so deeply, in the current film *Lady Sings the Blues.*" In this article we have one of the earliest attempts to counter the emerging victim narrative. "The current legend of Billie Holiday—the cinematic tale of The Black Lady of the Gardenia, a latter-day Camille who burned her candle at both ends—leaves out the very essence of Lady Day: her music" (*New York Times Magazine,* December 24, 1972).

While many lamented the liberty taken with Holiday's life and while even more criticized Ross's Holiday, the simple fact of the matter is the film probably did more to assure the availability of Holiday recordings than did any prior effort to keep her in the public eye. The success of the movie immediately inspired the reissues of two Holiday compilations, *Strange Fruit* (Atlantic) and *Lady Love* (United Artists). Because of this, younger listeners who had not had access to Holiday's recordings found them available to listen to and to study. Those made curious by the film to find out more about the lady behind the myth were also able to turn to albums that may have previously been unavailable.

My own curiosity about Holiday was piqued by my father. When he died in 1972, the same year the film was released, my curiosity was quenched by the availability of articles and books about her, photographs of her, and reissues of her recordings (all of which were supplied by my mother and aunts upon my request). They were available in large part because of the film. I was allowed to read books and articles about her and to listen to her music because my mother considered these intellectual pursuits. However, she feared the power of the moving image on her daughter's dreamy psyche, so I was not allowed to see the film when it first appeared in theaters. Instead, I saw it on television when I was a teenager. By then, I'd read enough to have my own critique of the film and to distinguish between Diana Ross's performance and what I thought I knew of Billie Holiday's life.

Watching *Lady Sings the Blues* again almost thirty years after its release, I find myself less resistant to Ross in the title role than I was upon my first viewing. Having gotten over the misimpression that this is a film about Lady Day and seeing it instead as a vehicle to showcase Ross, one can appreciate her performance much more. She is stunningly beautiful, and she is a very capable actress. In fact, as reviewers insisted at the time, she is the best thing about this otherwise bad movie. She is in every scene and she manages to carry them well. She rises above a mediocre script and poor direction. I am, however, even more conscious of the low-budget settings juxtaposed with the expensive gowns and the saccharine, fictional love story into which the Holiday/McKay relationship had been turned.

I also value the film because I recognize that by being one of the first black women to have her life portrayed in a feature-length film, Holiday set yet another standard, opened yet another door. Given the dearth of material available to black actresses, the lives of black women entertainers are thought to possess all of the drama and passion actresses seek in their roles. The lives of Josephine Baker, Tina Turner and Dorothy Dandridge have been the bases of dramatic films starring Lynn Whitfield, Angela Bassett and Halle Berry respectively.

All of the works discussed in this chapter—the media coverage of her arrests, her autobiography and the film—are important elements in the history of Holiday's persona. All fight to situate a version of her life as THE version. Even as these versions and counterversions are launched, we are simultaneously both closer to and farther away from Holiday. The characters become clearer, but their roles grow blurry. For example, for biographer Donald Clarke, the lawyer Earl Zaidins was a loyal, beloved friend at the end of Lady's life. For biographer

Stuart Nicholson, Zaidins exploited Holiday by providing her with drugs and forcing her to sign contracts that were not in her interest. The more we claim to pull back layers, the more we expose contradictions and complexity.

Very early in her career, Holiday, like most celebrities, presented versions of her life to the press. As her fame grew, she created a stage persona whose life story we have come to know as the story of Billie Holiday. Stuart Nicholson insists that Holiday's "persona and person [had become] interchangeable, and . . . she had become dominated by her legend." It is because of this conflation of persona and person, because of the domination of the Holiday legacy, that others fear being compared to her and that I fear the tale told by the myths of Lady Day. Perhaps those aspects of her legend that we most fear are not lies but instead dimensions of a larger truth.

Exploring versions of Holiday in an attempt to discover her, I wonder if she was able to maintain a sense of wonder and discovery in the woman who unfolded as the years went along. Ultimately, Billie Holiday was a creative artist who left behind a substantial body of work. While we might hear addiction in the voice as it ages or the failed romances in the rendering of the lyric, always in the work we meet a woman who, through the creative process, discovers and rediscovers herself, time and time again. One need only listen to her various renditions of "God Bless the Child" for evidence of this.

Holiday is listed as the song's cowriter along with Arthur Herzog. She claimed to have written it after a dispute with her mother. Herzog claims she only supplied the title. First recording it for Columbia in May 1941, she would record it numerous times over a period of almost twenty years. The Columbia version is lovely and lyrical. It is light and she sings it more quickly and higher than the other renditions. Lady leaves the listener thinking that it is a statement of independence and empowerment: "He just don't worry 'bout nothing, cause he's got his own," ends on an up note. During a trip to Los Angeles in the spring of 1950, she recorded a version of the song for Decca. Though it is perhaps the best-known version, it is also one of the more controversial.

Ordinarily, Milt Gabler produced her Decca sides, but he didn't accompany her on this trip, so Gordon Jenkins produced it. The version is immediately recognizable because of the string accompaniment and the Gordon Jenkins singers who open it and provide background vocals. Lady's voice is deeper, richer and fuller. The song weighs heavy as her voice tries to establish itself in the midst of the lush arrangement of flutes, strings and other voices. It seems inappropriate. Gabler says "I would have killed the opening." Of Jenkins, Gabler notes, "He had such taste. The only thing he didn't have was a black taste for that intro, and it doesn't belong there." But apparently Lady wanted the strings. She'd heard and liked Charlie Parker's recordings with strings, so this was probably an instance of her wanting to try something different, to place herself outside of the box that had been erected around her as a jazz vocalist. The entire piece doesn't quite work, but we hear a very different story in the lyrics as a result of its setting and of its rendering. There is a live version of the song from a 1953 episode of the television broadcast *Comeback Story*. Here we get Holiday the storyteller. She is accompanied by Jimmy Raney on guitar, who plays beautifully behind her. The voice is not full and she seems to be talking more than singing, which is fitting with the context of the "this is your life" theme of the television show. When she recorded the song for Verve in May 1956, her voice was more raspy but also more wise. It hasn't the upbeat optimism of the Columbia version nor is it the sad dirge of the Decca side. Here she is hip, knowing, sharing a life lesson that seems to say "That's just the way it is." This one was recorded to accompany the release of the autobiography. While in Los Angeles in 1950, Holiday also filmed a short for Universal Studios with members of the Count Basie band. Though the film is staged as a nightclub set and she appears to be lip-synching, it is an extraordinary piece of footage, especially in comparison with the Diana Ross film. During the filming Holiday was reported to have been addicted to heroin, yet there is no evidence of this in her performance. She is beautiful, full bodied and sensual. Dressed in an off-the-shoulder dark satin gown, she is both vocalist and actress. The subtleties of her movement lend to the tale she tells, arm bent just so, finger snapping to keep the rhythm, the raise of an eyebrow, the tilt of her lips, the slight, appreciative bow at the end—all work together to give a fuller sense of Lady Day in performance and a more multidimensional rendering of the way she chose to tell her own tale.

Listening to Holiday's music, especially to more than one version of the same song, lends complexity and depth to the stories told by newspaper reports, biographies, the autobiography, the documentary and the Holiday film. No one of these things gives us a truer, more real Holiday. They do help to create a much stronger sense of who she might have been, and certainly who she continues to be in our own time.

Respectable and refined, an angel walking through the clouds
(or, a smoldering songstress in a smoky nightclub).
(Herman Leonard, 1949)

3

Ebony Lady and the Politics of Respectability

Wisdom . . . is obtainable only by the breaking of a taboo
and . . . the price of knowledge is the end of virginity
and innocence. As with Eve and her apple of knowledge,
Prometheus and his gift of fire [Makeda, Queen of Sheba
and Solomon's riddles], and Pandora and her box, the way to
full human knowing lies through transgression and the body,
through bliss and suffering, through birth and death.

—JANE HIRSHFIELD,
WOMEN IN PRAISE OF THE SACRED

UPON HEARING OF my admiration for Billie Holiday, my elegant and respectable grandmother exclaimed: "That woman was a freak!" I had never heard such language from the mouth of the family matriarch. Of course this made me even more intrigued by the mystery Lady. Apparently, at one time, the two of them, my grandmother and Lady Day, occupied suites at the famous Teresa Hotel in

Harlem. My grandmother never explained why she believed Holiday was a freak but she clearly wasn't talking about physical deformities.

My grandmother and her youngest daughter, my mother, prided themselves on being ladies: feminine, soft-spoken and well groomed. Though they both smoked cigarettes, they never did so in public. (My favorite aunts, however, would light their cigarettes the minute they walked out the door.) On occasion a "damn" or "hell" might slip from their perfect mouths but never, ever the more "vulgar" profanities. They left the room when the other adults listened to Redd Foxx albums. With the exception of an occasional glass of champagne or a fruity mixed drink, they did not drink alcohol. My immediate and extended family respected their status, put them on pedestals, and never swore in front of them. They were admired, respected, protected. Interestingly, they were not churchwomen, nor were they middle class. In fact, my mother was the only one of her sisters never to have worked as a servant in a white woman's home. In that way, she, like Billie Holiday, refused to be "anybody's damn maid." She was one of that first generation of black women to gain employment in the garment industry. Her skill as a seamstress gained her quite a reputation. My mother's talent, along with my aunts' ability to purchase exquisite, quality clothing in second-hand stores and consignment shops, provided all of us with beautiful, fashionable wardrobes.

"Lady"—this was the highest compliment you could pay to these black women, for it was a moniker that had been denied them for so long. "You must be a lady at all times," they instructed me. In their relentless efforts to make a lady out of me, there were constant directions about how I should behave, speak, walk, sit, and dress. They also determined the degree of my involvement with the opposite sex: as little as possible. "Boys and books don't match," was my mother's mantra. Ladylike behavior combined with my intelligence—virginity plus brains—were to be my ticket out, my path to upward mobility.

After I told my mother that my grandmother called Billie Holiday a "freak," I asked, "But why did they call her Lady?" My mother's response: "Because she always carried herself that way in public." What she did in her private life was one thing, but she was always a lady in public. They [white people] didn't treat her that way. They treated her terribly. But we [black people] loved her. "She was so regal."

These encounters with the women in my family, their notions of private versus public behavior, of good girls versus bad girls, of ladies versus freaks, always left me wondering about their obsessions with ladylike behavior and respectability. It also left me questioning the obvious ambivalence toward Billie Holiday. It is good and important that you want to know about her; please don't grow up to be like her.

Any black American writer approaching the subject of Billie Holiday must confront the weighty legacy of "respectability." How do you talk about her in a manner that honors her complexity in a context where negative stereotypes about black women's sexuality continue to justify inequality and oppression? These stereotypes justified the sexual violation of slave women by claiming black women were so sexual it was impossible to rape them. Even today they ensure a man is far less likely to be convicted of raping a black woman than he would be had the victim been white or Latina, and that once convicted, he will serve one half the time he would have served had his victim been a white woman. Such stereotypes allow black women's sexuality to be discussed openly in the halls of Congress as well as academia. They continue to plague us from without and limit our creative and sexual expression from within.

This is the quagmire into which contemporary hip-hop artists (particularly the males who refer to women as "bitches" and "ho's" and the young women who refer to themselves in this way and sing homage to their "ill na na") find themselves stepping. These young people know that the subject matter sells records. They also know that "politics of respectability" can lead to the harshest kind of criticism from black elders and black leaders.

For African-American leaders and intellectuals, the politics of respectability first emerged as a way to counter the images of black Americans as lazy, shiftless, stupid, oversexed and immoral in popular culture and the racist pseudo-sciences of the nineteenth century.[45]

Even earlier than that, as I have mentioned, Thomas Jefferson wrote of the intellectual deficiency of black people and the sexual promiscuity of black women in particular. Today, popular culture portrayals of Jefferson's relationship with his teenage slave Sally Hemings depict her as the flirtatious, coy aggressor. The politics of respectability emerged in a sincere attempt to address the conditions of black people both internally and externally. It marked an attempt to instill dignity and self-respect while also challenging negative, stereotypical images of African Americans. Paradoxically, the more black leaders embraced the politics of respectability to counter racist discourse, the more they conformed to the standards and prejudices of the larger society.

The politics of respectability seeks to reform the behavior of individuals, and as such takes the emphasis away from structural forms of oppression such as racism, sexism and poverty. The logic is as follows: We will get our rights if we prove we deserve them. Positive images of us will ensure a better ground on which to fight for our rights. The politics of respectability was at work during the Harlem Renaissance, when influential intellectuals such as W. E. B. Du Bois and Alain Locke called for fictional portrayals of upstanding, proper middle-class blacks in contrast to representations of the black working class, their blues, their sexuality, their artistic forms.[46] The politics of respectability was at work when civil rights leaders decided not to organize a bus boycott around a young, unwed, pregnant black woman, Claudette Colvin, and instead waited for the proper, hardworking Rosa Parks.[47] In the case of Holiday, the tyranny of the politics of respectability abounds. There is a lovely photograph of Billie Holiday with schoolchildren that was taken while she was in Kansas City in the mid-fifties. On the back of the photograph someone has written "Not the best image at this time." Although the photo is undated, it was probably taken around the time of the NAACP's school desegregation cases.

In other words, the politics of respectability tells oppressed groups to put their best face forward. (The most recent instance of the politics of respectability is evident in the gay movement's shift from calls of sexual liberation to demands for gay marriage and rights to adopt children.) It demands conformity to standards set by the dominant society.

Such a politics fails to recognize the power of racism to enforce itself upon even the most respectable and well-behaved black people. It also polices the unconventional, the nonconformist and the poor.[48] Many members of the black middle class or those with middle-class aspirations are haunted by negative images of the black poor. As much as they protest the racism that allows white Americans to lump all black people together, many also hold the black poor in contempt and disdain for "playing into the stereotypes." The obsession with respectability reveals the fissures and class divisions between the black elite, black middle class, working class and the black poor.

In an ethos governed by the politics of respectability, there is no place for the black bad girl. While she may be tolerated as long as she remains unfamiliar to white Americans (there has always been room for Millie Jackson), her crossover is a threat. Bessie Smith in her day, Little Kim in ours. Interestingly, unlike Bessie Smith or Lil' Kim, Holiday never sang lyrics that could be construed as vulgar. Unlike Lil' Kim or Foxy Brown she never dressed in ways that exposed her body or emphasized her sexuality. Her stage persona was that of a Lady—though a charismatic, sensual one. It was the exposure of her personal woes that proved to be such a problem. However, her personal woes are also what made her seem so vulnerable, so desperately in need of protection. The promise of protection is an extension of the politics of respectability. In this worldview, respectable black women require the protection of masculine black men.

Ebony Lady

IN AN ATTEMPT to counter press reports of her as a low-life junkie, Holiday, her handlers and many subsequent historians of her life and music have tried to fit her into narratives of respectability. However, the politics of respectability leave little room for an individual such as Billie Holiday. Nowhere is this more evident than in an *Ebony* cover story about Holiday. The article utilizes the terms of respectability to present a version of her to the black middle class. In July 1949, seven years prior to the publication of her autobiography, Billie Holiday appeared on the cover of *Ebony*. The article was titled, "I'm Cured for Good," and it fits into the conventions identified above. It represents one attempt at defining a public image of Holiday that both coincides with and yet differs from her more familiar autobiography of 1956. The text and photographs reveal the way that the medium of publication and the intended audience shape the image that Holiday seeks to fashion. The article is an explicit bid for black middle-class respectability.

Founded in 1945 in Chicago by John H. Johnson, *Ebony* magazine asserted itself as the *Life* for black Americans. In many ways it was also the *Ladies Home Journal* for blacks, although it is more politicized than either of those mainstream publications. It featured countless stories of black success—celebrities and their homes, pools and wardrobes; civil rights leaders; black people abroad; stories of racial passing and light-skinned models. In fact, brown- and dark-skinned models didn't find their way into *Ebony* until the mid-sixties. By 1950 the magazine had a circulation of over 500,000 and it reached more black readers than any other publication, black or white.

According to historian Jacqueline Jones, the *Ebony* "brand of image-making" included "its portrayal of women," which hardly reflected the economic status of most black women. In features about female celebrities, "although photographs conveyed the glamour of show business, texts frequently emphasized performers as homemakers." Pianist and wife of Adam Clayton Powell, Hazel Scott, was "a typical housewife" who darned her own stockings. International opera diva Marian Anderson "found peace in her new Connecticut home with her husband." Lena Horne—a favorite *Ebony* cover girl—was "a working mother." In addition to being glamorous homebodies, all of

Billie Holiday with children in Kansas.
(*Library of Congress*)

the women were featured as civil rights activists as well. Since its founding, *Ebony* has been a primary vehicle for the expression of black middle-class aspirations as well as a major vehicle for the articulation of a liberal black civil rights agenda. With its push for domesticity, *Ebony* joins many other American publications of the postwar period.[49]

In the fall of 1947, Holiday pled guilty to drug possession and she was sentenced to one year and a day in the Federal Reformatory for Women in Alderson, Virginia. She was released on March 16, 1948.

Eleven days later, on March 27, 1948, she appeared at Carnegie Hall to a warm, enthusiastic standing-room-only crowd.

On January 29, 1949, she was arrested for possession of opium in San Francisco. She beat those charges, as there was no evidence to link the opium to her. She always contended that narcotics agents had framed her; the jury acquitted her after deciding she had been framed by her lover/manager, John Levy. Subsequent FBI records note that there was "no definite information of any narcotics, but presumed that since they [Holiday and Levy] were together they probably possessed some narcotics." Nonetheless, by all accounts she had begun to reuse heroin.

The *Ebony* story is a clear effort to counter negative publicity, and it follows the narrative design of an earlier article by Larry Newman titled "Lady Day's Comeback," which appeared in the August 1948 issue of *Negro Digest*—also owned by *Ebony* proprietor John H. Johnson. The Newman piece documents her "fall from grace, her addiction, and her cure culminating in her Carnegie concerts" (Nicholson, 170). Unlike the Newman article, the *Ebony* article is written in the first person. Nonetheless, it is highly unlikely that Holiday wrote it. Throughout her career Holiday agreed to sell the story to various tabloids and black publications. These articles were often written in the first person. It is in this context that we must read the *Ebony* article.

The photographs that accompany the article are selected from several publicity stills and previously published images. The first group of images creates the visual story. The largest is a disembodied image of Holiday's head floating above the text; it dominates the page. She appears with very respectable, conservative makeup, a fashionable head of short curls—there is no false ponytail nor the gardenia for which she had become famous. Thus, the look of artifice associated with show people is gone.

Beneath this photo there are four others. The first, a reproduction of Holiday being awarded an *Esquire* music award from Arthur Godfrey early in her career—the *Ebony* caption reads "Peak of Career" and notes her best-known song, "Strange Fruit," as "moving." The image invokes Holiday during a moment of accomplishment and her recognition by white institutions and celebrities. Furthermore, by citing the anti-lynching song "Strange Fruit," the caption links her to the tradition of black art as protest against American racism and identifies her as a spokesperson against racial terrorism.

Later, there are photographs of Holiday with such jazz luminaries as Louis Armstrong as well as the photo of the fur-clad Holiday at her arraignment with John Levy. The caption beneath it succinctly covers her downfall and her triumphant return: "Jailed for using heroin, Billie was sentenced to a year and a day in federal reformatory. She was released with 72 days off for good behavior. Gained 30 pounds in prison, gave concert of 32 songs at Carnegie Hall 11 days after release."

The last photo in this part of the spread features a series of Herman Leonard photographs, staged shots of Holiday and her dog, the boxer Mister, seated in domestic bliss in front of a fireplace as dog and mistress pretend to read a magazine. The caption reads: "Anxious for peaceful home life, Billie resents hounding of narcotics agents. She spends much time reading in off-hours. She prefers light fiction, reads comic books by the dozen. She cares for Mister, 4-year-old boxer, with motherly solicitude." It appears the dog stands in for the child that Holiday tells readers she wants and also the ominous "hounds," the agent dogs at the door.

Peppered throughout the rest of the article are photographs showing Holiday with "second husband" John Levy and Dickie Wells. Because Levy, whom Holiday never married, looks white, the article stresses that he is her manager and that she believes it important to have a black manager. Again, the fur-clad Holiday of this photograph appears the epitome of sophisticated glamour. In contrast to the earlier photo, where white officers surround her, here she sits safely ensconced between two protective and prosperous-appearing, light-skinned black businessmen.

In the accompanying article Holiday speaks little of her artistry, using phrases like "sing my heart out" and "sing the songs that people like to hear." These are in striking contrast to the highly descriptive musical passages that characterize the autobiography. Her *Ebony* audience includes many individuals who do not appreciate the music she sings and some who have a great deal of ambivalence toward and even disdain for it. This ambivalence and disdain were born of a desire to distance themselves from the sources that gave birth to and nurtured the music. Jazz was often associated with brothels, jazz musicians with drugs and other things deemed negative. Other readers of *Ebony* were probably jazz fans because the jazz of the thirties was America's popular music—swing. Billie Holiday gained notice while singing with two swing bands in the thirties, Count Basie's and Artie Shaw's. For these readers, she would have been remembered as a rising star of that era.

Instead of focusing on the music, the article engages in a kind of written testimony. (In the African-American religious tradition, testifying is the practice of publicly narrating the low point of one's life and God's power and grace in bringing you through the dark times.) "Sure I made a mistake, a serious one, and I paid for it. Being on a drug habit is a fantastically costly predicament. In the year preceding my imprisonment, I spent an average of $500 each week to satisfy this deadly craving." She describes the conditions of her incarceration: "It was strictly the 'cold turkey' treatment, and let me tell you it was rough. The first 19 days were sheer hell for me." Out of this experience she even becomes more committed to fighting racism. Alderson was segregated, and Holiday says: "I came out of that place with a greater determination to fight against discrimination." *Ebony* Lady stresses that she has paid her dues and is ready to earn respect both "as an artist and as a woman," and she wants to earn her living.

However, she is confronted with obstacles that make earning this respect difficult: "There have been barriers placed in the way of my return to my profession and obstacles thrown up to revert my living again as a free citizen in this great democracy of ours." Here Holiday affirms one of the missions of the young magazine. *Ebony* is a publication born of the Great Migration—that massive movement of African Americans into Northern, urban centers—and the political optimism that characterized the aspiring and emerging Northern, urban black middle class. Having participated in the War for Democracy, they have come back to a civic life that refuses to extend the basic tenets of democracy to black citizens. They stand poised to initiate a new phase of the civil rights movement—through the courts, through legislation and through direct action. As such they call into question the nation's commitment to an egalitarian democracy. Holiday taps into this when she says:

> I wanted a new home somewhere in the country close to New York; I wanted to escape from the old, oppressive environment which had caused so much tragedy in my life; I wanted to buy a complete new wardrobe and see how I would look in the New Look. I wanted to enjoy a quiet home life, to enjoy the pride of motherhood. . . . Above all I wanted to work, to sing my heart out and make people happy.

The list of middle-class accoutrements—suburban home, new clothing, "quiet home life," motherhood—includes all of the things that are praised and paraded in the pages of *Ebony*. Motherhood is central to many early *Ebony* articles. For example, in 1947 the magazine published an article titled "Good-bye Mammy, Hello Mom," heralding the day when black women could leave domestic service and take care of their own families, even though large numbers of them continued to be employed as domestics. Finally, when Holiday says she wanted to escape from her old oppressive environment, she seems to be assuring readers that she wanted to leave that low life, the life of negative images, of fast women, hustlers and drugs.

The closing paragraphs describe the routes Holiday has taken to get to her present state. First, she contacts a Catholic priest for spiritual guidance. We might read this as "I refound Jesus." Then she says, "I spent some $30,000 on new clothes, gowns and a wonderful fur coat. I bought a new Cadillac, sleek and pea green. I bought a little piece of land in Morristown, New Jersey, and started to build my 'dream house' there." Religion, consumerism and private property are the epitome of the American dream.

Nonetheless, just as this talented black woman reaches the American dream, evil forces intervene in an effort to destroy her. This, of course, is a familiar tale to her audience. The federal narcotics agents, local police and drug peddlers harass her. Most significantly she is denied a cabaret card, and thus a major way to make a living. Furthermore, like Judas, "certain Negro newspapers forgot their responsibility as public institutions and dreamed up some pretty fantastic yarns. They made some grim predictions about my future. It was rumored that I was 'back on the stuff,' that I couldn't stay away from it and was doomed to a life of drug addiction." Readers familiar with black autobiography, and especially the slave narratives, will recognize this sequence of events: the narcotics agents like the fugitive slave agents of old and the black newspapers and dope peddlers like those blacks who gave information to slave catchers for their own benefit.

All of this drives Holiday to contemplate suicide, but visions of her mother ("My mother's face came back with all of its sweetness and Christian strength"), the love of her audiences, the intervention of a psychiatrist, and John Levy, her lover/manager, help her to overcome such tendencies.

Although friends, acquaintances and biographers tell of Levy's cruelty to Holiday, his physical and psychological abuse of her and his use of drugs to control and manipulate her, here she says: "In John Levy, my personal manager, I have a wonderful loyal friend who has stood by me through all my recent trials. I have turned over my entire life to him and I think he is managing it all right. I don't know how I'd have survived without his help and guidance. He knows what I want. I feel that other performers of my race who want to get to the top should have a Negro manager." (Ironically, a *Down Beat* article of July 15, 1949 [the same month of this *Ebony* story] reported: "Broke and alone after her manager, John Levy, left her to face the trial here at which she was acquitted, Billie Holiday decides to go back to work." This certainly is not the image of Levy painted in the *Ebony* story.)

The article closes with the following lines: "I want peace of mind. I want to sing. I want a home of my own. I think I have picked out the right man to share it with. Is that asking too much of life? I don't think so. It's what every woman wants." This is very similar to the way her autobiography ends. Holiday always expressed the desire for a conventional domestic life.[50]

Interestingly, around the same time as the *Ebony* article came out, a similar newspaper story written by Wambly Bald appeared as well. Here we have the same vocabulary used in the *Ebony* article but with an interesting twist: "I bought a piece of land last week, and it's right next to the Tuckers [Bobby Tucker]. It'll be my first own home, and do you know who'll be in it? My husband, Jimmie Monroe." She continues, "We got separated three years ago and he scrammed down to California, but he's just come back and looked me up, and we are going to be together and we're to have a home and a baby and contentment."[51]

The Holiday of the *Ebony* article is written into the history of persecuted black people. She becomes the black woman who is born again into a life of middle-class respectability. However, as is the case with many middle-class blacks, she continues to be plagued by racism, police harassment and a continued connection to those who insist on remaining in the low life. Holiday calls out for sympathy and empathy. The letters to the editor that appear in following months suggest she was successful. However, because *Ebony* always seems to have had an editorial policy of publishing only positive commentary, we do not know if they received any adverse mail.

The *Ebony* article was part of an effort to regain and broaden Holiday's audience and to gain a base of support in the black community. No such article appeared in the mainstream white press. Holiday did have a popular following, especially after the release of her more pop-oriented torch songs on the Decca label (1944–49). However, that following certainly was not as large as that of Frank Sinatra (who subsequently admitted her influence on him) and later, Peggy Lee (whom it is said Billie Holiday disliked for her blatant imitation of her).

During this time Holiday seems to have addressed a white audience in print only in the jazz press. These readers were the hipsters, whites who were themselves just a little left of mainstream America. For instance, following her arrest in 1947, Holiday consented to an interview in *Down Beat*. The interview opens with a quotation from Holiday: "When you are writing, straighten them out about my people. Tell 'em I made my mistake, but that show people aren't all like that. Whatever I did wrong, nobody else but me was to blame—and show people aren't wrong. . . . Sure I know about Gene Krupa—but don't forget he's white and I am a Negro. [Krupa was a white drummer whose arrest for possession of drugs was highly publicized.] I've got two strikes against me and don't you forget it. I'm proud of those two strikes. I'm as good as a lot of people of all kinds—I'm proud I'm a Negro. And you know the funniest thing: the people that are going to be hardest on me will be my own race." She ends the interview, "Don't forget, though. I just want to be straight with people, not have their sympathy." In this quotation, Holiday rejects victim status. She wants respect, not pity. Interestingly, her "people" are artists and entertainers, not necessarily black people. It is quite significant that she thinks black people will be hardest on her.

The *Ebony* article is Holiday's attempt to address these black people. It seems to be an unspoken rule for black celebrities: When you experience scandal, come back to the black community. One is here reminded of similar efforts by celebrities as diverse as former Miss America Vanessa Williams, following the publication of nude photographs of her in *Penthouse,* Michael Jackson following allegations of child sexual abuse, and O.J. Simpson following his notorious trial for the murder of his wife and her friend. Prior to the scandals that engulfed their lives, all three of these celebrities distanced themselves from black Americans and had been identified by mainstream Americans as persons who transcended race. Following the scandals that plagued them, all three made highly publicized visits to black public events and black institutions. Many black people were willing to forgive them in light of what appeared to be racist condemnations of them. I think that the community also has a sense that the allegations of these scandals brought celebrities down to earth, reminded them that there is no transcendence of race in the U.S. It is important to note that unlike the celebrities listed above Holiday never, ever distanced herself from black people. Instead, the comparison is only to demonstrate the role of the black press and other black institutions in helping "fallen" black celebrities gain support from black people. Perhaps Washington mayor Marion Barry is a better comparison. Both Barry and Holiday were scorned by many middle-class blacks; both maintained a sense of identification with and loyalty toward working-class and poor black people who identified with their plight and with the harassment they suffered from police.

Black institutions such as *Ebony,* the NAACP Image Awards and now the television channel BET are prime locations for fallen celebrities to rescue their public images and gain black audience support. In Holiday's case, it is especially significant that she agreed to have her handlers participate in the construction of this *Ebony* Lady—the persecuted middle-class black woman.

The *Ebony* article attempts to manipulate an alternative image of black women as ladies, homemakers and race women. This is an image built in opposition to the mammy, the beautiful, sensual but tragic mulatta, the domineering, angry Sapphire, and perhaps the most modern and enduring of these, the black female drug addict.

However, as is clear from this article, the Lady image is also very confining, for it allows only for a Holiday who is first and foremost a homemaker, who prefers a life of taking care of her husband and longs for children and a suburban home. While all of this may in fact have been true, there is no room whatsoever for the woman who also happens to be a highly gifted jazz artist, who prefers the fast life, who indulges in her appetite for pleasure, and who practices and refines her artistry not simply as entertainment but as a form of creative expression. As is the case in most constructions of the lady—whether she be a middle-class black woman or a white Southern belle—the pedestal is high. The terms of staying on top are set by those who create and define it, not by she who occupies it.

Billie Holiday was not one to maintain the pretense of "respectability." Yet she was not unaware of her deviation from the "good" image, even as she seemed to revel in aspects of her bad girl reputation. While many "respectable" people may have found her an embarrassment, the black poor and working class, particularly, identified with and claimed her as their own. Critic Clyde Taylor remembers seeing her at the Apollo when he was a child: "Billie was ours; she belonged to us."[52]

Lady in G-flat

ON MONDAY, August 22, 1955, Billie Holiday, pianist Jimmy Rowles and bassist Artie Shapiro met at Shapiro's home in Los Angeles to rehearse prior to an August 23 recording date. Both Rowles and Shapiro were white musicians who worked with Holiday throughout her career. Rowles first worked with her in 1942, and he continued to be one of the most well respected pianists, especially among singers until his death. Norman Granz, who produced Holiday's recordings for Verve during the last third of her life, hired Rowles to accompany her on the recording date.[53]

As Rowles tells the story, he retrieved a drunken Holiday from her hotel room so that they could rehearse, "set the keys and figure out if there was anything special she wanted to do with the chords."[54] He took her to Shapiro's home because he knew there was a piano there. According to Rowles, neither he nor Holiday realized Shapiro had turned on the tape recorder. Portions of the rehearsal tape first surfaced in 1973; they were later reproduced on the Paramount album *Billie Holiday: Songs and Conversations*. The recording is now available on *The Complete Billie Holiday on Verve 1945–1959*, produced by Phil Schaap. Though not entirely unmediated (it is edited, sequenced, transcribed and interpreted by Phil Schaap), the tape is perhaps the closest we get to Holiday in her own words, her own voice, her own shaping of her tale. In this tape she comes forth as a figure quite different from the tragic songstress of her autobiography or the bourgeois matron of *Ebony* Lady.

Here, hers is the grainy voice of a woman who has spent a lifetime in the fast lane, seeking pleasure, drinking and smoking till dawn. It is a voice that is street-smart yet loving, at times vulnerable and self-doubting and most often in control—clapping out rhythms, setting the key, directing the other musicians, as leader, collaborator and peer. Here is a Holiday who talks, shares stories, gives her personal history, plays with her dog.

The conversation between Shapiro, Rowles and Holiday is wide ranging and gives insight into yet another Holiday. Much of the quarreling between her and Rowles might be attributed to the nature of the relationship between accompanist and vocalist: there are negotiations concerning who is in charge, who leads and who follows.[55] In a later interview Rowles said: "When Lady made those 78s with Teddy Wilson, she was just a vocalist. The records were issued under Teddy's name, and she only sang a chorus. But on the records we made together she was the artist—even though she just acted like one of the guys."[56] Later in the interview, he notes "She was just like a sister." Clearly, the two musicians came to this rehearsal with a history, a shared past, an affection for each other, and a sense of her seniority.

Early in the tape Holiday runs through a version of "Nice Work If You Can Get It." Afterwards the musicians discuss the approach to the song:

SHAPIRO: You got Jimmy working in that key you know.

HOLIDAY: Yeah.

ROWLES: You goddamn bitch, you've come up with the god-awfulest key in life.

Here, taken out of context—away from the responses of the other musicians that precede and follow it, taken from the run-throughs that try to pin down what it is that she has just done, some hear an abusive statement, said by a white man to Lady Day. We who are familiar with the history of black women in the United States, those of us who have witnessed the popular culture representations of the power dynamics between slave and master, stereotypical Southern sheriff and black man or woman, representations that are by now clichés, will hear this as inappropriate and disrespectful, to say the least. We can even construct our own narrative around it, one that is familiar, that we know from our image of big white overseers, Klansmen, Southern jailers, state troopers, those who yell "black bitch" to a cowed and bowed black woman. She—head down, lacking dignity, accepting the abuse as though she has come to believe she deserves it. For us, it's enough to bring tears to our eyes, to make us pick up a gun and kill the "cracker."

Maybe . . .

But let's keep listening, just a little while.

Shapiro tells Rowles, "That's all right, it's a good key, I like that key." Then Lady says "and write the lyrics out too, underneath of that, because I won't remember it tomorrow. . . . See, I'll be in a different mood." And Rowles responds, "Well, we'll make it." She sings a few phrases, he tries to notate it and they move on through "Mandy Is Two," "Prelude to a Kiss" and "I Must Have That Man."

Now, what are we to do with that? Of course, those of us who are less familiar with the playful banter and colloquialisms of jazz musicians might think "So what, he ain't had no business calling her a bitch." But I am less interested in Rowles here. What are we to do with the Lady? I am not entirely inclined to believe that she is like an abused child who has come to accept the abuser's definition of her.

The politics of respectability—that paradigm that insists members of oppressed groups need always put the best face forward, especially in racially mixed company—would have us dismiss her as either abused victim or as a vulgar low-life. There is no other space within the confines of respectability for a woman who in this instance might be neither lady nor victim, for a woman who doesn't skip a beat, who does not ask for or seek protection. Let's listen a little more.

She runs through "Jeepers Creepers" three times with Rowles, telling him "You can speed it up here with the rest of the cats." She snaps it out, claps when he doesn't get it. As he struggles with it, she turns to Shapiro and says:

> You know, when I met this cat, he was a little goddamn boy, scared to death—out there at the Trouville. He was a little boy, a little goddamn, little piss-ass boy, and he wasn't scared to go through a man, so what is this shit now? . . . He was a little piss-ass and you know. And he was a gray, you know. Me and Lester put the eye on him right away. Lee's thing. And you know, sure, be like that now . . . I forgot there was another colored cat who played piano at that time. Lester had eyes for him, you know, and for Red. And this cat was sitting there, always with them dark glasses on, you know. We couldn't even seen how he looked.

Having urged Rowles to take charge of the session, she now accuses him of not stepping up to the plate to her satisfaction. She then puts him in his place. She was a 27-year-old seasoned musician in 1942 when they met, and he was "a goddamn boy, scared to death . . . a little goddamn, a little piss-ass boy"—21 years old. Then she reads him: "And he wasn't scared to go through a man, so what is this shit now?" A reference to his sexuality, perhaps? She says he was gray—a white boy—she calls him Red.

They go on, he gives her the key and says, "I'll play in this key." Later Rowles says "You sing in G-flat all the time. You know that? She sings in G-flat. . . . It's a beautiful key. I wish I'd been playing it in the last year."

Now here we are, back to where we started—back to the key, to that which makes her unique, that which challenges those around her, and when they get where she is taking him, he realizes it's a beautiful place. A place where he wishes he had been artistically.

My friend musician/composer Salim Washington tells me G-flat is one of the hardest keys in which to play, especially for those who are used to playing in the key of C or the C-major scale. However, the key has a long history with blues and jazz musicians. Washington says G-flat is an especially difficult key for those who learned to play by reading music as opposed to those who learn to play by ear. "This opposition between literacy and orality is significant in this case because those who learn to play by reading music invariably learn from a paradigm which contains no sharps or flats: the key of C. Those who learn to play by ear, depending upon their instrument, do not necessarily (and most certainly not invariably) learn from a paradigm key."[57]

Furthermore, he feels that musicians who play by ear (particularly those who come from a black church tradition) "not only do not find one key easier or harder than another, they are able to transpose (that is, switch a song from one key to another) instantly" and without the difficulty experienced by musicians who are trained by reading music. Holiday did not sing in the church, but she did learn by ear, and many of the musicians with whom she apprenticed first started playing in black churches.[58]

Bill Lowe, another scholar/musician/composer, concurs. Lowe notes that Rowles, who is an experienced jazz musician, should have been aware of what Lady was doing, should have recognized the key. In fact, she might even have been in the key of C and simply decided to glide into an unexpected G-flat before returning to C.[59] In this instance the G-flat would be the flatted or diminished fifth—the blue note. This is the beauty of much of Billie Holiday's music: it's in the anticipation. She never goes where we expect her to go. When she shifts to G-flat, we sit in hushed anticipation. Is she going to return to the key of C or is she going to a whole new scale?

Granted, this must be somewhat frustrating for an accompanist. In a later interview, Rowles explains, "She used to come up with some awful keys—six flats unfurnished." Pianist and musicologist Guthrie Ramsey notes that Rowles's choice of the word "unfurnished" suggests lacking adornment or smoothness. There is something rough and raw, something impoverished in these notes.[60]

However, for a group of musicians who are on the same page, this shift to the key of G-flat might even be expected. In fact, the jazz version of "Nice Work" is often played in this key. For Washington, G-flat is a "very dark and lush" key. And here, in this setting, at this rehearsal, it is the key of Lady Day. Eventually the mood shifts, the two musicians caress each other through their work, she bringing him along to a special dark-and-lush place.[61]

When they get to "I Don't Want to Cry Anymore," she encourages Rowles: "You ain't got one part that's kind of puzzling you, and it's hard, Jack. This is a hard tune, that's why nobody fuck with it." She goes over it with him until he is where she wants to be. "I love the changes here, she got you playing it," Shapiro tells Rowles.

After he gets the key right, Holiday tells him about the mood, about how she wants him to swing:

> I want that son-of-a-bitch jumpin' because you know
> everybody else would make it pretty, you know. I want, I
> want to tell that cat "I don't want to cry; it's all I can do
> every time I pass by your house I want to throw a stink

bomb at that son-of-a-bitch." You have to live with my tunes. When I sing a song, it's got to mean something to me.

She tells him, and by extension us: Listen not only to what I sing, but how I sing it. This ain't no longing and missing you, sitting at home. No, this is I am violently pissed, I want to enact violence on you for fucking with me.

In other words, in the rehearsal—unlike the interviews in which she performs idealized versions of herself, or published writing attributed to her—in the creation of the music, you get Lady in her complexity, which spills over the categories that have been created for her. Throughout the rest of the rehearsal, the two musicians work together as collaborators in an atmosphere of mutual respect and friendship. At one point, toward the end of the tape, Rowles begins to reassure Holiday about her voice. When they discuss "Ghost of a Chance," she says, "Picked you another hardy, didn't I? But I like it." To which Rowles replies, "Well, it's an easy song, but the key is kind of rough, you know."

> HOLIDAY: Yeah, that's what I mean; me and my old funny keys. That's what I'm talking about.

> ROWLES: That's all right. Love that key. I just haven't been playing it.

> HOLIDAY: I'm telling you, me and my old voice, it just go up a little bit and come down a little bit. It's not legit. I do not got a legitimate voice. This voice of mine's a mess, a cat got to know what he's doing when he plays with me. (*Laughter*)

> ROWLES: Well, know what I'll do see, I'll scribble these changes down and we'll all be straight.

In the recordings following the rehearsal, Rowles and Holiday make beautiful music together. He is actually one of her best accompanists; in all likelihood because they were both talented professionals who also had a trusting personal relationship.

NOW, WOULDN'T IT BE NICE if the story came to an end here, with two musicians who love and admire each other? Well, not one to believe in nice, neatly tied closures, I don't want to end here in 1955. With a figure like Holiday, it is never that simple.

Let us fast-forward to 1994. The rehearsal tape is available on the CD. In the academy, Harvard historian Evelyn Brooks Higginbotham has published her book *Righteous Discontent,* which defines the reasons for and pitfalls of "the politics of respectability." Black feminists have challenged the field of African-American Studies for adhering to a "politics of respectability." Black lesbians have challenged heterosexual black feminists for adhering to heterosexist paradigms. Scholars of the black left have challenged the field for adhering to elitist forms of analysis. We witness the emergence of a more inclusive form of scholarship. At the level of popular culture we have a frontal assault on the politics of respectability in the form of "gangsta rap," and even Janet Jackson takes her clothes off and sings of sex. Both gangsta rap and the tradition of black women, from the classic blues singers to Millie Jackson, eventually lead the way for female rappers like Lil' Kim and Foxy Brown, who flaunt the sexuality of their stage personas in ways Billie Holiday never would have imagined.

I read an interview with Jimmy Rowles that accompanies the Verve collection. In it Rowles expressed regrets over the availability of the tape. "I've only listened to that tape once. I was disgusted that it was released because Billie was pretty loaded and it seemed like I was trying to catch up with her. She had gone through a whole bottle of vodka before I could get her dressed." He seems somewhat protective, concerned about her reputation but also, and perhaps especially, concerned about his own. He asserts that he was an experienced and skilled professional. He had no problem keeping up with her musically—in fact, he had to get her together. Or is he saying that the tape makes it seem like he was on his way to the same state of intoxication that she inhabits? Surely all of this is probably true.

Holiday on my mind, I tell my friend Cornel West that I want to write a book on her, and he encourages me to do so and then says, "You know, I just read about this new biography that was recently published about her."

"You mean O'Meally's?"

"No, this is supposed to be the definitive biography. I haven't read it yet."

I look and look for the book, and of course it has not yet been published in the U.S. but the ever-cosmopolitan Dr. West sends me a review of it that appeared in the *London Review of Books*. I run to Borders on Walnut Street in Philadelphia and place an order for Donald Clarke's *Wishing on the Moon*.

Donald Clarke's *Wishing on the Moon* is the most highly problematic of the three recently published biographies of Billie Holiday. It is fundamentally a decent biography, but it is deeply flawed by its author's obsession with every minute detail of Holiday's sexuality and drug use. Clarke's closing pages are illustrative of this tendency and contribute greatly to the book's problems. Clarke decides to give the last word of the biography to our "little piss-assed boy," Jimmy Rowles. Why, I still don't know, but he does nonetheless. Rowles relays a story of one of the last times he saw Lady Day. She is loud and foul-mouthed and probably drunk. They purchase Chinese food and then he accompanies her home. And then:

> I get her in the car, take her home, get her into her room, put her into bed, tuck her in with her food—"There's your shrimp, your foo young, you've got it all here. Now you're straight, now good night, you lovely bitch. (*Kiss.*) Talk to you

tomorrow; now eat your goddamn food, drink the rest of your gin." Then she'd get coy. She's in bed, and her titties are sticking out and all that shit. "Louis is out of town, you know." I know it. I wouldn't ball her, because I wouldn't spoil it for anything. I'll fuck her after I die. If I'm playing for them, I don't want to be fucking them. Oh, I did it a couple of times, but that was different. That wasn't permanent.

With Lady Day, you thought permanent.[62]

That's it. The last word; followed not by analysis or discussion but by the index. Here we have the last word given to Jimmy Rowles—a white male musician;[63] locker room narrative legitimized by its privileged space in a biography, "a definitive one" written by a foremost "authority" on jazz, published by a major press, and widely reviewed in the most prestigious literary publications. It is this, more so than Rowles's statement (though I do wonder why a man who claims to have loved her would have felt compelled to tell this story), that I find most offensive. Furthermore, Leslie Gourse chooses to close her valuable *Billie Holiday Companion* with the Rowles selection as well, thereby further reenforcing its power in defining Holiday.

Once again, the question of cultural politics and Holiday's legacy is much larger than the relationship between two individuals, Holiday and Rowles. Clarke's authorial choice to end his book this way suggests that he is particularly invested in providing a voyeuristic glance into her sexual habits and her drug addiction at the expense of her musical legacy. What might it have meant for him to end the book on a musical note instead?

IF THOSE OF US who write about black people insist on ridding ourselves of the oppressive politics of respectability, we must create a viable alternative—an alternative that would have us not rush to the defense of Lady Day by proving what a lady the "real" Billie Holiday was. Instead, we need an alternative that is aware of the workings of history and power that have defined us for the world, and to some degree for ourselves. We cannot replace the politics of respectability with paradigms that see every act of nonconformity or transgression as resistance. It means that our analyses need always be accompanied by a historically informed structural critique of the very things that called a politics of respectability into being—violent physical, religious and intellectual assaults on our humanity. If the politics of respectability still polices us intraracially, it does so because of the larger overarching structures that continue to oppress us externally.

Analyses informed by these factors allow us to call Billie Holiday by the name she preferred: "Lady." This is a term that is constantly redefined, and as such, it is historically determined. In its truest form it is a title of social distinction: a woman of property, rank or authority, of supreme social position, of refinement. This does not mean that the woman does not swear or drink or have lovers. We need only recall the antics of any number of "Ladies" from the House of Windsor to testify to this. Perhaps, Lady Day challenges us to redefine the term away from its basis in class ranking—to instead define it as a woman who earns the title by living up to her potential, by sharing with the world what God has given her, and being generous enough to take us along for the journey.

Holiday once told William Dufty, "Many a time I had the last word in a dressing room argument when I went onstage, threw out the list of songs I was supposed to do, and told the piano player to start off with 'Ain't Nobody's Business If I Do.' This is more than a song to me; it spells out the way of life I have tried to live, personal freedom, to hell with the what-will-people-think-people and all that." Of course, later on in the lyrics she sings, "I swear I won't call no coppa if I'm beat up by my papa," and "I'd rather my man would hit me, than for him to jump up and quit me. Ain't nobody's business if I do." These are phrases that haunt those of us who want to view her as a strong, independent black woman. Later artists such as Dianne Reeves revise these lines. Reeves sings, "I know my man better not think about hittin' me." But Holiday's persona is a woman who would suffer the abuse of her mate rather than lose him or call for state intervention. The song, like Holiday, forces us to reckon with her contradictions as well as ours.

"NEW MUSICAL EXPRESS"
LTD.
present (by arrangement with Harold Davison)

BILLIE HOLIDAY

AND

JACK PARNELL & HIS ORCHESTRA
Royal Albert Hall — Sunday, Feb. 14, 1954

Program book from Holiday's appearance at Royal Albert Hall, London.

(From collection of Jack Surridge)

4

European Holiday

LTHOUGH I HAVE long been a student of African-American culture and history, I pursued much of my education on my own or under the guidance of nonacademic intellectuals. As a college student at Harvard, my formal study of my people began. At that time, in the early eighties, there were few courses devoted to the intellectual and creative work of African Americans, and even fewer were devoted to black women. Classes that claimed to survey American life still often omitted people of color. After all, this was the beginning of the canon wars. Fortunately for me the esteemed historian Nathan Huggins taught history and Werner Sollors introduced me to nineteenth-century texts by black writers other than Frederick Douglass. Eileen Southern, the only black woman on the faculty, taught courses in black music, and extraordinary visitors and speakers made themselves available to curious young thinkers.

Visiting scholars helped to round out a strong core curriculum in African-American studies. One such scholar was the French literary historian Michel Fabre. In Fabre's class we encountered the myriad number of black intellectuals, activists and artists who found audiences, appreciation and inspiration in Europe. According to one version of the story, white Europeans were less prejudiced against black Americans, although they maintained a disdain for the people of color from lands they'd colonized. Still, they seemed less guilty of the white supremacist assaults on black beauty, intelligence and morality. Although this view of the relative innocence of Europeans was questionable, it certainly did seem that they were more welcoming and appreciative of the contributions of black Americans. And yet, as I have since found in my travels throughout the world, Europeans (and Asians and Africans) cannot help but share some of the misconceptions of white Americans because they are most often the purveyors of information about us. For my final paper in Fabre's class, I wrote an essay titled "Paris Noir: Black Women in the City of Light." I wanted to include Holiday, but at the time there was little information on her Paris visit. In her autobiography she favored the British over the French.

Nonetheless, when I was 22, a place where a black woman could find appreciation for her much-maligned beauty as well as her intellect seemed worth checking out. Josephine Baker and Nina Simone had gone to France; Barbara Chase Riboud and Andrea Lee were living in Italy; there was talk that Tina and Chaka were moving to England. And, yes, Lady had gone as well. Consequently, a month following my graduation from college, I left for Paris with $500 and a return ticket. Almost a decade later, this book provided me an opportunity to return to Paris and to my interest in Holiday's European travels. In April 1996 the W. E. B. Du Bois Institute at Harvard and the Collegium for African American Research, an organization of European scholars, sponsored a conference on black music in Europe. "April in Paris" was held at the Sorbonne. Research for my presentation revealed the importance of European, particularly British, intellectuals to writings and analyses of Holiday's life and work.

One work that continues to influence contemporary perceptions of Holiday is John Jeremy's documentary *The Long Night of Lady Day,* this but one of the latest representations of Holiday to come from Britain. To watch *The Long Night of Lady Day* is to witness a parade of white male authorities, many of whom were men who actually controlled Billie Holiday's career throughout her life. There are other voices, of course, including a young Michele Wallace, a black feminist who did not know Holiday; Sylvia Syms, Holiday's close friend; Alice Vrbsky, her maid throughout the last days of her life; and a priest, Father Peter O'Brien, who later managed jazz musician Mary Lou Williams and who speculates on Holiday's Catholicism.

But for me, it is the white men who stand out. They are so knowing, so authoritative. Even though I am sure some of them were friends who helped her out on occasion, their authority angers me. Leonard Feather, Earl Zaidins, Milt Gabler and John Hammond. The only one missing is Joe Glaser, her manager. For years I have been uneasy about this documentary because of the preponderance of white male authority.

And yet when I first saw it during my final year in graduate school, it was a documentary that fed my hunger for Billie Holiday. It finally offered an alternative to Berry Gordy's film and, most important, it provided live footage of Lady Day in performance. For those of us who never saw her in person, live footage is the closest we will get to seeing her perform. Until Robert O'Meally wrote the script for the documentary *Lady Day: The Many Faces of Billie Holiday,* I found myself returning to *The Long Night* again and again. On the one hand I was compelled by the images of Lady and anything that purported to be about her, that took her seriously, and on the other hand, bothered by the white men who claimed such authority during her life. I have since realized that much of what I find attractive about Jeremy's documentary, the seriousness with which it deals with her as an artist, is deeply related to its British origins. What angers me most is the authority granted the white men who controlled her life and in this instance seem to be in control of her memory as well. Holiday's relationship to

Europe and to European intellectuals is a microcosm of the history of black artists and entertainers in Europe.

European Holiday

BY THE TIME her plane landed in Copenhagen on January 11, 1954, Europeans had long been familiar with Holiday through her recordings and through the European jazz press. The London-based *Melody Maker* had documented her triumphs and failures from as early as 1933. The first story to appear about Holiday, which I have already cited, was written by John Hammond and published in the April 1933 issue of *Melody Maker*. In it, Hammond wrote:

> This month, there has been a real find in the person of a singer called Billie Holiday . . . though only eighteen she weighs over 200 pounds, is incredibly beautiful and sings as well as anybody I ever heard. (Chilton, 6)

The story posits Hammond as the white male discoverer of something massive—both the size of her body and the size of her talent. She is body, beauty and voice; he is explorer of this Dark Continent and the first to construct her for and insert her into the European imagination. As such, he precedes and provides the way for the subsequent reception of her records and the creation of the "European" Holiday. From 1933 to 1954, *Melody Maker* published more than eighty-five stories mentioning Holiday, almost all of which were written by John Hammond or by the British critic Max Jones. Stories reported, "Billie Holiday Has Ptomaine Poisoning" (1936). Other stories documented her bouts with drugs and the U.S. legal system. As early as 1936, *Melody Maker* assured her fans that she was headed to Britain.

So when Lady Day and her European fans first encountered each other in the winter of 1954, it was not only an encounter between a woman and a group of diverse individuals. Instead, it was the meeting of two long-standing myths with their own individual histories and their own relationship to each other.[64] During her three visits to Europe in 1954, 1958 and 1959, the "European" Holiday went from a beloved and admired artist to a beleaguered, tragic ghost of her former self, booed off stage and singing for a percentage of the gate. Any discussion of the meanings of Billie Holiday as icon requires us to consider both her trips to Europe as well as the role that European intellectuals, especially the British, have played in the invention of "Holiday." This is so because this "Holiday" continues to influence contemporary portraits of her life.

Furthermore, turning our attention to Europe allows us to see the international dimension of her art as well as the international circulation of her music. While that music certainly circulated in parts of Africa, Latin America and Asia as well, she never visited those places, and it is more difficult to document what people have said about her there. Cape Verdean vocalist Cesaria Evora cites Holiday's influence on her as she grew up singing her country's traditional "mournas."[65] And actress/singer Dolly Rathebe was often referred to as the South African Billie Holiday, although the title probably ought to have been given to vocalist Sathima Bea Benjamin. Benjamin recalls listening to Holiday in the fifties and reading her autobiography before it was banned. Finally, the magazine *DRUM,* a kind of African version of *Ebony,* published several articles on American jazz, a few of which mentioned Holiday. So readers on the continent were certainly familiar with Lady Day. However, I have yet to identify a specifically African or Asian discourse related to Billie Holiday.[66]

During her tours, Holiday visited Sweden, Germany, France, Italy and Britain. Here, I focus on Britain for three reasons: 1. British intellectuals have engaged in jazz criticism since the form's founding and were among the first to write about Billie Holiday. 2. Because it is written in English, the British version of Holiday is more influential in the United States than that of other European countries. 3. Of all the European countries where she performed, Great Britain was Holiday's favorite.

Because Holiday's autobiography was published prior to her last two trips, her version of Europe serves as yet another uncritical portrait of the continent as an oasis for black artists. Holiday and/or Dufty contributes to the larger African-American narrative about Europe. The chapter of *Lady Sings the Blues* that is devoted to the Jazz Club USA Tour of 1954 is titled "Dream of Life." The Jazz Club USA tour was organized by critic and promoter Leonard Feather, himself a Brit. The tour grew out of Feather's *Voice of America* radio series. It should not be confused with the State Department jazz tours, which took many jazz musicians abroad during the Cold War.

In a sensational book that largely documents the pain and difficulty of her life, this chapter stands out for its humor and its indictment of the United States. The opening paragraph situates Holiday's longing for Europe in the context of the stories she has heard about it: "I guess every Negro performer dreams of going to Europe. Some of them have gone over and never come back. Ever since I got to be a name, I had thought about it too."

Throughout the entire chapter, Holiday relates some incident or anecdote that is indicative of European cosmopolitanism or progressive stance in race relations, health care, the treatment of drug addicts and the press. Each of these assertions is followed by an indictment of the United States. As such, the chapter is ultimately more about the United States than it is about the various European countries she visited. Following the tale of a Danish doctor and his 12-year-old daughter who meet her at the airport and take her home to attend to her cold, Holiday writes: "If anybody ever met me at La Guardia Airport, I'd expect them to say send the bitch back where you got her" (172). In this statement there is the sense, experienced by many African Americans, that she is an unwanted foreigner in the land of her birth. Holiday was warmly welcomed wherever she traveled in Europe. In Germany she was surprised by the enthusiastic reception she received and the high regard the Germans had for jazz.

Europe emerges as far more humane, cultured and politically progressive than the United States. As such, *Lady Sings the Blues* joins a tradition of American artists' and intellectuals', especially African-American artists' and intellectuals', representations of Europe. Frederick Douglass, William Wells Brown, Harriet Jacobs, Jessie Fauset, Josephine Baker, Miles Davis and many others have written similarly of Europe in their autobiographical musings.

What the autobiography adds to African-American portrayals of Europe is the comparison of national policies toward drug addicts. Throughout the text, she warns young people against experimentation with drugs and pleads for more humane treatment for those who are addicted. In this chapter, Britain provides a national model for the speculative recommendations that pepper earlier chapters. Most important, Europeans recognize and value the cultural innovations and contributions of jazz musicians. In addition to painting Europe as a "freer space," Holiday praises the European press for their understanding of the music and their appreciation of her as an artist and an icon: "These European writers dig more music. They were hip; they had ears. The big brains, the writers and jazz authorities in America catch up with what's going on in jazz ten years after it happens" (180–181).

Holiday's description of her European tour joins reports about her trip from the road in the jazz and black press. All help to posit Europe as a respite from American racial provincialism. The African-American press and the U.S. jazz press echoed this sentiment in their coverage of the Jazz USA tour. The February 25, 1954, issue of the African-American weekly *Jet* ran a photograph of Holiday as its Week's Best Photo. In the photograph, Holiday, decked out in ski gear, has fallen and sits in an awkward, almost comic pose, her skis crisscrossed though still on her feet. The caption beneath it reads "While satisfying her newfound enthusiasm for skiing, singer Billie Holiday—now touring Europe—takes a spill in Zurich, Switzerland." As such the photo and the caption tell the folk back home that their beleaguered but talented Lady Day is afforded a life of leisure and pleasure, and yet the fact that she cannot ski assures that she is still "just folks." I think it might also imply the difficulty of navigating this very foreign and very white landscape.

The same week, famed critic Leonard Feather, writing in *Down Beat* (February 24, 1954), reported the difficulty the tour encountered; but about Holiday he wrote:

> From the second night on, Lady Day has been thrilling everyone, looking prettier and singing better than she has for years. She's been getting an even bigger hand since she started to use "Strange Fruit," which her fans know from the record, and the constant aura of applause, bouquets, photographs and autograph hunters has done for her morale what a trip like this could do for many a despondent American artist.

During her long-awaited first tour in 1954, Holiday performed in Denmark, Norway, Sweden, Holland, Switzerland, Italy, France and her favorite, Britain. Press reviews were favorable, at times even laudatory. The Danish critic Harold Grut wrote: "She held the audience at Copenhagen's vast KB Hall spellbound" (Chilton, 152). In *Melody Maker*, Max Jones, who along with his wife was to become a friend, reported, "Onstage she looks calm and dignified but she also looks warm and sounds warm and her whole attitude seems spontaneous and very, very hip." The Jones quotation is especially interesting. Holiday "looks calm and dignified." The phrase is not one often associated with black performers, particularly black women, of her day; perhaps only Marian Anderson was spoken about in this way. Yet he goes on to reassure his readers that she looks calm and dignified—untouchable, unapproachable perhaps, but in fact she also looks, and most important, she sounds, warm and her attitude is "spontaneous" and "hip." The passage moves from describing her restraint to assuring her spontaneity and hipness. Don't be taken aback, it assures readers, she really is black (spontaneous and hip). In fact, Holiday was all of these things.

As with so many African-American women, Holiday was so used to explicitly negative press that she welcomed the acknowledgment of her beauty and her artistry. Of the British press, she would later write:

"The stuff they wrote about me in Europe made me feel alive. Over here some damn body is always trying to embalm me. I'm always making a comeback, but nobody ever tells me where I been." Europe gives her life: a notion reminiscent of the abolitionist of old who spoke of being able to breathe "free air" for the first time in Britain.

Throughout her tour, Holiday sang songs for which she'd become famous, including "Strange Fruit." We must understand the context in which Holiday chose to sing "Strange Fruit" for her European audiences and in which she is so critical of the United States. Following World War II, America emerged as the dominant world power and it began to engage in an ideological turf battle with its former ally the Soviet Union—the Cold War. The Cold War had a tremendous impact on African-American leadership, resulting in a split between persons such as Paul Robeson and W. E. B. Du Bois and the more mainstream bourgeois leadership represented by organizations such as the National Association for the Advancement of Colored People. In her important book, *Race Against Empire: Black Americans and Anticolonialism 1937–1957,* Penny M. Von Eschen argues that African-American liberals constructed a civil rights agenda during the Cold War that insists that racial discrimination need be eliminated at home in order to legitimize the United States' place as leader of the free world. At the same time, the U.S. State Department tried desperately to export positive visions of American race relations to Asia and Africa. Also, the U.S. government repressed anticolonial activists within these countries and those African Americans, such as Robeson and Du Bois, who dared speak out against the U.S. in a national arena.[67]

It is in this context that we must place Billie Holiday's critiques of the United States while she was abroad and her publication of these critiques in her autobiography. Furthermore, we must remember that this was the era of Senator Joseph McCarthy's nationally televised hearings as well as the State Department tours in which jazz musicians such as Dizzy Gillespie and Louis Armstrong participated throughout the world as goodwill ambassadors of sorts for the United States.

"Strange Fruit" is a strong indictment of American racism in any context, but what must it have meant for Holiday to sing it to European audiences? The European whites were not the direct objects of the indictment. And, oddly enough, they could hear it for its critique of the United States, but in no way were colonial and racist histories of Europe explicitly implicated in the song or by the performer. Interestingly, the anti-lynching activist Ida B. Wells also took her crusade to Europe. Unlike other African-American artists, Holiday never mentions Europe's relationship to its own colonized people of color. John Chilton notes that Holiday's planned three-week stint at Paris's Olympia Theater in 1956 was interrupted when the Algerian crisis caused the French to close down the halls. Biographer Stuart Nicholson writes that Holiday had "discovered a new generation of admirers in the African Nationalist movement in Paris: tough cosmopolitans with whom she shared many bitter experiences of racism" (219). Hazel Scott later wrote that Holiday referred to her as Queen of the Mau Maus. "She meant this as a compliment," wrote Scott. "She said it because of the affection and esteem the African students of Paris hold for me."[68]

One photograph of Holiday during her second European trip depicts her with a pair of African mask earrings. This is the closest we get to any awareness on Holiday's part of Africa or an African aesthetic. Yet Holiday makes no mention of meeting Africans in Paris, and as such her documentation of that trip remains one unmarred by the complexity of Europe's own racial situation. It is quite possible that given her own troubles with the law, she might have been aware of the censorship that befell black artists and intellectuals who openly expressed admiration for or solidarity with African colonials.

While Holiday's first trip to Europe was indeed a triumphant one, subsequent visits were not nearly as successful. In 1958, Holiday returned to Europe, and her first stop was Italy. There, for the first time, she encountered booing and hissing at the Smeraldo Theater in Milan. So disappointed were the audiences with her performances, management canceled the rest of her engagements. The producer Mario Fatoria, an Italian fan, booked one of the smaller halls at La Scala for Holiday to perform for invited guests. The Italian failure was indicative of the rest of the trip. Fans and critics in France were equally disappointed. Gone is the "spontaneity" and "warmth" of the earlier visit.

The last image we have of Holiday in France comes from Hazel Scott, the famous African-American pianist and former wife of black congressman Adam Clayton Powell. In a much-cited article, "What Paris Means to Me," originally published in *Ebony* and reprinted in the November 1961 issue of *Negro Digest,* Scott recounted her own years of exile in France. According to Scott:

> Paris is Billie Holiday, too. . . . Sitting there in the Mars Club in Paris, listening to this woman who represents so many years of my life . . . I was overcome by all the tragedy, all the greatness and all of the beauty of her life.
>
> I had my own problems, too . . . I began to cry. Billie stopped, gripped my arm and dragged me to a back room and slammed the door. "The next time you begin to feel like this," she said, "just remember that you've got Skipper, and Lady only has a little chihuahua, and Lady's making it. And another thing: Never let them see you cry." (See endnote 68)

Scott's reminiscence is significant not only for what it says, but also for its circulation and as such its influence on subsequent versions of Billie Holiday's last encounter with Europe, particularly with France. First of all, as is almost always the case with stories about Holiday, this one is more about the teller than it is about Lady Day. Her presence, her voice, triggers something in the teller of the tale, something that reminds them of a sense of hopelessness or loss in their own lives. Interestingly enough, here that "something" is countered by Holiday herself who insists that her friend "never let them see you cry." Even within the context of this narrative, over which she has no control, she is fighting against being associated with her own misery but particularly that of others. However, ultimately the Holiday of this story is sad, alone, despondent and a long way from home. The story has been quoted by most of Holiday's biographers (with the exception of Robert O'Meally) and it was reprinted not once but at least twice in publications owned by the Johnson Company (which also owned *Jet*).

The story participates in two types of myth-making. For a general audience, it paints a portrait of the demise of a great artist. For a black audience, it also counters the myth of Europe as a haven for black Americans. It seems to expose a "dirty little secret." In the black American press there is always the counter-narrative, which suggests that those who choose exile and abandon the black struggle in the U.S. do not always lead lives of luxury in their chosen lands. Particularly by the early 1970s, this is an image of black exiles that starts to become dominant. In the final chapter of *From Harlem to Paris,* Michel Fabre notes the African American's changing conceptions about Paris and the very notion of expatriation during the Black Power era.

Holiday's last days there were anything but triumphant. By the end of her time in Paris, she was singing for a percentage of the gate in Parisian nightclubs. Still, she continued to hold Britain in high regard. Just five months prior to her death (1959) Holiday returned briefly to London to tape an appearance on the television show *Chelsea at Nine.* Of that performance, she said, "I was so nervous out there, I could have died. Everything is a little different from American TV. I do hope that people like it." It seems, however, she had given up on living in London. *Down Beat* reported, "Lady Day not to move to London, she will buy a house on Long Island." She did neither; she died in July 1959.

If Holiday continued to perpetuate the century's old myth of Britain as a site of black freedom, British-born or -based critics and writers have had an enormous influence on the development of a myth of Holiday. Leonard Feather, originally from north London, and Stuart Nicholson and Donald Clarke, recent biographers of Holiday, are all critics with bases in England. Interestingly, instead of opening his brilliant biography of Holiday in Baltimore, as do most, Nicholson opens *Billie Holiday* by recounting her appearance at Paris's Mars Club during the week of November 24, 1958. Max Jones, one of the most sympathetic and understanding of the critics to have written about Holiday, reported on her career extensively prior to her visit in 1954. Subsequent to that trip, he and his wife became her close friends. Even the noted social historian Eric Hobsbawm penned Holiday's obituary for the *New Statesman:*

> What sort of middle age would she have faced without the voice to earn money for her drinks and fixes. Without the looks—and in her day she was hauntingly beautiful—to attract the men she needed, without business sense, without anything but the disinterested worship of aging men who had heard and seen her in her glory.

Hobsbawm's assumptions about Holiday paint a life for her that she never lived to experience. Discursively he creates her ending and asserts that an early death is actually better than the life she would have led. In some ways this is the kind of romanticization that happens whenever celebrities have early deaths. As singer Deborah Harry of the group Blondie—who modeled her stage persona after the iconic figure of youthful death, Marilyn Monroe—sang: "Die young; stay pretty." Especially interesting, though, is the self-indictment of the last sentence. The phrase "disinterested worship" is almost an oxymoron, and yet it is a perfect description of a fan's momentary adoration.

Largely due to the efforts of The Billie Holiday Circle, Holiday's legacy has been kept alive in Britain. Established in 1946, the Circle continues to have an active international membership. It publishes a newsletter five to six times per year, listing reissues of her recordings, books about her, and news of members. The society also maintains an up-to-date Web site. The late Jack Millar, one of the founders of the Circle, started with a listing of Holiday titles and a network of individuals who would buy and swap her records. His *A Discography of Billie Holiday* continues to be one of the most comprehensive discographies of her work.

One of the Circle's most distinguished members, Jack Surridge, actually began a correspondence with Holiday in 1939. He wrote to her care of her record company; she replied with a note and a signed photograph. He recalls her performance at Prince Albert Hall as if it were yesterday:

> Billie appeared very beautiful in a kind of cream or off-white evening gown, long white gloves and as I remember, she seemed taller than I had always imagined. She had a mesmerizing power over the audience, due not only to her singing, but her beauty and graceful stature, a true lady. . . . She sang beautifully as always and with such feeling and conviction, her elbows swaying gently in time to the music. As I remember, the spotlight on her was soft and the rest of the podium was in semi-darkness.[69]

At Prince Albert Hall, Holiday sang to an audience of over 6,000. Though their correspondence ended with the war, Mr. Surridge phoned Holiday at her hotel. Much to his surprise, she remembered him and asked to come hear him play. He explained that he had given up playing, to which she replied: "Never, never give up playing." Interestingly, more than forty years after her death, Holiday has brought together the author, a woman who never saw her but has grown to love her nonetheless, and this long-standing European fan and admirer. Mr. Surridge has been my link to a version of the European Holiday that lives on through his efforts and those of others like the late Jack Millar.

The Billie Holiday Circle, Jack Surridge, Leonard Feather, Jack Millar and Max Jones are among the British fans, friends and intellectuals who affirmed Holiday's beauty, artistry and cultural contribution. Long after her death they have kept her legacy alive.

It is not surprising that these Englishmen would have been among the first and the most consistent to pay serious attention to Holiday's life and career. As she knew, they always took her more seriously than Americans did. This much of the myth, at least, is based in fact. These intellectuals also sought to provide an historical, psychological and sociological ground upon which to place Holiday. While this resulted in a much more complex understanding of Holiday than that made available in the United States, at times it also focused on the sociological pathologies of American race relations in ways that diverted attention from any notion of the black joy that exists even within the confines of American racism.

As I have noted, one of the most significant mediums for influencing notions of Holiday outside of her own autobiography and the Diana Ross vehicle of 1972 is the BBC documentary by Englishman John Jeremy, *The Long Night of Lady Day*.[70] The documentary presents Holiday's life in the most solemn tones. It is also ironic that, given its focus on the destructive nature of Holiday's personal choices and the racial environment of the United States, the documentary posits white males as the primary voices of authority. While anecdotes about her often refer to her penchant for no-good black men, pimplike lovers, managers, drug suppliers and husbands, few talk about the white male publicists, managers, club owners, critics, booking agents, narcotics detectives and judges, who had as much if not more influence on her. Significantly, in *The Long Night of Lady Day*, this latter group is presented as heroic authorities on the life and legacy of Lady Day. While two of her contemporaries, Sylvia Syms and Thelma Carpenter, her maid, a young Indian vocalist she met in London, the bassist Milt Hinton, Ray Ellis and black feminist Michele Wallace all make appearances, the central figures of authority are Father Peter O'Brien, Leonard Feather, John Hammond, Milt Gabler, Artie Shaw and Earl Zaidins. While the others offer personal anecdotes about her, these men do so while also speculating about the meaning of her life, her psychology and her music.

Michele Wallace is provided the opportunity to do the same at the close of the documentary, demonstrating that Jeremy was certainly aware of the need to posit a black woman as analyst as well, but the fact that these men knew and worked with Holiday and she did not, lends greater credence to their opinions. Furthermore, they can speak in terms of decisions they made about the direction of her career. Only the absence of her manager, Joe Glaser, makes the gathering incomplete.

Father Peter O'Brien narrates the film. In fact the work is framed in terms of Holiday's Catholicism, which O'Brien analyzes and with which black Catholic Michele Wallace closes the film. John Hammond, the politically liberal integrationist, jazz writer, record producer and concert promoter who claims to have discovered Holiday, makes several appearances. British jazz journalist, composer/musician and producer Leonard Feather offers his opinion several times. Composer Artie Shaw, who was the first white bandleader to tour with a black vocalist, Billie Holiday, provides insight into the difficulties she faced traveling with a white band. Barney Josephson, owner of Café Society, Milt Gabler, who produced "Strange Fruit" and other Holiday recordings for his independent label, Commodore, as well as for Decca, and Norman Granz, who recorded her Verve sets, are among the other white men who appear in the documentary. Of all of these, Feather and Hinton are the two who might have called themselves her friends. Granz and Gabler were extremely sensitive to her artistic needs.

Hammond was central to her early career. His writings about her introduced her to a larger jazz public in the U.S. and abroad. He produced her first records for Columbia and introduced her to Café Society. Also, he hated "Strange Fruit" and discouraged Columbia from recording it. Hammond claims responsibility for breaking up what seems to have been a romantic relationship between Holiday and a wealthy Manhattan socialite because he believed association with Holiday would ruin the socialite's reputation. Holiday socialized with a great many well-known wealthy New Yorkers, many of whom indulged in the same practices of smoking opium and experimenting with other drugs. One source claims that when the wealthy women of Hammond's set became addicted they were sent to sanitariums, while Holiday was sent to prison. I offer none of this to deny Hammond's importance to the music nor his commitment to racial justice. It is simply to say that his relationship to Billie Holiday in particular and black artists in general is more complicated than the documentary would suggest. If he had had his way, he would have had Holiday singing the same types of songs in the same style that she did when he first recorded her in the early thirties. While his choices were sometimes perfect, they were not always so, and he sometimes had a very limited vision when it came to the artists he produced. Mary Lou Williams notes that he discouraged her own musical growth and experimentation. This is the same man who offered Aretha Franklin her first record contract, thank God. But he tried to force her into the jazz vocalist mold, thereby undermining the unique contribution that she would later make when freed from the limiting arrangements he placed upon her. Through his writing, producing and promoting, Hammond had a very strong influence on the presentation and interpretation of black music, especially jazz, for decades.

Unlike Hammond, Milt Gabler didn't shy away from encouraging Holiday to pursue a different style in the late thirties and early forties. In fact, he is largely responsible for the selection of materials that would turn her into a torch singer, and therefore he is responsible for many of her hits. Furthermore, it was Gabler, through his independent label, Commodore, who recorded "Strange Fruit" when Holiday's record company refused to do so. Norman Granz, who also produced classic sides for Ella Fitzgerald and Frank Sinatra, produced Holiday's later recordings for Verve. In these he returned her to small, intimate settings with stellar musicians. In 1947 he organized a benefit concert for her to cover her debts, but Joe Glaser thought it would be bad publicity and forced her to donate the money to charity.

This is ironic, given that Glaser has been accused of skimming money from his performers. It was Glaser who advised Holiday to appear in court without legal representation and was therefore partly responsible for her incarceration. While she was in prison, he never visited her, never provided statements of her earnings and rarely responded to her request for money to purchase toiletries and cigarettes. Helen Hironimus, Lady's warden and friend, begged Glaser not to force Holiday back to work immediately upon her release out of fear that she would return too quickly to an atmosphere saturated with drugs. She wrote him: "How would you feel if you were being released from prison without funds, and clothing that did not fit you? Suppose you had a manager who withheld your checks and gave you no reason for doing so?"[71] At one point, when Holiday signed with another agent, Glaser refused to release her gowns. Of all the white men in her life, Glaser was clearly one of the most manipulative.

Although Glaser is not in the documentary, the man who makes him look like a saint is: the lawyer Earl Zaidins made himself indispensable to Holiday during the last years of her life. Zaidins appears in the documentary as Lady's protector from abusive black men like her husband, Louis McKay.

In other instances McKay accuses Zaidins of supplying Holiday with drugs and sexually molesting her. According to McKay, once she became dependent on drugs, Zaidins had her sign documents giving him power to make decisions in her name. He had her sign with another manager while on her deathbed, and after her death he claimed she owed him $12,000 in legal fees, which he forgave in exchange for 10 percent of her estate. Though McKay signed the agreement, he did fight it in court, where it was reversed. But in the Jeremy video, Zaidins's authority is even greater because he sits in a judge's chamber in his judicial robes—if we are to believe some accounts, a man who exploited her terribly is now a member of the system that harassed her and exploited her as well.

Perhaps the greatest irony of the Jeremy documentary and of the various white men, British and American, who wrote and spoke about Holiday during her life is that she never could have returned the favor. Nor would she ever have been granted the authority to analyze their lives, their work, their value as thinkers, writers or human beings.

This discussion of the Jeremy documentary provides an appropriate transition into the following chapter because it emerged following her death and because its version of Holiday is in direct opposition to the version posited by some of the most influential black American intellectuals. Nowhere is the above contest more evident than in two clips from two different documentary biographies of Billie Holiday. As noted above, in February 1959, just months before her death, Billie

Holiday appeared on the British television program *Chelsea at Nine*. She sang three songs. Both the Jeremy documentary and Robert O'Meally's *Lady Day: The Many Faces of Billie Holiday* make use of the *Chelsea at Nine* footage but in very different ways.

Jeremy uses the footage of a serious, gaunt-faced Holiday singing "I Loves You Porgy." The Holiday of this clip is sad, painfully thin, drawn, and pleading with a lover for protection. O'Meally's documentary seems to be in direct dialogue and debate with the Jeremy documentary. O'Meally also uses sections of the *Chelsea at Nine* tape. He excerpts Holiday singing "Strange Fruit" and "Please Don't Talk About Me When I'm Gone." The latter choice serves as a form of signification. A jubilant and playful Holiday tells all of us not to "scandalize her name," so to speak. This is even more noteworthy in that the clip is preceded by an interview with Albert Murray, who chides those writers who insist on focusing on the sordid details of her life.

In many ways it is the Holiday of the Jeremy documentary, as well as that of the movie *Lady Sings the Blues,* that African-American critics such as Albert Murray, Amiri Baraka and Robert O'Meally try to counter in their portraits of Lady Day. They emphasize her elegance, her musicianship, and her artistry, and they resist efforts to contextualize her life in the tragedy of American racism, drugs and bad love affairs only. Instead, these writers have chosen to emphasize Holiday's remarkable transcendence of the circumstances in which she found herself. For them, that transcendence is evident in the music. And in the music they hear a variety of stories about the woman and about black artists in general. In Holiday, they have located the complicated meaning of the blues. Certainly there were many abusive and exploitive black men in Billie Holiday's life; however, these black male critics are chivalrous lovers and protectors of their Lady.

Part Two

Alternative Myths

Myth, Mystery and Mourning. She had just finished singing "Strange Fruit" when Robin Carson took this, the most memorable of portraits of Lady Day. *(Robin Carson, 1945)*

5

Lady's Men and a Woman's Day

*H*OW DO YOU RESPOND to the call to write about black music? Indeed, it is a daunting and intimidating task. First, there is the enormity and diversity of the music: spirituals, sacred hymns, the blues, gospel, jazz, rhythm and blues, soul, funk, hip-hop—and even within these categories an even greater diversity exists. Second, the weighty genius of those who created the music as well as of those who have written about it overwhelms the would-be writer. Finally, there are the various ways of approaching the topic: as historian, musician, musicologist, poet, novelist, essayist, critic. Where to begin?

Of course, you must immerse yourself in the music, trying to learn as much as you can about it and those who play. Then, as with the musicians themselves, you turn to those who have come before, who have mastered the form of jazz writing. You study every word and argument. One thing you learn from them is that it is a never-ending process of learning, trying to dig deeper, exploring further. Next, you quote them in your own attempts to communicate your vision. Eventually, if you work hard enough and are blessed with a little talent, you acknowledge them, pay homage, critique, deconstruct or build upon what they have left you, but most important, you try to tell your own story within the grand and contradictory tale. If you are fortunate, there may be an ancestor figure—writer or musician—through whom you are led to your own voice. Billie Holiday has been the conduit through which many singers have discovered their own unique sound. She has certainly played a similar role for me, for to write about her is a constant state of discovery. She accompanied me through my early efforts as an aspiring writer, through my academic training, and now she has become the subject that allows me to enter the world of writing about the music I love. She has done so for others as well.

I first felt compelled to write about black music in college. During that time, the music helped me keep a sense of balance, and I greatly admired and sought to emulate the dedication and discipline of many black musical artists. By the time I entered graduate school in the late eighties, this desire grew into a preoccupation. At that time, black feminists such as Michelle Russell, Hazel Carby, Daphne DuVal Harrison, Deborah McDowell and Angela Davis were writing about blues women (especially Ma Rainey and Bessie Smith) and positing them as black feminist icons.

For the most part, the major critics of jazz were men. This is probably why male instrumentalists have received so much attention. Also, there is a way that music subcultures, not unlike athletic ones, are like fraternities. Young men are encouraged to pick up the instruments most often associated with jazz—the horns and the drums, even the piano, though this has been the instrument that has most given women access to the form. Think of Alice Coltrane, Lil Harding Armstrong, Marian McPartland, Carmen McRae, Mary Lou Williams, Amina Claudia Meyers and Geri Allen.

During the early years of the art form, most jazz innovators were black Americans, while the vast majority of critics and commentators were white men. Consequently, in telling the story of jazz, they shaped perceptions about the music and the musicians—perceptions that many found condescending and patronizing at best, racist at worst. Prominent black male intellectuals began to challenge white dominance by asserting the brilliance and elegance of the players as well as situating the music firmly within an African-American cultural and political milieu. Interestingly, today we are witnessing a backlash of certain white critics who are even suggesting that while greatly influential, black musicians were not the sole founders of the form nor were they its only technical innovators.

Some black male intellectuals—including Amiri Baraka, Langston Hughes, Albert Murray and Ralph Ellison—were among the most significant to engage in the debate about the meaning of jazz music. In spite of their differences, critics such as Baraka, Stanley Crouch, Leon Forrest and Robert O'Meally have also focused on Billie Holiday and have sought to "rescue" and "protect" Holiday from the sensationalizing myths that obscure her contributions as a major artist. Truth be told, some of them seem to be a little in love with the Lady.

Though few black women have engaged in jazz criticism, it is not surprising that black women artists and intellectuals have been drawn to Billie Holiday.[72] Michelle Wallace, Alexis De Veaux and Ntozake Shange are among the most prominent women to write about Lady Day. The latter two have chosen creative writing as the forum for their discussion of Holiday's meaning. The stakes are particularly high for black women artists and intellectuals. Holiday is a foremother, a beloved and respected ancestor. When she is called out of her name, so are we. When she is judged by everything but the genius of her body of work, we recognize and fear that it might happen to us as well. And yet, we also fear sharing the end of her life: to have given all you have to the world only to leave it alone, broke and harassed by a racist state. Not surprisingly, Holiday is often the means by which black women thinkers enter into and engage jazz criticism.

Angela Davis is one black woman critic who has extensively engaged Holiday's legacy. She both builds upon and corrects Baraka's notion of Holiday, in order to construct her as a political and social figure whose art raises questions about intraracial gender relations as well as race relations in the United States.

Before moving on, let me here say certainly, black intellectuals have not been the only ones to write about the meaning of black music with intelligence and sensitivity. Nat Hentoff, Ingrid Monson, John Szwed, Paul Berliner, Geoff Dyer and Linda Dahl are but some contemporary nonblack writers who have done so.[73] However, I have decided to focus on a selection of black intellectuals, those who write from within the circle and still suffer the consequences for doing so, for a few reasons. One, all too often their intellectual work is devalued or ignored. Two, I find it especially compelling that black intellectuals have devoted such care and time to the meaning of Lady Day's legacy; that they have sought to rescue her from the realm of popular media representations and to emphasize her intelligence, artistry and importance to many black Americans. My third reason is more personal. I feel a sense of community with this group of writers who love the music, who believe it to be fundamental to our racial and national identity and in some instances to our spirituality and humanity as well. Like Lady, I join those other black women writers who insist upon "sitting-in" with the cats. What is it about black music, about jazz, about Billie Holiday in particular that moves us to write about them as if we were called to a vocation? What lessons do black intellectuals derive from Lady's life and legacy? How does her example provide me a model of how one enters the largely male terrain of jazz criticism? How does her model provide me the opportunity to insert my voice into the chorus, singing the critical praise song of Lady Day and consequently of black music?

IN THE BEGINNING, Frederick Douglass posed the question, What does it mean? In so doing, he set off over a century of debate and discussion. In his narrative of 1845, Douglass wrote, "The songs of the slave represent the sorrows of his heart; and he is relieved by them, only as an aching heart is relieved by its tears." Douglass was among the first to counter the observations of slave owners and travelers who said black singing was illustrative of the slave's happiness with his or her condition of servitude.

At the dawn of the twentieth century, W. E. B. Du Bois responded to Douglass's call by naming the spirituals "the sorrow songs" and identifying them as the gift of the Negro people to the world. In *The Souls of Black Folk* Du Bois posits not only the sorrow in the songs but also a sense of hope as well: "Through all the sorrow of the Sorrow Songs there breathes a hope—a faith in the ultimate justice of things. The minor cadences of despair change often to triumph and calm confidence. Sometimes it is faith in life, sometimes a faith in death, sometimes assurance of boundless justice in some far world."

Ever the iconoclast, Zora Neale Hurston countered Du Bois's analysis of the meanings of the spirituals: "The idea that the whole body of the spirituals are 'sorrow songs' is ridiculous. They cover a wide range of subjects from a peeve at gossipers to Death and Judgment."[74]

So while many of us situate the origins of the debate about the meaning of black music with Ralph Ellison and Amiri Baraka, in fact the conflict is much older. However, while Douglass, Du Bois and Hurston focused on the meanings of the spirituals, Baraka and Ellison turned their attention to the blues, the form which emerged as the single most influential musical form of the twentieth century, sparking countless other new forms of music.

In 1963, the year of Du Bois's death and my birth, Amiri Baraka (LeRoi Jones) published what continues to be one of the most influential and enduring studies of African-American music, *Blues People:*

The Negro Experience in White America and the Music That Developed From It. At the time, Baraka was already a well-respected poet, editor and music critic. He would go on to become a major playwright, director, anthologist, and political activist as well. As a measure of its significance at the time of publication, *Blues People* garnered the attention of the prestigious *New York Review of Books,* where it was reviewed by the esteemed African-American novelist and essayist Ralph Ellison. Ellison critiqued Baraka for paying attention to politics and ideology at the expense of art and poetics. For Ellison, this did a great disservice to the blues. The two competing philosophies of black art to emerge from Baraka's book and Ellison's review have become one of the most significant debates within African-American cultural and intellectual history.

Baraka's insistence that the creation of black musical forms was a direct result and reflection of the position of African Americans in the United States became the dominant stance of many intellectuals, writers and musicians during the 1960s—a decade of intense political activity and of efforts toward black self-determination. He wielded influence beyond the written page into the very presentation and reception of jazz during the decade. Baraka organized jazz festivals featuring the New Music, including artists such as Archie Shepp, Albert Ayler, Sun Ra, Betty Carter and John Coltrane among others. According to Aldon Nielsen, one of the concerts was "held as a benefit for Baraka's joining of the new movements in black music, poetry, and politics."[75]

In addition to the music, Baraka provided a venue for avant garde poets and musicians to share their innovations and provided a space where activists and artists were in dialogue with each other and where they could cross-fertilize each other's efforts. Along with Larry Neale and A. B. Spellman, Baraka also published *Cricket,* "a black music magazine intended to counter the white-dominated world of magazines like *Down Beat.*"[76] In short, he was not simply an historian, critic or artist, he was an institution builder as well. Baraka's institutions were situated outside the mainstream of American culture, but outside of the mainstream of jazz criticism and performance venue as well. Baraka and his institutions were oppositional to white America and to some of the black bourgeoisie as well.

Although *Blues People* continues to be widely read, the Ellisonian position on jazz emerged as the dominant and most influential. This is especially apparent if we consider the lineage from Ellison to his contemporary and fellow traveler, Albert Murray; from Murray to his protégés, critic Stanley Crouch and musician/composer Wynton Marsalis—the first jazz composer to be awarded a Pulitzer Prize and the Director of Jazz at Lincoln Center. Jazz at Lincoln Center marks the institutionalization of jazz as a "classical" American music. Few of today's avant garde jazz musicians perform at the Jazz at Lincoln Center events. Furthermore, it is this interpretation of jazz history that informs Ken Burns's epic documentary *Jazz*.

While Ellison's position seems to have won in the public arena, in the realm of theory Baraka's political understanding of the music remained influential. Houston Baker, who saw the blues as a lens through which to understand and analyze all of black cultural production, also refined it. The tools of poststructuralism allowed him to see the politics of form. Baraka also influences most studies of hip-hop.

Significantly, the differences between the Ellison and Baraka stances are nowhere more evident than in differing images of Billie Holiday and her legacy that emerge in the writings of Baraka and of those intellectuals who can be termed "Ellisonian." While Ellison did not write about Holiday, Murray and Crouch have. Also, two younger intellectuals, who to differing degrees might be considered Ellisonian, have written extensively about her: the late novelist Leon Forrest wrote the beautiful essay "A Solo Long-Song: For Lady Day"; critic Robert O'Meally (whose first book was on Ralph Ellison) wrote the extended essay *Lady Day: The Many Faces of Billie Holiday*. Although he did not mention her in *Blues People,* Amiri Baraka has written at least three beautiful pieces about Holiday: the poem "The Lady," the prose-poem/liner notes "Dark Lady of the Sonnets" and a statement that he planned to read in Jeremy's documentary *The Long Night of Lady Day.*

In all of these, Baraka's Lady Day emerges as a black poet of longing who expresses the collective desire of black people. She is both an artist in the tradition of black culture and a spokesperson in the tradition of black struggle. She carries tradition in her art and her person; she also shapes and helps to create that tradition. Because black music is so deeply rooted in black experience for Baraka, Holiday as woman and artist comes to be representative of the experiences, needs and thwarted desire of black people in this land called America. Baraka's Lady does not transcend history; she is mired in it, carries the weight of it in her voice and her being. She is not a "symbol" of black oppression but a full-dimensional aspect of it. And even in the lightness and joy, there is an underlying blue darkness of that experience. In this sense she can grow from the light, bouncy artist of her early recordings, to the communicative woman of her middle period, to the poet rendering a reading at the end of her life.

Baraka is not the first to view Holiday in this way. In his autobiography, Malcolm X claims to have been one of Lady's close friends during his days as a young hustler in Harlem. In a pivotal section of the book, he recalls going to see her perform prior to his confrontation with the older hustler West Indian Archie: "Billie, at the microphone, had just finished a number when she saw Jean and me. Her white gown glittered under the spotlight, her face had that coppery, Indian-ish look, and her hair was in that trademark ponytail" (128). After dedicating a song to him, she joins Malcolm and his date at their table and inquires after his tense disposition. Following his description of their evening, he notes:

> That was the last time I saw Lady Day. She's dead; dope and heartbreak stopped that heart as big as a barn and that sound and style that no one successfully copies. Lady Day sang with the soul of Negroes from the centuries of sorrow and oppression. What a shame that proud, fine, black woman never lived where the true greatness of the black race was appreciated! (129)

Malcolm mourns Holiday, a genius whose voice embodies the struggles of black Americans. Furthermore, he suggests that she might have survived had she lived in a society that valued black people; the vision of such a society is that to which he would devote his life shortly following that fateful meeting with her.

In contrast to Baraka and Malcolm X, Albert Murray gives us a different Holiday. In *Stomping the Blues,* Murray insists on distinguishing between the blues as feeling and blues music that seeks to chase the blues feeling away. He wrestles the blues from Baraka's realm of the social and political and situates it instead in the realm of ritual, poetry and the great achievements of Western civilization. In light of this he works with what I term the "Western Civ Simile," whereby the blues and great composers and musicians of the blues tradition are defined in terms of the Western canon—*Oedipus Rex, Hamlet*—or great canonical American writers such as Melville, Emerson, Whitman, Twain and Hemingway.

When he does write about Holiday (no women receive the extensive attention given to the male instrumentalists; his discussion of Holiday is limited to an extended caption for a photograph of her), Murray emphasizes her musicianship and artistic achievement. He first situates her by describing her pedigree. Here, the emphasis is on her role in the black musical tradition, not the collective social history of African Americans. He relegates the tragedies in her life to "sensational publicity" and her choice of material—"torch songs"—instead of racism, sexism or drug addiction.

To differing degrees, Stanley Crouch and Robert O'Meally have helped to disseminate Murray's version of Holiday and thus his theory of a blues/jazz aesthetic as poetry and ritual. While O'Meally has not done so uncritically, Crouch is perhaps the most faithful adherent to Murray.

Although Crouch is a self-avowed disciple of Albert Murray, the Ellison-Murray version of Billie Holiday finds its most eloquent elaboration in Robert O'Meally's *Lady Day: The Many Faces of Billie Holiday.* O'Meally had already established a respected reputation as an

Ellison scholar before turning his attention to Billie Holiday. His 1991 "biographical essay" is a labor of love and an exquisite companion to the numerous Billie Holiday CDs currently available. O'Meally makes no pretense toward objectivity—he is a Lady's man. Furthermore, his is perhaps the best exploration of Holiday's development and achievement as an artist. Although O'Meally stresses the artistic over the social, he does not entirely dismiss the Baraka position. He never goes so far as to dismiss the weight of racism in her life. Most important, O'Meally's Holiday is a woman who underwent a rigorous period of training and apprenticeship before emerging as one of the most significant artists of her time. Robert O'Meally's Billie Holiday is the creation of Eleanora Fagan, that young, precocious Baltimore girl who decided first that she would not be a maid, and later that she did not want to be a whore. So she chose the third option available to black women of her generation: singer. Furthermore, she picked her name, chose a personal style and dedicated her life to the development of her craft. She is a woman of her own creation.

In the exquisite "A Solo Long-Song: For Lady Day," novelist and essayist Leon Forrest credits his mother with introducing him to Holiday and claims that Holiday's voice was the mother's milk on which he was weaned. He writes of her art as "literature" and discusses her impact on his development as a novelist. In the first part of the essay, he compares Holiday to Hemingway and identifies both of them as quintessential American artists. While the first part of the essay seems to be driven by the Western Civ Simile, the second part situates Holiday as the foremother to such black women writers as Toni Morrison and Gayl Jones. Citing Holiday's storytelling ability, Forrest identifies her as one of the first black women to create beautiful, complex narratives out of the life experiences of black women. "Before the recent rise of those gifted signifying black female writers, led by Toni Morrison, it was really Lady Day, more than any other cultural carrier, who spoke in an avant-garde, sophisticated manner—on the national stage—concerning the themes of heartbreak in romance, the perils of sentimentality, the ways of men, and the ransom of heartache, sexual victimization, racism, the wounds of loneliness, all of which were forged from the injustice engraved upon the black female perspective. This dimension of Lady Day's art forced you to contemplate deeply the plight of the condition of the African-American woman's tragic situation, in ways that were both contemplative, intellectual and soul searching" (376–77).

Significantly, it is this aspect of Holiday that has most interested black women writers, many of whom, like Forrest, claim her as a literary or intellectual ancestor. Interestingly, the brilliant Ntozake Shange has Holiday appear as a guiding ancestor in her novel *Sassafrass, Cypress and Indigo*. Holiday, as ancestor, appears to chide Sassafrass, an artist, about neglecting her creativity:

> Who do you love among us, Sassafrass? Ma Rainey, Mamie Smith, Big Mama Thornton, Fredi Washington, Josephine, Carmen Miranda? Don't ya know we is all sad ladies because we got the blues, and joyful women because we got our songs? Make you a song, Sassafrass, and bring it out so high all us spirits can hold it and be in your tune. We need you, Sassafrass; we need you to sing best as you can; that's our nourishment, that's how we live.[77]

My own interpretation of Billie Holiday's legacy adheres to Shange's. For that reason I chose the passage cited above as one of the epigraphs to this book. For Shange, Holiday is not only ancestor to the contemporary black woman artists, she is also representative of a host of women of color who did not receive the acclaim and attention they deserved during their lifetimes. In this instance, it is the role and responsibility of the black woman artist to sing her own song, create her own body of work, as a means of giving voice to the legacy of her female ancestors. Black women vocalists such as Carmen McRae, Miki Howard and Abbey Lincoln also sing songs as nourishment for the spirit of Lady Day. Interestingly, many black women intellectuals, both creative and critical, also focus aspects of their work on Holiday.

Angela Davis, Patricia Hill Collins and Michelle Wallace have offered feminist analyses of Holiday. Davis shares with Baraka a concern for the political implications of Holiday's music, but she provides an inherent critique of his masculinist and at times boldly sexist understandings of black music by offering a feminist Billie Holiday.[78]

Angela Davis provides the most in-depth and extensive example of what is at stake when we try to write about Billie Holiday, the meaning of her legacy and of her music. Although I disagree with some of the assertions Davis makes about the feminist implications of Holiday's performances, we do share the project of a black feminist reclamation of Billie Holiday.

Davis's greatest contribution to our understanding of Holiday is to be found in her powerful, historically grounded discussion of "Strange Fruit" and the contexts in which it was performed and debated. Here, Davis does not have to claim Holiday as a proto-feminist, but instead works to rescue her from critics and biographers, especially white men, who have claimed that she was too stupid to know what she was singing when she first performed and recorded the song. John Chilton wrote: "At first, Lady was slow to understand the song's imagery, but her bewilderment decreased as Allen patiently emphasized the cadences, and their significance." Barney Josephson, owner of Café Society, claimed: "She looked at me and said, 'What do you want me to do with that, man?' And I said, 'It would be wonderful if you'd sing it—if you care to . . . [she said] 'You wants me to sing it, I sings it.'" According to Donald Clarke, "Lady was nonpolitical; when she looked at 'Strange Fruit' she didn't know what to make of it. She never read anything but comic books . . . and she was used to learning songs, not reading poetry."[79] (Miles Davis is reported to have loved comic books as well.)

To those who question Holiday's ability to understand the lyrics of "Strange Fruit," Davis responds:

> I have considered these conflicting accounts of the genesis of Billie Holiday's "Strange Fruit" because they reveal—even in the narratives of those whose relationships to her

should have afforded them special insight into her musical genius—the extent to which her stature as an artist and her ability to comprehend social issues were both disparaged and defined as results of plans conceived by savvy white men. Chilton's, Clarke's, and Josephson's stories capture Holiday in a web of gendered, classed and raced inferiority and present her as capable of producing great work only under the tutelage of her racial superiors. (187)

The major significance of a black feminist project of reclaiming Billie Holiday lies in its seeking to restore her to her complexity, her gifts and her courage in the face of powerful claims to the contrary. Davis is joined in this project not only by writers like Ntozake Shange and myself, but by artists such as Cassandra Wilson and Abbey Lincoln.

The myths about Holiday's inability to understand the lyrics to "Strange Fruit" surfaced in September 1998 and the spring of 2000. David Margolick's article for *Vanity Fair* on Lewis Allen and "Strange Fruit" and his book *Strange Fruit: Billie Holiday, Café Society and an Early Cry for Civil Rights* repeat some of the inane comments about Holiday's initial failure to understand the lyrics of the song. So even today, these stories continue to circulate. Interestingly, Hilton Als's foreword to the book counters these charges of her stupidity.

Billie Holiday was a musical genius, but she didn't have to be a genius to understand a song about lynching, particularly in 1939. At the beginning of the decade over twenty black men were lynched. In addition, black newspapers carried vivid photographs and descriptions of lynching. Even children's rhymes referenced lynching as the fate of black men who desired white women.

In "Strange Fruit," Holiday left us a powerful and enduring song of protest against racial violence—protest that has been cited by each succeeding generation of black singers to follow her from Nina Simone to Abbey Lincoln to Cassandra Wilson and Dee Dee Bridgewater. It is not necessary to claim that all of her songs possess such a political impact. Historian Darlene Clark Hine argues that Holiday's version of "Strange Fruit" helped to establish and maintain a political consciousness among black people about lynching. In so doing, Hine argues Holiday built upon the work of anti-lynching activists such as Ida B. Wells by assuring that the issue remained at the forefront of black American consciousness. While Albert Murray claims "Strange Fruit" was a song for the white liberal left and not for Harlem, over three generations of black Americans have claimed the song as their own. Leon Forrest notes the song's influence on his first novel, *There Is a Tree More Ancient Than Eden*. According to Forrest, the novel "has at its artistic epicenter, a horrific lynching, which in turn was directly influenced on a primary level by my own attempt to play out Lady Day's most haunting and memorable long-song . . . 'Strange Fruit'—in narrative form."[80] Even as I write this book, Dwayne Wiggins sings "What's Really Going On? (Strange Fruit)," a song inspired by "Strange Fruit" and used to express discontent over contemporary instances of racial profiling, police harassment and brutality. "Strange Fruit" has become an indelible part of the African-American cultural landscape.

But we need not look to her most overtly political song to claim her genius or her political consciousness. The genius of Lady Day lay also in her ability to articulate the broadest range of experience and emotion and therefore the humanity of our lives as black people and as women.

Neither Nor but Both

THE AWKWARD and contradictory phrase "neither nor but both" exemplifies my understanding of Holiday's artistic legacy. It is neither only aesthetic, nor only political, but both.

Musicians are part of the political and cultural ethos of their time. To claim that they as individuals transcend it is nonsensical. They are also artists; the best of them are on a constant quest to refine their craft, create meaning and beauty, and communicate to those willing to listen, read or see. If they are successful, the art forms they create will be part and parcel of the times in which they live and also contain an element of universality that speaks to generations and cultures beyond their immediate context.

Billie Holiday came of age in Harlem in the thirties, the Age of the Popular Front, Scottsboro, the rise of fascism in Europe.[81] It was hardly possible to live in Harlem at this time and not be aware of these things. In Harlem she participated in the May Day Rally of 1941 and the Golden Gate Ballroom Rallies for black communist politician Ben Davis in '43 and '44.[82] Furthermore, she matured as an artist at Café Society. In a conversation with Robin Kelley about Holiday at Café Society, he reminded me that "Even if it was just to get a gig, the air of revolution was there. And so was repression, which Holiday experienced first hand." Furthermore, those who knew Holiday personally note her allegiance to the black poor and working poor. While she never became as politically involved as Paul Robeson, Lena Horne or Hazel Scott, Horne notes: "Hazel Scott and I . . . we'd go to hear Billie together, and that's one time we would settle down and not fight. Because here was this voice speaking for the people." Josh White, who also sang a version of "Strange Fruit," said that Holiday was "more race conscious than people thought."[83]

The question isn't whether Holiday's art is political. It is. The interpretation of her work as a political form changes over time and that says more about the interpreters and their times than it does about Holiday and her music. Ralph Ellison's is an ideology for conservative times. This is why, though it was articulated and attacked earlier, it emerged as dominant following the demise of the Black Power movement, during the emergence of the right wing administrations of Ronald Reagan and George Bush. It is no coincidence that Amiri Baraka's position was dominant during the 1960s, for his is a position that can be nurtured during periods of sustained political activity on the part of our society's marginalized classes. Angela Davis's version of a political analysis of art is very much indicative of postmodern attempts during this more conservative time to sustain the political if only at the level of textual readings.

The cultural work of both Holiday's art and her icon is not political in the way that an activist or an organizer might be. Her icon insists on her genius in spite of the barriers posed by a racist and sexist society. At the level of form, Billie Holiday deconstructs and rewrites melodies. In so doing she influences the direction of American popular music. Art is a model of what can be done—it provides us with a vision of possibility, not simply its content, but also its form.[84]

All art forms can help to support the status quo or to challenge it by offering alternative visions and possibilities. Instead of turning to Billie Holiday's versions of popular love songs or to her most politically explicit song, "Strange Fruit," I want to focus on a formal blues written by her: "Billie's Blues."

First recorded for Columbia in 1936, "Billie's Blues" went on to become one of Holiday's most famous songs: she frequently performed it and between 1936 and 1956 she recorded at least five versions of it. The lyrics are most often recorded as follows:

Billie's Blues

I love my man I'm a liar if I say I don't
I love my man I'm a liar if I say I don't
But I'll quit my man I'm a liar if I say I won't

I been your slave ever since I been your babe
I've been your slave ever since I been your babe
But before I be your dog
I'll see you in your grave

My man wouldn't give me no breakfast
Wouldn't give me no dinner
Squawked about my supper
and then put me out of doors
Had the nerve to lay a matchbox on my clothes
I didn't have so many but I had a long way to go

I ain't good-looking and my hair ain't curled
I ain't good-looking and my hair it ain't curled
But my mama she give me something
It's gone carry me through this world

Some men like me cause I'm happy
Some cause I'm snappy
Some call me honey
Others think I've got money
Some tell me Billie
Baby you're built for speed
Now if you put that all together
Makes me everything a good man needs

The 1936 version differs slightly:

Lord I love my man Tell the world I do
I love my man Tell the world I do
But when he mistreats me makes me so blue
My man wouldn't give me no breakfast . . .

The differences are significant because by the time she records the song for Decca in 1944, she has added the lyrics about being treated like a slave but being unwilling to be treated like a dog. The persona of the second recording is more defiant, aggressive and assertive. This difference in the lyrics is echoed in the differences in performance as well. In the first version Holiday sings two choruses, taking her turn between the solos of her fellow musicians: Bunny Berigan, Artie Shaw, Joe Bushkin, Dick McDonough, Pete Peterson and Cozy Cole. By the second recording she has added more verses and is clearly the leader who is backed by other musicians (Heywood, Simmons, Catlett, Dickenson, Davis and Walters). They provide a foundation from which she sings. Consequently, she is the leader and she is more aggressive and assertive musically as well.

There are two ways of reading the lyrics of the 1944 version. (These are the lyrics of subsequent versions as well.) In one the persona is talking about what she will and will not take from her lover. She loves him but there are limits. She will be his slave (work for nothing, be at his beck and call) but not his dog. In fact, she will kill him if he treats her as such. She then lists all of the abusive things he has done to her. She knows her own limitations but also recognizes her strengths—strengths she inherits from her mother. Men find many things attractive about her, so she can find a new man, a good man. This is a warning: "I will leave you if you don't treat me right."

On another level, audiences might hear the song as spoken from a black person or black people to an American society that refuses to allow them entry as full-class citizens. We have been your slaves and concubines, but we will not be treated as if we are not human. If you continue to abuse us, we will take up arms. The next stanza lists all the ways that black people have been dispossessed; they are homeless—lacking food, shelter and clothing. Following this, the persona says, we don't meet white supremacist standards of beauty: my hair is nappy; but as a people we have many attributes and our own codes and standards for judging them. Given the context and the mood of her performance, audiences might hear either one or both of these messages.

Holiday's recordings of this tune are filled with fun and humor. The musicians who accompany her engage in a playful dialogue, setting up important lines with a dramatic lead and keeping silent when she delivers them. In most of the recordings there is a brief piano introduction, which Lady follows with the sentence beginning "I love my man." By the time she begins listing her attributes, the other musicians remain silent while she builds up the tension by singing:

Some men like me cause I'm happy (piano and drums
= Stop Time)
Some cause I'm snappy (Stop Time)
Some call me honey (Stop Time);
Others think I got money (Stop Time)

The piano and drums are the commas that punctuate her articulation of her attributes. They also help to build the tension. When she resolves the tension with "Some tell me Billie, baby you're built for speed," all of the other musicians join her and carry her through to the last line: "Now if you put that all together, makes me everything a good man needs." She stretches the word "needs" and the band carries her through to the end, followed by one of the horns, which finishes about two beats after she does.

The 1946 Verve recording of "Billie's Blues" is of the live performances of Jazz at the Philharmonic. She is accompanied by Joe Guy, trumpet; Georgie Auld, Illinois Jacquet, and Lester Young, all tenor saxophone; and Kenny Kersey on piano. In this version, the drums and piano play the same role, but the chorus of horns plays behind her throughout the entire song, with what I imagine is Lester Young playing a more dominant role, emerging from the background in what is almost a duet with Lady. This is the concert that took place prior to Holiday's imprisonment for drugs and her frequent appearances in the press that covered her various bouts with the law.

On November 10, 1956, after several years of arrests and having had her cabaret card taken from her, Holiday recorded another live version of this song at a Carnegie Hall concert. Roy Eldridge accompanied her on trumpet, Coleman Hawkins on tenor sax, Carl Drinkard on piano, Kenny Burrell on guitar, Carson Smith on bass and Chico Hamilton on drums. The bass and guitar join the drums and the piano in keeping the rhythm and providing punctuation between Billie's phrases.

As described in Chapter Two, during this concert the journalist Gilbert Millstein read the most dreary selections from her autobiography between performances of her best-known tunes. Just prior to "Billie's Blues," he reads the section of her autobiography where she talks about her decision to be neither whore nor prostitute and her beginning quest for employment as a singer. After Millstein finishes the passage in a rather dry monotone, the familiar piano introduction of "Billie's Blues" starts and is immediately met with an enthusiastic round of applause and approval. When Lady begins to sing, it is clear that the audience is with her. She plays with them, teases them, stretching the first "I" of "I ain't good-looking" over six beats. Millstein recalled that she was high when she arrived at the hall, went through minimal rehearsal, and could barely dress herself, but was adamant about the musicians who would accompany her. When she walked on stage, even the musicians applauded her. He noted that "they loved her," and that the audience did as well, adding that they could not have cared less about his readings. According to Millstein the audience constantly interrupted her with applause and she had at least six encores; she responded to all of them.

Although Millstein reads the most tragic portions of her autobiography and although the song is preceded by "Lady Sings the Blues" and "Ain't Nobody's Business If I Do" and followed by "Body and Soul," her performance of "Billie's Blues" is not a sad, low down blues. Instead it is one that functions as Murray suggests, to blow the blues away.

In both of these live recordings (as well as a third, recorded in Germany in 1954) it is evident that "Billie's Blues" marks a light and fun part of the evening. Her audience laughs with and encourages her. One can almost hear them saying "Yeah right, Billie" to her "I ain't good-looking." There is a great deal of laughter from the audience, and their call-and-response encouragement is evident throughout. The musicians are like her girlfriends, giving her advice and the strength to take action.[85]

However, the song also has a political dimension, and in this instance the laughter it provokes might come from a shared understanding between audience and performer of the conditions to which she refers. It is a laughter of the "you got to laugh to keep from crying" variety.

Ralph Ellison notes that the blues is "a chronicle of a personal catastrophe expressed lyrically." He is emphasizing the artistry and the formal qualities of the blues that allow artist and audience to transcend the mundane materiality of their lives. However, we should remember that catastrophe is usually the result of an imbalance of power over nature, death, fate, a lover, a family member, one's boss. . . . Imbalances of power are political, if even the personal politics of romantic relationships. The ability to express the catastrophic lyrically doesn't change the fact of its disastrous nature.

Even if there were no political dimension to Holiday's art, she is important both for what she gave us musically and for her existence as a social being in a world of racial, gender and class inequities. That she performed the Carnegie Hall concert with such professionalism and grace, given her addiction and the fact that her livelihood was limited because of the loss of her cabaret card, is evidence of the strength of her will to create even in the face of tremendous obstacles and odds—odds that might not have been set against her were she not black in America. Add to this the fact that what little money she was able to make probably went directly to the men who were her dealers, her husbands, and her manager, Joe Glaser, then her statement "I've been your slave" takes on a different dimension. No one was more aware of this dynamic than Holiday herself, who compared the circuits and clubs in which she performed to plantations and on more than one occasion referred to herself as a slave.

Holiday's example shows us that art is not merely a reflection of the social and political context out of which it arises, but that it is informed by that context and helps to shape it as well. Her artistry pronounces a constant will to survive with dignity and grace, a stance that marks much of black America's response to its oppression in the United States. Holiday did not have to fight assaults only from the men in her life, but from the vicious racism she encountered at every turn. She was hunted by the police because of her addiction and harassed by federal authorities because she chose to sing songs like "Strange Fruit" and "The Yanks Aren't Coming." And yet she continued to give voice to the concerns of millions of people, especially to the day-to-day concerns of blacks in the United States.

Our Lady of the Store Window, she of the gardenias who makes us long for the music, the pleasure, the bad-girl beauty lurking just beneath that mischievous smile. *(Murray Korman, 1941)*

6

Longing for Lady

ILLIE HOLIDAY'S voice evokes longing, loss and desire. In her lifetime she was a woman desired by both men and women. Though she often sang sassy, upbeat songs, she is best known for her torch songs—songs of a deep and dark longing. After her death, she continues to distract us, make us hunger for her, to follow her in her search for fulfillment. Lady Day gives voice to our yearnings for love, recognition, personal fulfillment and justice—for some of us, connection to a higher power, something larger and outside of ourselves. She is a seductive one, calling us with her siren song, promising discovery if only we follow her to the other side.

Is it any wonder that those who want to tap into our yearning find in Holiday's voice a most effective tool for doing so? Among the most successful are two disparate groups: corporate advertisers and poets have been attentive to Lady Day's capacity to evoke longing, to encourage us to follow her as children followed the Pied Piper. When an icon such as Holiday is placed on an object or in a poem or story, she communicates a number of messages. Her image becomes part of our memory of that object, poem, story or song, and when we see it or hear it or read it, we desire it. Advertisers want a Holiday who represents a longing for sex, beauty, hip blackness and luxury goods. Artists want a Holiday who inspires their own creativity.

Holiday Sales

IN THE SUMMER OF 1995, Knit Wit, a very chic clothing store in Center City, Philadelphia, exhibited three flat cardboard mannequins. Each wore blue linen slacks or skirt and different styles of crisp, white linen blouses. A black-and-white photocopy of Murray Korman's 1941 portrait of Billie Holiday was attached to the head of each mannequin. In one folded, cardboard arm each mannequin held a different Holiday biography: Robert O'Meally's *Lady Day: The Many Faces of Billie Holiday*, John Chilton's *Billie's Blues* and Donald Clarke's *Wishing on the Moon*. The words "Lady Sings the Blues . . . Lady Wears the Blues" were stamped on the windowpane.

By their choice of photograph, the store's proprietors evoked a mood and an image. Clearly there was the expectation that passersby would recognize the face, the signature gardenia, the phrase "Lady Sings the Blues." Given the prevalence of "heroin chic" on the pages of *Vogue* and *Harper's Bazaar* that summer, perhaps they would identify her with heroin as well. The clothing store, situated as it is between Borders to the left and Ann Taylor on the right, is chic, expensive, hip, slightly funky. These adjectives also describe this particular image of Holiday. How different it might have been had they chosen another of the many Holiday photographs currently in circulation—consider, for instance, the 1959 Milt Hinton photograph that depicts a tired and aged Holiday, head down, eyes watering, glass in hand (see Figure 2). Our Lady of the store window is the Holiday of "Swing It Brother, Swing," not the Holiday of "Good Morning Heartache."

How do we get from Holiday as a highly gifted musician with severe problems in her personal life, to Holiday as the poster child for various forms of victimization, to Holiday as muse for numerous poets, novelists and musicians, to Holiday as commodity representing all that is cool, urbane, upscale and hip—our lady of the boutique, coffee shop and J. Peterman catalogue?[86]

Advertisers have gotten hip. The jazz audience has always been a sophisticated one. Now there are many, not necessarily jazz fans, who associate the music with hip sophistication. Billie Holiday is jazz royalty. She also, in death as in life, sparks desire. This has always been the case, but something has changed to bring all of these elements to the attention of corporate advertisers. The identification of jazz as a music that sells high-priced items is related to the changed image of the music and its practitioners.

Noted critics such as Albert Murray and Stanley Crouch seek to emphasize the professionalism, elegance and discipline of the jazz musician in contrast to the downtrodden, drugged-out genius stereotype that dominated mainstream perceptions of jazz musicians. I should add that William "Billy" Taylor, pianist and ambassador of jazz as "America's classical music," has also argued for similar understandings of jazz.[87] Through lectures, concerts and a regular segment on CBS's *Sunday Morning,* Taylor has been equally responsible for helping to spread the good news about jazz.[88] But it is Wynton Marsalis's cultural work as musician, composer and founding director of Jazz at Lincoln Center that has helped to ensure that this version of jazz emerged triumphant.[89]

Had Marsalis not struck such a conservative stance, whereby some of the most innovative practitioners are left out of the jazz canon, it is highly unlikely he would have been able to acquire the resources necessary to do the kind of work on behalf of the music that he has done. Marsalis has used a vocabulary of European classical music to describe jazz to people who otherwise might have refused to acknowledge the seriousness and importance of the art form.[90] His own talent, success and elegance have made him a favorite of advertisers as well. Marsalis even appears in an advertisement for Movado watches. According to Scott De Veaux, Marsalis is the contemporary image of jazz "young, black and hip but fiercely committed to ideals of tradition, artistic discipline and education."[91] His is an image that sells, but certainly not the only one. Cassandra Wilson sells Coach bags; Sarah Vaughan, Gap khakis; and Dinah Washington, luxury cars. Advertising images even influence the way musicians present themselves. Cassandra Wilson appears in the booklet accompanying her CD *Traveling Miles* seated in a pair of classic khakis. The photo looks like an earlier photograph of Miles Davis sitting in a recording studio, a photograph of Miles that was later used for a Gap khaki ad.

Yes, Billie Holiday's image and voice have been attractive to corporate America as well. Holiday the commodity falls within a wide range of elements of black life and culture that the mainstream culture both fears and desires. These elements or individuals are constructed as commodities so as to contain their threatening traits and apparently make available for sale those characteristics that consumers desire. Consumers desire that which they never have. You can have the beauty, the romance, the risk, without the danger. What factors contribute to the making of Our Lady of the Store Window? First, of course, is the transformation of the public image of jazz during the last two decades of the twentieth century. The second is the profile of the jazz audience members who also constitute a market. To whom are advertisers addressing their ads? I think there are actually two overlapping target groups: the first made up of the contemporary jazz audience, the second, a broader group, not necessarily jazz fans, but those who have a sense of jazz as something both classy (like opera and Western classical music) and perpetually hip.

The National Endowment for the Arts (NEA) has funded four Surveys of Public Participation in the Arts—SPPA: 1982, 1985, 1992 and 1997. The studies have sought to identify the "size and demographic characteristics of the jazz audience: those adult Americans who attend jazz events, participate in jazz through the media, perform jazz, or simply say they like the idiom."[92] (It is important to note that they did not distinguish between straight-ahead, avant garde and smooth jazz.)

In 1997 approximately one third of the surveyed American adults reported they liked jazz. Five percent reported they like it best of all musical genres. Twenty-five percent expressed a desire to attend jazz performances more often than they do now. Ten percent attended a jazz performance during the previous year. The survey concluded that the jazz audience is nearly as large as that of classical music.

What are the demographics of the jazz audience? Most are under forty-five years old. The SPPA also found that nearly half those attending jazz performances earned at least $50,000 per year. They are ethnically diverse, though most are affluent males and many are black. In 1998 *Blue Note* commissioned a similar study, which revealed a racially diverse audience, "made up of 35- to 49-year-old college graduates who earned at least $75,000 a year. Some 40 percent of those surveyed said they owned or planned to buy a luxury car or sport utility vehicle within the next year."[93]

Advertisers will use this information, the jazz fan's desire for a luxury car or sport utility vehicle, as a means to help make their products more attractive. Consequently, jazz provides the soundtrack for commercials for Cadillacs, Mercedeses and Jaguars. On one commercial you can hear a voice that sounds like Billie Holiday's. You think it is Lady until the vocalist hits a note outside Holiday's range, thereby jarring the true Holiday fan. But it is the familiarity of the voice that calls attention to the commercial. "Is that Lady Day?" I ask. My attention turns from the book, the dishes, the telephone, to the television, to a commercial I might otherwise have ignored. Suddenly I am drawn into a scenario where I am inside a beautifully upholstered car, riding down a tree-laden road. Were I not primarily interested in Lady's voice, I might even miss that point where the vocalist distinguishes herself. (The vocalist is Madeleine Peyroux.)

In an article on advertisers' use of jazz, Valerie Gladstone writes: "Advertisers often turn to . . . music houses, companies that produce music for commercials, because the cost of using original recordings is so high. They start at $200,000 and can go to $2 million for a signature song by Nat (King) Cole. In contrast, such companies charge from $50,000 to $100,000 to create a composition in the style of one of the masters." I don't know if cost drove the choice cited above, but it is clear that the vocalist's resemblance to Holiday influenced that choice.

What does Lady's voice invoke for the person in search of a new luxury car? Certainly not criminality or substance abuse. No, the targeted group knows her to have been a bearer of the jazz tradition. She is beautiful, laid back, hip but not flamboyant. Because most buyers of luxury cars are men, she appeals to them not just as a singer, but as a woman as well. Peter Greco, a senior vice president at Young & Rubicam, says he turns to jazz because it evokes classicism. Lisa Kirschner of Ogilvy & Mather cites the music's timeless quality. Eric Korte of Saatchi & Saatchi says, "Bottom line, jazz has integrity. It's never corny. It moves. And its percussive quality, its energy, livens up anything connected to it."[94] Lady Day is a member of jazz royalty. She is timeless, she has integrity and she swings. Commercials promise: you too will be classy, timeless, have integrity and the ability to swing, not by talent or discipline but by purchasing a product.

There is a commercial for BV wine that uses a recording of Holiday singing "As Time Goes By": her voice singing one of our best-known love songs, a song linked to a classic couple, Bogie and Bergman, the epitome of romance, exotic locale, mystery and intrigue. The two-and-a-half-minute commercial depicts a couple in for an evening at home. Clearly we are to think that the couple will make love later in the evening. Faces are forgettable, but the wine, the promise of sex and the voice are not.

Not all advertisements using Billie Holiday are directed at affluent hip men who drive luxury vehicles and drink fine wine. Some are directed at their companions, or at least the women they imagine as their companions or who imagine themselves that way as well. Two of the most interesting of these are print advertisements, neither of which uses Holiday's voice or image to sell the products. In 1999, the J. Peterman Company advertised two dresses in its catalogue, one under a heading "Lady in Autumn" and the other simply "Lady Day."

The Peterman catalogues were mini-books, which provided their commodities with personal histories through brief narratives that accompanied drawings of the item. There was no model, rarely did the drawings have faces, many had no heads and the full image of the product itself was drawn as if it were on a woman's body, but the body was not there. The dress or slacks or blouse hang there as if a sensual, elegant but invisible ghost might be wearing them. This way, women were not distracted by some ideal they couldn't meet. They could imagine themselves as the figure wearing the article of clothing. The narrative tells you that if you purchase the dress, you can be the heroine of the tale. The clothing was often associated with a celebrity or the character she played in a film, such as Audrey Hepburn and Grace Kelly. The figures had to be recognizable to the people who browsed through the catalogue, so while Dorothy Dandridge was beautiful and sexy, one would not have found a Dandridge or even a Carmen Jones dress, because she and her most famous character were not as easily recognized. Madonna wouldn't be there because though she provides the perfect heroine for a Peterman narrative—adventurous, unconventional and independent—her image does not provide the same sense of nostalgia or romance, though that of Evita Peron might. But Billie Holiday is a perfectly fitting choice: their version of her is beautiful, sexual, talented and slightly dangerous. And, most important, like Kelly and Hepburn, she is a recognizable icon, with a distinct style.

The Lady Day Dress—a below-the-calf length, sleeveless, "silk georgette, chiffon-lined" dress with a "high waist and fitted bodice" with a flounce at the bottom, in "a muted tan, cream and green floral print"—sold for $250. If you so desired, you could also purchase the Lady Day Sweater—in natural or black—for an additional $75. Three narratives accompany the image of the dress. The first and longest develops the character and the setting. The two that describe the garments give additional scenarios.

Lady Day

She steps into the spotlight with a gardenia in her hair, puts her head back, closes her eyes.

Talk stops. Waiters stand still.

Her voice, that voice, emerges like a small silver bell. It flirts, bubbles, rasps, turns ironic.

She reshapes ordinary moons and Junes into something fresh and wonderful. As for songs like "Love for Sale," well . . .

A Philadelphia nightclub owner recalls that in one week, 27 fights broke out when wives didn't like the way their husbands were looking at her.

It doesn't matter that she grew up in the streets. It doesn't matter that her body is a map of needle scars.

Up there Billie Holiday is Lady Day, secure in the perfect world she sings.

Listen to the records. You'll see.

The main narrative does not even mention the product. Instead it serves a pedagogical function. It introduces Lady, paints a picture of the intimacy and sensuality of her performance. The passage tells those who just don't get the fuss what she does. "She transforms ordinary moons and Junes into something fresh and wonderful." She had it hard, grew up rough and was a junkie, but none of that really matters. All that matters is the world she creates onstage. If you associate yourself with her by purchasing this dress, you will not be entering the street life but that beautiful one where voices sound like silver bells and men forget their wives because of you. Wouldn't you like to have that impact? The narrative closes by giving you an assignment. Listen to the records. If you want to be the woman of this advertisement, you need to not only wear our clothing, but you should have some knowledge of the things that give you some cultural capital—in this case, jazz.

Having set the scene and taught the lesson, the advertisement now turns to the product and to the consumer. The Lady Day Dress: "What the greatest jazz singer who ever lived wore onstage." Can't you just see yourself in it, onstage, gardenia in hair, singing? The Lady Day Sweater: "For appearances at Carnegie Hall. Or sitting at the bar with Prez, about 4 a.m., feeling the chill come on." Now that you've been schooled, you're hip enough to recognize the references. You know Prez is Lester Young, brilliant tenor saxophonist and Lady Day's creative soulmate. Is the chill coming on because it's getting chilly or because her habit is coming down? That's all part of the mystery.

The Lady Day Dress is a summer frock. When the seasons change there is Lady in Autumn. An asterisk follows the title of this one and points you to a footnote: "Worth looking for: 'Lady in Autumn,' 1946–59, Verve Records." This is part of your continuing jazz education.

The narrative:

Lady in Autumn

No one on earth like her. Winsome and wise. But risky. A fool for love. An irresistible force (taught Orson Welles a little more about jazz and still got him to the set by 6 a.m.).

It was chilly in Berlin. She went anyway, because they loved her. They came from both sides of the Wall. She dressed as they expected: fragile beauty but sensible. Sensible enough to pull on a long-sleeve sweater, under her fur, over her classic dress. It got very hot and very cool.

Here is a second installment of lessons on Lady Day. She is one of a kind. It's not only nameless husbands who fall for her, but cinematic geniuses as well. The ad says she "taught Orson Welles a little more about jazz and still got him to the set by 6 A.M. With Orson Welles, she is in control. Teaching him about jazz until 6 A.M." suggests "jazz" is here used in the way it was before it became music. To jazz was to have sex. She did not just sing in Philadelphia. She was an international star who broke through political boundaries. Her German fans didn't only expect to hear her sing, they had expectations of her clothing as well. The outfit is the Lady, both sensible and no-nonsense. And yet she is emotionally fragile, so very, very sensitive. Like the Lady in the song "The Lady Is a Tramp," Lady Day is not pretentious. Yes, she has a fur, what star wouldn't? But for warmth she puts on a long-sleeve sweater. She is both hot as in passionate and cool as in hip.

The Bordeaux (burgundy) print dress "is the lush life. Floating, heavyweight silk. Fully lined. High fitted waist (not empire; no faux-pregnant billowing). Elegant bateau neckline. Worldly innocence, a golden time. No need to explain." In this dress you can become the Lady who is worldly, street-smart and yet in possession of that little girl innocence in need of protection. Not to worry, the dress isn't tight, but it isn't so loose as to make you look pregnant. For those in the know, there are allusions to Billy Strayhorn's "Lush Life" and to Lady Day's famous song "Don't Explain." Wear this dress, and you won't need to say a word—it speaks for you. You don't have to just long for Lady; every time you wear this dress, you can be her.

Advertisers take this desire for Holiday, decontextualize the image from the lived life, marry the Holiday image to particular products or services, and in doing so, create desire for the latter. Lady makes you long? For what? Advertisers want you to long for this luxury car, this stereo, this wine, book, dress, magazine, and so on and so on. All in all they want you to long for a lifestyle of which these things are a part. The ads make promises that the products cannot deliver.

Poets make no such promises. They, too, agree that Lady evokes longing for something unattainable but worth reaching for because in the process you gain something else—something both abstract and real. Their Lady is no closer to the historical Holiday than is that of the advertisers, but she does not promise to satisfy your longing. Instead, the Dark Lady of the Sonnets leads us to our own creativity: creativity born of yearning.

Dark Lady of the Sonnets[95]

Poetic language is language owning up to being an orphan.

—Nathaniel Mackey

POET AND CRITIC Susan Stewart provides an apt starting point for exploring the connection between longing, poetry and Billie Holiday. In *On Longing* Stewart writes of the available metaphors for talking about "the relationship between language to experience or . . . the relations of narrative to its object." She asks, "How can we describe something? What relations does description bear to ideology and the very invention of that 'something'?" (ix). Here, Stewart identifies the impossibility of representing anything (or, for our purposes, anyone) as it is or was.

The act of representation is at best one step removed from that which one desires to "represent." There is always a distance between the "thing" as it is and the language used to describe it. Because the representation is not the original, one has to choose the way of describing. Which words work best? What metaphor, sound or image best renders the "thing"? These choices bear ideological consequences, because words and definitions necessarily challenge, reflect, embody or sustain existing ideologies. Whenever we describe or attempt to represent something, we construct or invent something else—something related to, but distinct from, the original. Given the circulation of this new thing, it may also become more ubiquitous than the original. This is especially the case with poetry and prose, because unlike a living being, texts have a greater chance of achieving immortality.

Billie Holiday, or her absence, generates a longing expressed in writing. This writing results in a new thing—a new Holiday, a new poem, or both. She becomes part of the poem, the new thing, which then becomes part of the lexicon that defines her. Because we have access to the poem and not to "Holiday," the poem transforms the very meaning of Billie Holiday.

Poetry—unlike biography, music criticism, commercial film and journalism—makes explicit its effort to represent the object of its inspiration without claiming to be that object. In this instance, Lady Day is the melody upon which the poet improvises. This improvisation, complete with references to, and quotations from, other improvisations, teases us with an image, version or glimpse of Billie Holiday.

MANY POETS are attracted to and mourn the loss of Holiday because she was a poet herself. As I asserted in Chapter One, if we think of music as a language, then Holiday's careful juxtaposition of chosen notes structured into phrases, which give both beauty and meaning, makes her a poet as well.

In addition, Holiday's rendering of lyrics, especially toward the end of her life, often sound more like a poet reading than a vocalist singing lyrics. On *Lady in Satin,* she offers dramatic recitations of the lyrics as if she were an actress. If Holiday delivers a lyric like a poet reading verse, many poets seek to emulate her phrasing. It is as though they long for the most identifiable characteristic of her singing. In this way, poets are not only attracted to Holiday's tragedy but also to her art. In losing her, they mourn one of their own.

There are perhaps more poems written in honor of, about or mentioning Billie Holiday than just about any other jazz artist, save John Coltrane. In his *Bibliographic Guide to Jazz Poetry,* Sascha Feinstein cites more than sixty poems about Billie Holiday; in addition he cites twenty-one that name her and four in which she is mentioned. My reading of Holiday poems suggests they fall into six overlapping categories:[96] elegies, poems that are specifically about her music, poems that borrow from lyrics of songs she popularized, "Strange Fruit" poems, poetic biographies, and poems that construct an image of Holiday in order to trigger something else that the poem contemplates. This list is certainly not an exhaustive one.[97]

The most famous Holiday poem, Frank O'Hara's "The Day Lady Died" is one extraordinary example of the elegiac nature of many poems about Holiday, especially the last two stanzas:

and for Mike I just stroll into the PARK LANE
Liquor Store and ask for a bottle of Strega and
then I go back where I came from to 6th Avenue
and the tobacconist in the Ziegfeld Theatre and
casually ask for a carton of Gauloises and a carton
of Picayunes, and a NEW YORK POST with her face on it

and I am sweating a lot by now and thinking of
leaning on the john door in the FIVE SPOT
while she whispered a song along the keyboard
to Mal Waldron and everyone and I stopped breathing

The poem chronicles the mundane minutiae of a city dweller on his way to the suburbs for dinner. Suddenly the casual pace is disrupted by the *New York Post* headline announcing Holiday's death. He then is taken back to a breathless moment when he heard Billie Holiday cast a spell over "everyone." Because none of the twenty-eight lines preceding the last one has a period, the reader also experiences a sense of breathlessness by the time she reaches the final line. Consequently, the poet provides us the experience of hearing Holiday; accordingly, we also feel the power of the loss of Lady Day.

While this is the most famous of the poems dedicated to Lady Day, it is not the only one to evoke the tremendous loss embodied in her voice and invoked by her death. Even in those poems where Holiday is a minor presence, she is nonetheless a significant and necessary image. Her appearance usually marks a departure point for the persona to begin a kind of self-reflective pondering. When the persona of Betsy Sholl's poem "Don't Explain" thinks of Holiday, it triggers a series of memories and contemplative moments about her parents and her own relationship to her father's memory. In other instances Holiday is a sign for any number of things, ranging from social injustice to artistic accomplishment. This is the case in Amiri Baraka's poem "The Lady," where Holiday represents the longing of an oppressed people.

The O'Hara, Sholl and Baraka poems are three of my favorites. I find the most satisfying those Holiday poems that, like Holiday's live performances, create an atmosphere of intimacy and request the kind of quiet that demands the listener's attention. Like Cassandra Wilson's blue velvet voice wrapped around "Harvest Moon," the best poems whisper: "Come a little bit closer, there's something I have to say." The poems that most move me all seem to share a sense of longing for something that it is utterly impossible to possess. Perhaps this says more about me than it does about Holiday poetry, given the relationship between my own paternal longing and my early engagement with Holiday.

THE LADY

The Lady said of her life here that she 1st
heard part of her own voice, (Bessie & Louie),
in a whore house; but she wasn't the only one
  The Lady said
But also that the whore
house
was the only place where
there was even a semblance
of democracy
People say
no one says the word
"Hunger"
"Love"
  I want to remember

Amiri Baraka (1987)

With the poem "The Lady," Amiri Baraka immortalizes Billie Holiday by quoting statements attributed to her in his construction of something new—the poem. In addition to direct quotations from Holiday, he also evokes her phrasing by his repeated use of two or three consecutive stresses: "life here"; "whore house." The fourteen lines of the poem mimic the standard fourteen-line form of the sonnet. The title "The Lady" draws upon the phrase "our Lady," whether it is "our Holy Mother" or the inaccessible lady to whom the poet pays homage. Baraka situates Lady Day within a tradition of black art and longing. From the spirituals, which speak of a longing for home, freedom or death, much of black art is an art of longing.

Because these feelings of longing are universal, Holiday, though grounded in an African-American tradition, serves the same purpose for artists outside that tradition as well, as seen in the poetry of Betsy Sholl. "Don't Explain" is the title poem of Sholl's prize-winning volume of poetry published in 1997. Although it is named for a song Billie Holiday wrote and popularized, Holiday is a minor, though important figure in the poem. "Don't Explain" is a narrative: it has a protagonist, a plot, a moment of crisis when confronting an unexpected antagonist—in this instance, the discovery of her father's bigotry. Holiday's voice on a discarded cassette tape reminds the poem's persona of her father, whose memory exists in her mind like a reel-to-reel tape. Both figures are ghostlike and inaccessible, the reproductions of their voices and images flawed at best. Holiday's voice helps the persona of that poem come to terms with her own father's racial bigotry and reveals to her the dawn of a more tolerant and inclusive vision. In Sholl's poem, Holiday's voice insists on life and articulates loss and longing. It is a voice from the other side, a haunting voice. This articulation of loss and longing is transferred from the singer to the listener. The persona, the listener, reads the loss of Holiday's song and of her voice not as death but as the triumph of life—its insistence on breaking through artifice, much like flowers that grow between the cracks of a cement pavement. Holiday's voice awakens in the persona a sense of vision and the possibility of a life free from the dehumanizing vision of her father.

Of all of the myriad Holiday poems, Rita Dove's "Canary" is one of the most beautiful and the one from which this book takes its title.

Billie Holiday's burned voice
had as many shadows as lights,
a mournful candelabra against a sleek piano,
the gardenia her signature under that ruined face.

(Now you're cooking, drummer to bass,
magic spoon, magic needle.
Take all day if you have to
with your mirror and your bracelet of song.)

Fact is, the invention of women under siege
has been to sharpen love in the service of myth.

If you can't be free, be a mystery.

RITA DOVE (1989)

The word "canary" can have two meanings in the context of Dove's poem: 1) the name given to the "girl-singer" who sings in front of a band of "real" (male) musicians, and 2) the little songbird, indigenous to the Canary Islands off the coast of Africa, caged and kept as a pet. "Canary" might also bring to mind the bird sent into the coal mine to gauge its safety. For many black thinkers, black people have been a metaphorical canary sent into the coal mines of America. The canary is the sacrifice. Finally, for some of us, canary, the caged songbird, also brings to mind Paul Laurence Dunbar's poem "Sympathy" with the oft-quoted line, "I know why the caged bird sings." All of these are relevant here.

A description of Lady's voice opens the poem. The sentence is in the past tense; the burned voice "had as many shadows as lights." This refers both to the cadence and tone of her singing voice and to the mood it evokes. As many shadows as lights; neither one nor the other, but both. In this stanza, her voice and her signature gardenia are the things by which we remember her, the sound and image that can invoke her presence. The voice is burned—it lacks materiality. The face is ruined. Both "ruined" and "burned" are verbs in the past tense. They are also adjectives that suggest things are over, past and destroyed.

The second stanza is contained by parentheses much like the caged bird, like Holiday encaged by her habit that is described here. "Cooking" again has two meanings. One musician commenting on the ability of another to swing; or heroin cooking in a spoon to be taken up by the hypodermic needle. The penultimate stanza is a magnificent statement of society's need for tragic women. They are invented, not born. There is an investment in their being under siege by drugs, fame, men. They are necessary for the myths we construct about our lives and ourselves.

The final line stands free from the other stanzas. It is a directive to the readers, one learned from Holiday. It opens out telling others to choose mystery if you cannot have freedom. Who is the "you" here? Holiday, the reader or both? "Free" and "mystery" rhyme and are therefore joined. The caged bird isn't free, Holiday isn't free. Choosing to be a mystery is the one way to maintain a semblance of control, to keep your inner self to yourself. This is an act of agency for the unfree. Mystery is the thing we do not know, cannot solve. The caged bird's song is a mystery; the "real" Holiday is a mystery. In spite of the familiarity with her autobiography, it is as though we know everything and nothing about her.

The OED offers several definitions for "mystery." Its theological uses include "a religious truth known only from divine revelation; usually a . . . doctrine of faith involving difficulties which human reason is incapable of solving." The nontheological uses include "a secret or hidden thing, unexplored, unimaginable, an enigma." Finally, and perhaps most significantly, "mystery" also means "the behavior or attitude of mind of one who makes a secret of things, usually for the purpose of exercising undue power or influence." All of these definitions are relevant to our Dark Lady of the Sonnets. She is inaccessible; to know her is an act of faith. She is a ghostly presence. She is like the Divine, which we are only capable of knowing through our own limited imagination. The Lady of the last line is also she who "makes a secret of things" in order to exercise power or influence over those who are obsessed with her. In this poem, she is in control; we can never grasp her. She is what Lewis Turco describes as "an unanchored abstraction," that which means nothing and therefore can mean anything we wish it to.

While Holiday in this poem is representative of the "invention of women under siege," women such as Marilyn Monroe, Dorothy Dandridge and Judy Garland, she again is connected to the history of black Americans. The allusion to Dunbar's poem that I spoke of earlier makes this clear. In 1899 Dunbar penned the following lines:

> *I know why the caged bird sings, ah me,*
>   *When his wing is bruised and his bosom sore—*
> *When he beats his bars and would be free;*
> *It is not a carol of joy or glee,*
>   *But a prayer that he sends from his heart's deep core,*
> *But a plea, that upward to Heaven he flings—*
> *I know why the caged bird sings!*

Here, the caged bird—black Americans, brought enslaved to a foreign land—seeks freedom. He mourns the loss of it; beats his wings in an unsuccessful bid to acquire it and then, bloodied and still enslaved, he sings. He sings not out of joy but out of a desire for freedom. However, like Holiday, he is not free and his song remains a mystery to all but those who share his predicament and "know why the caged bird sings." As is the case with the Baraka poem, this allusion to Dunbar links the Holiday of "Canary" to a tradition of black longing for freedom.

Interestingly, when Billie Holiday was literally encaged in Alderson Prison, she never sang a note.

Poems about Holiday tend to stress that she cannot be fully portrayed or represented. For many poets Holiday is that messenger from the other side, she is "our Lady"; she is an ancestor turned orisha (divine beings of the Yoruba pantheon) whom we cannot represent, but in longing for her we are inspired. Always, the result is something that both acknowledges her legacy and builds upon it.

Abbey Lincoln—vocalist, poet, lyricist and artistic descendant of Holiday—acknowledged her debt to Holiday. But her own work, especially her beautiful, poetic song lyrics, rejects much of the Holiday myth. "Caged Bird" calls upon the tradition cited above, but not satisfied with "I know why the caged bird sings," she writes, "Birds were meant to fly away/And birds were meant to sing." She rejects the agency of mystery for the agency of flight. In another song, "Bird Alone," she provides an alternative vision: "Bird alone, flying low/Over where the grasses grow/Swinging low, then out of sight/You'll be singing in the night." Poet Alexis De Veaux says, "Jazz gave Billie the power of flight." Thanks to these black women artists, the bird alone singing in the night is yet another version of Lady Day and those who follow her.

The birds who live in cages
never spread their wings.
They sit with ruffled feathers
on the tiny swings.
—"Caged Bird"

7

Abbey Lincoln:
The Dawn of a New Day

ONE NIGHT in the spring of 2000 I went to Harlem's Aaron Davis Hall to hear Abbey Lincoln in concert with her trio. The hall was filled with an intergenerational, multiracial audience whose love for the singer was apparent even before she stepped onstage. For two hours she sang to us, taught us, seduced us, and provided spiritual nurturance. Her band was made up of three gifted young musicians; we watched as she chided, chastised and praised them. Giving them room for long, extensive solos, she would sit in a chair or stand off in the corner, smiling, nodding approvingly like a mother bird watching her young ones take flight. And then she would return center stage and soar, her audience borne aloft on her song.

Unlike the caged birds of Rita Dove's and Paul Laurence Dunbar's poems, Abbey Lincoln sings of birds not satisfied with their cages, birds meant "to fly away," and ultimately autonomous birds who glide, swing, fly and sing. In her art, Ms. Lincoln also has grown from the caged bird to the beautiful, complex "Bird Alone," "singing in the night."[98] This trajectory is evident in her choice of songs and in the lyrics she writes. Notions of flight and love dominate Lincoln's later work. If the theme of flight changes in the way described above, then love changes its very meaning as well. One hears a shift from the romantic love of the jazz standards, to the love of a people and a culture, to love of self, of the ancestors and the divine.

I am devoting the last chapter of this book on Billie Holiday to Abbey Lincoln because she provides one of the many alternative directions taken by those who inherit Holiday's legacy. I could have chosen Carmen McRae or Betty Carter, both of whom offer versions of the legacy from which all women and artists (male and female) can benefit. But I have chosen Ms. Lincoln because she most resonates with my own hopes and desires. While both Carter and McRae feed my aesthetic appetite, Lincoln's work speaks to me personally and spiritually as well. Also, as was the case with Holiday, my father introduced me to Abbey Lincoln; consequently, I link all three.

Abbey Lincoln has become yet another of those African-American women artists whose creativity and vision have helped to inspire, influence and shape my own. As with Holiday, I find myself turning to Lincoln's music time and time again. I listen to it to hear how she has grown as an artist and a woman. I am encouraged by her refusal to stop growing and taking risks.

Thankfully, her life has been long enough for her to have made the mistakes of youth, learned from and built upon them. She has entered her maturity with a dignity, grace and beauty that actually make me look forward to growing older. In my adulthood, Lincoln joins my own pantheon of artistic greats, providing one means of building upon and extending Holiday's legacy, life and art.

CAGED BIRD

The birds who live in cages
never spread their wings.
They sit with ruffled feathers
on the tiny swings, . . .
and tuck their heads in feathers
of a colorful array.[99]
—ABBEY LINCOLN

IN JUNE 1957, Abbey Lincoln appeared on the cover of *Ebony* magazine singing in front of a blue stage curtain. Her statuesque figure is swathed in a fire-engine red dress with spaghetti straps, a sequined bust and tight shirring to emphasize the curve of her hips. At the bottom of the photograph, a caption reads "Abbey Lincoln—The Girl in the Marilyn Monroe Dress."[100] Monroe wore the red dress in the film *Gentlemen Prefer Blondes*. The photograph of Lincoln is taken from the film *The Girl Can't Help It* (1956), starring another blond bombshell, Jayne Mansfield. The *Ebony* article features photographs of Marilyn Monroe juxtaposed to photographs of Lincoln imitating the blonde's poses: lots of cleavage, legs and derriere. Minimal text accompanies the photographs. In fact there is only one paragraph, and it reveals Lincoln's measurements (36-24-37).

Another story on Lincoln had appeared in an earlier issue of *Ebony*. "Miss Gaby Lee"[101] introduced her to *Ebony* readers: "The hottest new singer to hit Hollywood this season is a tall, shapely, torch-voiced lass who is billed as Miss Gaby Lee." The article went on to discuss Lincoln's appearance at the Moulin Rouge. Again there is little text and at least three cheesecake photographs. These two stories demonstrate the role for which Lincoln was being groomed. In the mid-fifties she was poised to inherit the mantle of black sex symbol, a browner version of the café au lait chanteuses described in the chapter "Lady-like." In fact, she took over the lead role in the musical *Jamaica,* which had once featured Lena Horne. The cheesecake photographs and nightclub persona suggest she would have fallen in line with Dorothy Dandridge as well.

It is not insignificant that the *Ebony* layout compared her to a white sex symbol. The film *The Girl Can't Help It,* directed by Frank Tashlin, features Lincoln as the nightclub act that Jayne Mansfield's character appreciatively watches. In both instances Lincoln appears as a kind of shadow of the white woman, imitating Monroe and instigating Mansfield's sexuality.[102] Later in her career, Lincoln would vehemently oppose standards of beauty that deified blond women.

While she sang only one song in the film, that same year Lincoln released her first album, *Abbey Lincoln's Affair . . . a Story of a Girl in Love,* on the Liberty label, produced by Russell Keith and arranged by Benny Carter. The album cover echoes the images in *Ebony* and in *The Girl Can't Help It.* She is lying down, smiling softly and dressed in a low-cut, cream-colored negligee that barely covers her breasts. The liner notes read: "As the cover of this album would indicate, Abbey Lincoln has been blessed with the lines, curves, arcs and semicircles in the tradition of classic beauty." Her image is more important than the contents of the album. Unlike subsequent liner notes, there is no discussion here of her style of singing, her choice of lyrics or of the musicians who accompany her.

The songs are all love songs, including two also sung by Billie Holiday: "Do Nothing Till You Hear from Me" and "Crazy He Calls Me." There is none of the emotion, originality or experimentation that would come to characterize her later efforts. Her voice is lyrical, clear, and predictable. Though there are instrumental jazz elements, especially the trumpet, this is not a jazz album. She is not in dialogue with any of the soloists, nor are any of the individual musicians named.

In a 1986 interview with jazz critic Francis Davis, Lincoln notes that following *Affair,* "I didn't yet think of myself as a serious artist or as a serious person either. All I wanted was to be thought of as beautiful and desirable." In the same interview she says, "I was on the road to loneliness and despair."[103] This concern with the outer shell at the expense of her inner substance resulted in dissatisfaction and depression. A social movement, a love relationship and Lady Day would lead her to herself.

By the time Lincoln appeared in *The Girl Can't Help It* and released *Affair,* she started to change the direction of her career and life. In 1956, at the age of twenty-six, Lincoln moved to New York and in 1957 she began writing her own lyrics and recording with Max Roach. She recalls in New York: "I met a circle of black musicians and other artists. It was the early days of the civil rights movement, and we were all asking the same questions" (66). In other words, the atmosphere she inhabited was a highly politicized and creative one. The choice to leave the path laid out for her was a choice of integrity, one that honored her desire for personal and artistic growth and one that was aided by this atmosphere. She was part of a context energized by militant political activism, creative originality and social change. The experience would have been similar to Billie Holiday's time at Café Society, though Holiday's political context there was the interracial Popular Front in bohemian Greenwich Village, while Lincoln's was primarily black in the black cultural mecca, Harlem. The most powerful force influencing Lincoln's changing sense of herself at this time was the social movement, which greatly influenced the musical world she inhabited. That world in turn greatly affected the social consciousness of the movement. While Holiday did come of age in the highly politicized atmosphere of Café Society, she did not have access to the militant politics of race that so deeply influenced Lincoln.

At this time Lincoln and Roach embarked upon a romantic relationship that would result in their marriage and one of the most incredible musical collaborations in the history of jazz. One of the first products of their collaboration was her second album, *Abbey Lincoln and the Riverside Jazz Stars,* released in 1957 on the Riverside label. Along with Prestige and Blue Note, Riverside was one of the most innovative independent labels producing jazz in the late fifties and early sixties. On Lincoln's first Riverside release, she was accompanied by a stellar group of musicians, including Sonny Rollins, Kenny Dorham, Wynton Kelly, Max Roach and Paul Chambers. Their names are listed on the front of the album. Lincoln begins to experiment with jazz phrasing, and the material she sings offers some insight into her changing persona. While she sings a few Holiday classics, including "My Man" and "Don't Explain," she also sings songs in praise of black masculinity, "Strong Man" and "Happiness Is a Thing Called Joe."

"Strong Man," written by Oscar Brown, Jr., is especially indicative of this mood. Lincoln recalls telling Brown: "I want a song about my father, my brother, not about a man who ain't nothing."[104] Brown offered her "Strong Man." He was a poet, lyricist and singer who is best known for his provocative political lyrics and performances. The song opens with Sonny Rollins's sax solo for 2 1/2 bars, and he carries her—her voice—across the threshold on the second beat of the third bar. Her strong man holds her with "great big arms muscled hard, dark and shining." His hair is "crisp and curly and cropped kinda close." His lips are "warm and full." On this song, when the trumpet solos, she is in dialogue with him. But the deep, rich sound of the tenor sax stands as the strong man on his own. She sings "It's easy to see why I love life when I'm loving my strong man and letting my strong man love me." Immediately following this lyric, Strong Man Sax enters and loves her for several more bars. She is a little freer on this album, a little more experimental in her phrasing, and we can hear a kind of raw edge in her voice that will become more apparent later.[105]

The album was marketed as her first as a jazz singer. Orrin Keepnews, one of the founders of the label, wrote most of the liner notes and produced many of the label's albums. Keepnews's liner notes focus as much, if not more, on the musicians as they do on Lincoln. The recording still emphasizes love songs and the cover still portrays her as an accessible sex symbol in a tight gown with one strap falling off the shoulder . . . yet there is a kind of playfulness to the glamour. The persona of "Strong Man" loves life when she loves him and he loves her.

It's Magic (1958), Lincoln's second Riverside album, marks the last stage of her transition from apprentice to jazz vocalist. Again she is accompanied by strong jazzmen: Kenny Dorham and Art Farmer on trumpet, Benny Golson on tenor sax, Curtis Fuller on trombone, Wynton Kelly on piano, and Philly Joe Jones on drums. Once again she sings love songs with another nod to Holiday and Bessie Smith in "Ain't Nobody's Business." Interestingly, she doesn't revise the line "I rather my man would hit me than for him to jump up and quit me." Subsequently, other artists such as Dianne Reeves chose to sing the line differently.

The album cover is quite significant. Although she is still beautiful, she is less conventionally glamorous, more natural and approachable. It is not a full-body shot, just shoulders and head. She is smiling. Her sweater and turquoise jewelry suggest a more bohemian glamour.

Jazz critic Nat Hentoff didn't like the album:

> Abbey Lincoln's second Riverside set is billed, like the first, as a jazz album. If one uses Billie Holiday and Anita O'Day as criteria, Miss Lincoln isn't much more of a jazz singer than any average night club performer. She, first of all, does not swing. Her phrasing is often gratuitously angular and her works lack subtlety of imagination and wit. There is also a hardness to her tone that this listener finds unattractive. Her determination to sing jazz and have jazzmen as her accompanists is admirable, but jazz may not be her line. (*Down Beat,* January 8, 1959)

Hentoff was a highly influential critic who seems to have had a particular investment in Holiday. In his failure to encourage Lincoln, he risks keeping jazz singing stuck in a series of imitations of past greats. Here, he is unnecessarily harsh. No, she is not Billie Holiday nor is she Anita O'Day. She is a young woman who stopped on the path to pop stardom, switched directions and seriously began to pursue a jazz calling. In the first number she sings the opening accompanied only by the bass and the drum. Here she is making an effort to be the third musician, setting the stage in much the same way that Rollins did on "Strong Man." The rest of the band joins her after she introduces the song. And while she doesn't have the brilliance that characterized Billie Holiday's early recordings, she is finding her voice and taking risks. Hentoff later became one of Lincoln's staunchest supporters.

(Schomburg Center for Research in Black Culture)

I know why the caged bird sings
and flaps its tethered wings.
Birds were meant to fly away,
and birds were meant to sing.
—"Caged Bird"

ANGRY BIRD

I know why the caged bird sings
and flaps its tethered wings.
Birds were meant to fly away,
and birds were meant to sing.

—FROM "CAGED BIRD,"
ABBEY LINCOLN

ABBEY LINCOLN entered the sixties serious about her art and her commitment to black culture and the black freedom struggle. This is evident in both her performances and her compositions, in her prose and poetry and in her movie performances. Just as Billie Holiday announced the emergence of a new image of black womanhood in the forties, and as Diana Ross would do in the seventies, so too did Abbey Lincoln in the sixties.

We begin to see this change as early as 1959, the year of Holiday's death and the year that Lincoln released *Abbey Is Blue* (Riverside). There are none of the traditional love songs that characterized the earlier albums. She tackles "Afro-Blue" and significantly, for the first time, she writes the lyrics, for "Let Up." The change in musical material is once again accompanied by a change in image, a change that did not go unnoticed.

In the December 4, 1958, issue of *Jet* a notice appeared titled "Abbey Lincoln Changes Act, Now Jazz Singer."

"Abbey Lincoln, the supper club thrush who gained fame as 'the girl in the Marilyn Monroe dress,' deserted the champagne circuit for jazz rooms." The article quotes Lincoln as saying: "I'm a black woman and I have to sing about things I feel and know about, blues and jazz. At the other places, something inside of me was not content. I didn't really fit in. It was an act." In the accompanying photograph, she wears her hair in a shortly cropped, non-straightened Afro, and we sense the emerging militancy and racial pride for which she would become known during the second stage of her career.

For many, Abbey Lincoln and Max Roach epitomized the new mood of the sixties—a decade of social unrest, black activism, militancy and pride. It didn't hurt that they were both physically beautiful and therefore made a striking couple. Significantly, as was the case with many of her contemporaries, Lincoln advocated a black nationalist politics where black women would finally have access to femininity, protection and domesticity. The couple lived in Harlem in a community of exciting artists, activists and intellectuals, including Maya Angelou and Malcolm X. During this time Lincoln wore her hair in braids and Afros; she was very outspoken about her racial pride and her critique of American racism. In addition to extraordinary collaborations with Max Roach and Clifford Brown, she released albums under her own name, made two important films and she began to write poetry and lyrics. She also developed as an intellectual, publishing "Who Will Revere the Black Woman?",[106] appearing at a symposium on black women at the New School and engaging in a heated debate about race and music in the pages of *Down Beat*. Only Hazel Scott before her gained such a reputation for being talented, intelligent, glamorous and militant.

Lincoln opened the decade with her appearance on husband Max Roach's *We Insist!: Max Roach's Freedom Now Suite,* featuring Coleman Hawkins and drummer Olatunji.[107] Though Hentoff did not like Lincoln's early forays into jazz, he was won over by her participation in this project. She attributed her growth to Roach: "I've also learned a lot from Max Roach in recent months about being me when I sing."

I have been tempted to see the recurrence of these statements as evidence of a young woman granting someone outside of herself all the credit for her growth as an artist. Listening to the change in both her voice and her material makes it necessary to refuse such temptation. Still, while Lincoln alone is responsible for the dedication and discipline it took to grow artistically, the influence of the gifted drummer and composer Roach is clear. In fact, upon close listening, it seems her two greatest influences are Roach and Holiday. No one is clearer on this than the mature Lincoln: "Max Roach was my mentor. I learned from him the ways of the music—theory on piano, and how to sing on the beat, not legato. He lent me understanding." Max Roach also attributes some of his own growth as a composer to her: "I began through her to discover the voice and began to write for and experiment for the voice."[108] In this way, the two shared an artistic partnership. In later years, Roach would say that while they had no children, the music they created together was their offspring.

The *We Insist!* project opens with Lincoln's strong voice on the work song "Driva Man," just her voice and the tambourine serving as the hammer that keeps time. This is the music at its most basic, at its source—born as a form to help get through the difficult work: simply the strong, confident voice, the first instrument, and the work tool turned into rhythm-keeping instrument. Lincoln's voice anchors the song in the tradition of black music. She and Hawkins's saxophone are the lead voices taking us through black social and musical history. The work song with which she opens provides the rhythmic backbone for Hawkins's solo, making the song span both the earlier folk form and the newer, complicated jazz whose era Hawkins helped to usher in. He soloing with the percussive background and a chorus of horns, she just with the tambourine and the bass. In "Driva Man" Lincoln's voice is not that of the coy feminine lover but that of the defiant black woman.

Perhaps the best-known piece on the recording is "Triptych: Prayer, Protest, and Peace." In "Protest," Lincoln's voice rises to a scream. In the scream I can hear the beaten slave woman, the mourning black wife or mother, the victim of domestic abuse and the rage and anger of contemporary black Americans.[109] Just as Aretha Franklin would later embody the demand of black America for "respect," here Lincoln gives voice to the fear, rage and release that would characterize much of the decade to follow.

Later, Lincoln said of the experience: "I learned from Max that I should always sound how I feel and that whatever I do, I should do it definitely. . . . Having to scream did a lot for me. It freed me up . . . it deepened my voice and made it more melodious. I'm not the kind of woman that screams. I tried, and I couldn't scream. Then my nephew showed me how. He screamed for me. Babies can scream even louder than we can. It's part of the protection of a woman that she can scream. I know that I've been screaming ever since."[110] Lincoln now says that she thinks she harmed her voice by screaming, because she did not know the proper way of doing it.[111]

The work closes on a Pan-Africanist note, with "Tears for Johannesburg." Percussionist Olatunji helps to make the connection between Africa and black America. The entire recording makes this connection, and with the stellar appearance of Coleman Hawkins, it links generations of jazz musicians as well.

We Insist!: Max Roach's Freedom Now Suite is an extraordinary artistic accomplishment and a gift to black people throughout the Diaspora from the talented composer, an equally talented lyricist and a group of extraordinary musicians, including an original vocalist. Speaking of Lincoln's performance on *We Insist!,* composer, musician and cultural critic William Lowe writes: "In the 1960 landmark recording, *We Insist!: Freedom Now* with master drummer/composer Max Roach, she was at once a strong member of the ensemble sound, an innovative soloist, and the narrative center of the presentation."[112] The collaborative efforts between Roach and Lincoln have extramusical consequences as well. Lincoln notes: "The collaboration was wonderful because for the first time it was a black man and woman. We have a hard time in this world as a couple."[113] This quotation resonates with Lincoln's essay "Who Will Revere the Black Woman?" and her comments at the New School forum.

While Hentoff didn't like her earlier efforts, he became an admirer and defender of her after *We Insist!* In fact, he wrote the liner notes, where he described her famous scream as "uncontrollable unleashing of rage and anger that have been compressed in fear for so long that the only catharsis can be the extremely painful tearing out of all the accumulated fury and hurt and blinding bitterness."[114] Critics were mixed about this album, but they seemed to have taken out most of their disappointment and rage on Lincoln in reviews of her fourth album, *Straight Ahead* (Candid).

Straight Ahead included five of her original contributions as well as two poems by canonical black poets: Paul Laurence Dunbar's "When Malindy Sings" and Langston Hughes's "African Lady." The album also features some of the most significant and innovative musicians of the time: Max Roach on drums, Eric Dolphy on reeds, Coleman Hawkins on tenor saxophone, Booker Little on trumpet, Mal Waldron on piano and Julian Priester on trombone. "When Malindy Sings" is forceful without losing its sass and humor, but it is the beautiful and moving "Left Alone" that stands out to me. Billie Holiday and her accompanist Mal Waldron penned "Left Alone." As Waldron tells the story, Lady came up with the lyrics and sang them to him on a cross-country flight; when the plane landed the song was done. Lady died before she was able to record the song. Lincoln records it accompanied by Waldron on piano, Hawkins, and Art Davis on bass. The song is minimalist but filled with intensity and drama, evoking a dark but exquisite mood. Hawkins's solo is masterful and lyrical. Lincoln is clearly influenced by Holiday but not imitative of her. With this song Lincoln attempts to make the most explicit artistic connection with Lady Day.

Of the recording, Charles Mingus said, "She lives it, every minute of it. As Billie did. She sings it hard because that's the way she lives it." Lincoln went on to say, "In a way, all of these tunes are about Billie." There is a danger in the Mingus statement. The young woman artist who believes she has to "live every minute of it as Billie did" is setting herself up for emotional disaster. It is significant that while Mingus links Holiday's harsh life with that which allows Lincoln to sing with such feeling, Lincoln herself does not. Instead, she says, "In a way, all of these tunes are about Billie. They are about all of us." Instead of making it her individual tale, she uses it as a way to honor an ancestor and to tap into a collective sensibility that characterizes much of black art: the beauty born from the pain and joy of being black in America.

Those who want to insist that the Lincoln of this period was only a creation of Max Roach clearly have not paid attention to Ms. Lincoln's other activities during the sixties. Lincoln emerged as an actress of substance and depth in such movies as *Nothing but a Man* and *For Love of Ivy*. In addition she organized and founded the Cultural Association for Women of African Heritage in 1962. According to Lincoln, the association was formed not as a political organization but as a vehicle for exploring the cultures of the African Diaspora. However, when Patrice Lumumba was assassinated, the organization protested at the United Nations, "the men in black armbands and the women in black veils." They entered the Security Council while Adlai Stevenson spoke, police were called and chaos erupted. Lincoln notes that when the media reported the incident, Chet Huntley "lied, saying we had bicycle chains and brass knuckles." She later disbanded the group because "some people like to be seen" more than anything else.[115]

Lincoln also held her own with such literary artists as Paule Marshall and Alice Childress. As mentioned above, in a symposium held at the New School on "The Negro Writer's Vision of America," Lincoln appeared on a panel titled "The Negro Woman in American Literature." Novelists Sarah Wright and Paule Marshall and playwright Alice Childress joined her. In her comments, Lincoln noted that even hostile white writers had to "take note of the depth and single-minded devotion of the love of the Negro woman for the man of her choice." While the other women discussed the stereotypes of black women created by both white writers and black male writers, Lincoln was careful to stress the unity of black men and women. This threatened unity had been the subject of her important essay, "Who Will Revere the Black Woman?", which first appeared in *Black Scholar* and later in Toni Cade's anthology *The Black Woman*. That it was reprinted in this volume is indicative of its status as an important manifesto of the time.

It is in the pages of *Down Beat* that Lincoln first demonstrates she is a woman of her own mind, capable of defending herself and her artistic and political choices. In his review of *Straight Ahead*, Ira Gitler expressed his disdain for Lincoln's militancy. It was Gitler's review that prompted the *Down Beat* debates between Gitler, Hentoff, Lincoln and Roach.

The article "Racial Prejudice in Jazz" appeared in two issues of *Down Beat* (March 15, 1962, 20–26; March 29, 1962, 22–25). These are actually a transcription of a conversation between Lincoln, Roach, critic Ira Gitler, trumpeter Don Ellis, composer/pianist Lalo Schifrin, critic Nat Hentoff and *Down Beat* editors Don DeMichael and Bill Coss. Gitler had negatively reviewed Lincoln's *Straight Ahead* in an earlier issue of *Down Beat;* the review seems as offended by her politics, the outspoken nature of her protest and racial pride, as by her rendering of the lyrics. In the review Gitler accuses her of being a "professional Negro" who exploits her race at the expense of her art. This is the same critic who dismissed John Coltrane's Impulse recordings and whom Frank Kofsky calls "a principal anti-Coltrane critic writing for *Down Beat.*" Clearly he was not a fan of the new black artistic experimentation and innovation.

Early in the discussion, Lincoln confronts Gitler for his ad hominem attack on her. He responds that he liked neither her lyrics nor her singing; he disliked the lyrics because of their overtly racial and political nature. Max Roach asks him, "Who is a good singer to you?" Gitler answers, "Billie Holiday," to which Lincoln replies:

Tell me, why is it that you never censured her for being an obvious masochist? Everything Billie Holiday sang was about unrequited love, nearly. . . . Why is it nobody got after her about her subject matter? She sang about what was most important to her. And I, Abbey Lincoln, sing about what is most important to me. And what is most important to me is being free of the shackles that chain me in every walk of life that I live. If this were not so, I would still be a supper-club singer.

Now tell me why you never censured her for this. . . . Well then, why do you like her so much, because she was really one-sided. Billie sang about "My Man Don't Love Me" and "My Man's a Drag." My Man, My Man, My Man.

Here we see the first instance of Lincoln distancing herself from the Holiday stage persona and using the political nature of her work as a means of doing so. She is trying to carve out space for herself as someone influenced by but attempting to move beyond Holiday in an effort to find her own voice. For decades to follow, critics would link Lincoln to Holiday, but here she is aware of the dangers inherent in that comparison. Indeed, it was her outspoken politics that caused the jazz establishment to censure her.[116]

According to Lincoln, she and Roach were unable to get work, but masters of the music treated them like royalty. She recalls that Duke Ellington would make the band stand up and bow at them when they entered a venue where he was performing. "But there was no work for us." Instead, they found new audiences abroad in Europe and Asia.[117]

While Lincoln did not record an album in the late sixties, she did not completely disappear. In 1964 she appeared in the independent film *Nothing but a Man,* directed and written by Michael Roemer, and costarring Ivan Dixon. A young Yaphet Kotto also had a role in the film. In fact, many of the actors in the cast were also members of the Negro Ensemble Company, and the set itself became a place for nurturing both her politics and her art. Founded in 1967 by Robert Hooks, Gerald Krone and Douglas Turner Ward, the Negro Ensemble Company was an innovative black theater troupe that provided opportunities for black actors, playwrights and directors. As with a number of newly formed black cultural organizations, the artists associated with the NEC saw a direct link between their work and the ongoing black freedom struggle.

Nothing but a Man is the story of Duff Anderson (Dixon), a young black man who works as a lineman on the railroad. Anderson meets, falls in love with and marries Josie (Lincoln), a twenty-six-year-old, college-educated schoolteacher and daughter of the town's most influential and accommodating black minister. Josie is the character who tames and domesticates the wandering Duff. She is also the victim of his outrage at the white South's assault on his manhood. Dignified, feminine, yet strong, Josie's character is her man's main support.[118]

While she is not successful in taming him, by the end of the film Duff returns to Josie with his son from a prior relationship. Because of the domestic space Josie provides, he garners the strength and the courage to stay put in the small town; he takes a leadership position in resisting the status quo. The black family is intact, and the struggle for the black nation is about to begin. Of Lincoln's role in this film, Hilton Als has written: "What is consistently striking about Lincoln's presence in such films as *Nothing but a Man* and *For Love of Ivy* was her reasonableness, the sweet rationale behind her gestures . . . thinking was Lincoln's actor's instinct . . . Lincoln's restraint [was] a hallmark of watchful intelligence."[119]

Lincoln's third film is a commercial feature costarring the biggest black star of the period, Sidney Poitier. She plays Ivy, a beautiful young maid to a wealthy white family. When she decides she wants to leave to live her own life, the son of the family (Beau Bridges) seeks a means to keep her happy enough to stay. He introduces her to hustler/entrepreneur Poitier. Lincoln is luminous in this role as a woman who is both innocent/virginal yet sexy. It is the kind as romantic comedy that never featured black actors, and there are few such films even today. At film's end, Ivy is rescued from the white household by Poitier's character, who clearly won't have a wife who works as a domestic. It is an ending you might expect of Doris Day and Rock Hudson.

These films are path breaking (though in very different ways) because characters such as the ones played by Lincoln and Poitier were new to movie screens. Josie is a character of emotional depth and quiet dignity, and Ivy is a beautiful, ambitious young black woman. Ironically, given her own insistence on wearing her hair natural, both roles required Lincoln to wear wigs. The films chart new territory, but are not particularly revolutionary with respect to gender. As was the case with

"Strong Man," with her comments at the New School panel and with her reflections on her collaborations with Max Roach, here again, Lincoln comes to represent the black woman as outspoken critic of racism and feminine supporter of black heterosexual relations.

Nowhere is this more apparent than in the essay "Who Will Revere the Black Woman?" In September 1966, two years after the release of *Nothing but a Man,* she published this short (five pages) but powerful polemic in *Negro Digest,* a journal of thought and opinion owned by *Ebony* founder John Johnson. Today the essay reads as both dated and timely. Her call for the protection of black women from systematic abuse joins a century-old tradition of writing by black intellectuals and activists.[120] Yet given the precarious social and economic position in which many black women still find themselves, Lincoln's words resonate with contemporary readers as well. A reprint of the essay appeared in Toni Cade Bambara's pioneering *The Black Woman: An Anthology* of 1970. In many ways Lincoln's is a founding text of the most recent renaissance in black women's writing.

Unlike later works such as Michelle Wallace's *Black Macho and the Myth of the Superwoman* or Ntozake Shange's *For Colored Girls Who Have Considered Suicide When the Rainbow Is Enuf,* the appearance of Lincoln's essay in a black owned and edited publication lessened any sense of divide and conquer that would characterize the writings of Wallace, Shange and Alice Walker.[121] The essay is a highly literate critique of white supremacy and of black people's (especially black men's) internalization of some of its most damaging tenets. Lincoln addresses those black men who believe that black women are "the downfall of the black man" in that they are "evil," "hard to get along with," "domineering," "suspicious" and "narrow minded." She notes that such men join whites in maligning, assaulting and negating black women's physical selves: "She is the first to be called ugly and never yet beautiful and as a consequence is forced to see her man . . . brainwashed and wallowing in self-loathing, pick for his own the physical antithesis of her (the white woman)" (82). Worse still, according to Lincoln, these attitudes fuel their mental and physical abuse of black women.

While black men are the explicit objects of critique in this essay, the implied object is the controversial Moynihan Report. In 1965 Senator Daniel Patrick Moynihan released *The Negro Family: The Case for National Action,* commonly known as the Moynihan Report. The report concluded that black poverty was a result of the breakdown in the black family during slavery and the creation of a black matriarchy in a society where patriarchy was the norm.[122]

Lincoln is also one of the first to publicly write about the pain and disappointment many black women experience when black men prefer white women aesthetically and sexually. While many ethnic groups experience these kinds of tensions, the legacy of white supremacy makes it especially painful for some black women. More than any other group of women, black women have been deemed unfeminine and the furthest from the white supremacist ideal of beauty.

If the big white man goes unnamed in the essay, then white women are relegated to parentheses in this paragraph and are later described in the kinds of derogatory terms with which black women had been labeled. Like Ida B. Wells before her, Lincoln argues that contrary to the stereotype, white women aggressively pursue black men: "White female rejects and social misfits are flagrantly flaunted in our faces as the ultimate in feminine pulchritude. Our women are encouraged by our own men to strive to look like the white female image as much as possible" (83). This sentence comes from a woman familiar with jazz musicians, jazz as a way of life and the jazz club scene, which one scholar describes as a site where "the male musician has more opportunities for meeting women than most men in other employment and more hope of exploiting those opportunities."[123] Anyone who has frequented clubs where jazz musicians jam has noted that often among the women who frequent clubs in search of black musicians, many are white.

Lincoln's statement also comes from a woman who had fully rejected a white supremacist aesthetic of beauty—a woman who stood as a symbol of an unlightened, unstraightened black beauty. When she tells black men that we "black, evil, ugly" women are a perfect and accurate reflection of you "black, evil, ugly men . . . For you are us, and vice versa," she anticipates rapper, multi-instrumentalist and poet Me'Shell Ndegeocello, who chided black men about their preference for "blond-haired, blue-eyed beauty without the hot comb," telling them, "I am a reflection of you."[124] As such, Lincoln expresses sentiments felt from the urban club scene to the Southern civil rights movement and shared today by contemporary young women of the hip-hop generation.

She reserves the most violent part of her disdain for white women, and in so doing gives her own answer to the question of whether black and white women can join in a movement for women's liberation. The essay stops just short of a black feminist statement. Lincoln begins to suggest the need for a more gender-based politics and organizing, but she is not speaking as a black feminist. She calls for black women to turn pain first into anger and then into action to "bring our men to their senses" (83). So, while she does call for black women to organize (and, as is discussed above, she helps to found a black women's political organization), it is not a call for them to organize for their own social and political rights, but instead a call for them to organize in order to enlighten black men. The essay closes not with a feminist vision but instead with a plea for protection:

> Who will revere the black woman? Who will keep our neighborhood safe for black innocent womanhood? . . . Black womanhood cries for dignity and restitution and salvation. Black womanhood wants and needs protection and keeping and holding. . . . Who will keep her precious and pure? Who will glorify and proclaim her beautiful image? To whom will she cry rape?

Each of these terms—precious, pure, innocent, beautiful and revere—are particularly important to black women because they are terms that have been equated with white womanhood and thereby with femininity—both privileged spheres in our society, spheres to which black women have historically been denied access. Poor and working black women, especially dark black women, have been excluded from the discourse of the precious, pure and protected.[125]

While protection has its benefits, it often comes at a tremendous cost. Often the pure and protected woman is also obligated to obey her protector. Years later, speaking of her marriage to Max Roach, Lincoln herself acknowledged this: "Max had been my teacher, my protector. He was willing to give me everything as long as I did what he said. I still loved him, but I didn't want to be married to him or to any other man."[126] In another interview she notes: "We lived together for four years. All I had to do was what he said. I was pretty good at that. After a while, though, my independent spirit wouldn't allow it, but he helped me. He saved my life."[127]

I have spent so much time on Lincoln's essay because I want to emphasize the intellectual nature of her life and her work, as well as the tenor of the times in which she came of age as a jazz artist. Thankfully, Lincoln has left a body of work, essays, poems, song lyrics, music, performances and interviews that will make it impossible for future writers to refer to her as stupid, illiterate and incapable of understanding her own complexity as they have done with Billie Holiday. This is one lesson learned from Billie Holiday's experience. As we shall see, Lincoln learned and put to use many such lessons in other aspects of her life and work as well. She emerged from these experiences with a mature sense of herself that would provide her with the foundation she needed for difficult times. In spite of her success as a film actress, she wouldn't find work in the cinema for another twenty years. As noted earlier, *Lady Sings the Blues,* the book, had been optioned for her but the project never materialized. Although the film *Lady Sings the Blues* was eventually made with Diana Ross, in the sixties it was optioned for Abbey Lincoln. Though initially disappointed that the Holiday project didn't materialize, Lincoln looked back on it as an important intervention in the direction of her life. "In a way, it's best that I didn't play Billie, because I don't know how to do anything halfway. I was in such a sorry state myself at the time that portraying Billie's sorrow might have killed me." She didn't work in film for another twenty years, but she notes "I watched Dorothy Dandridge die waiting for a movie."[128]

By the end of the sixties, Lincoln found herself blacklisted in the U.S. and undergoing a divorce from Max Roach. The divorce proved to be especially difficult for her: "Max and I were divorced in 1970 and I was like a wounded animal. It's very difficult recovering from a broken marriage, especially when it throws your career up in the air. I needed sanctuary, so I signed myself into a psychiatric hospital in upstate New York for five weeks, which turned out to be one of the best things that ever happened to me" (Davis, 67). The open honesty of this statement has much to teach us. Once again Lincoln finds herself on a road to self-destruction, but where in the past she was rescued by Roach and introduced to the jazz life, this time she rescues herself, choosing self-care over self-destruction.[129] (Interestingly, Holiday asked Joe Glaser to have her sent to a sanitarium so that she could undergo treatment for her drug addiction. Hospital staff tipped off the police that she was there, and she was arrested.)

Lincoln came out of her experience with the decision to stop "singing songs about no-good men who didn't know how to treat women. I discovered that you become what you sing. You can't repeat lyrics night after night as though they were prayer without having them come true in your own life."[130] This provides the perfect transition into the third stage of Lincoln's career—a stage that finds her making another choice: composing her own music and writing and singing lyrics that are prayers and affirmations for many of her fans. Lincoln takes this responsibility seriously. "If you stand before the people, in a way you are like a minister. You have a constituency, you have a following and you owe something to the people."[131] From Bessie Smith to John Coltrane, many black artists have recognized their role as spiritual guides for their communities. Lincoln now entered this phase of her career.

BIRD ALONE

Bird alone with no mate
Turning corners, tempting fate
Flying circles in the air
Are you on your way somewhere

Gliding soaring on the wind
You're a sight of glory
Flying way up there so high
Wonder what's your story

Bird alone, flying low
Over where the grasses grow
Swinging low, then out of sight
You'll be singing in the night

—ABBEY LINCOLN

"Now I don't feel rebellion against anything. I've grown. I've changed. There's a peacefulness about my world that's very right for me. I'm growing older. I want to live a contemplative and fruitful life."[132]

—ABBEY LINCOLN

IN THE CLOSING SCENES of Spike Lee's *Mo' Better Blues*, Abbey Lincoln appears as the mother of the protagonist, Bleek Gilliam. While the young Bleek wants to play baseball with his friends, she is the disciplinarian who insists he practice his instrument. In this way, she is the culture bearer, a title given to her by vocalist Cassandra

Gliding, soaring on the wind
You're a sight of glory.
Flying way up there so high,
Wonder what's your story.
—"Bird Alone"

Wilson. "Her importance goes beyond her technical achievements. She's a culture bearer. She represents a metamorphosis from singer as 'accessory' to singer as creator."[133]

During the period following her divorce from Roach in 1970 Lincoln moved to California, where she focused on painting and teaching. She taught acting during the times when she didn't record, and she appeared on the television shows *Mission Impossible, Name of the Game, ABC Movie of the Week* and *The Flip Wilson Show.*

Most important, Lincoln traveled to Africa and Asia. While Europe proved to be a significant turning point for Billie Holiday's sense of self, Africa and Asia were just as, if not more so, significant for Abbey Lincoln. (This is not to say she doesn't have a significant European following; she does. In France she is a legend.) While traveling in Africa as the guest of the talented and political South African singer Miriam Makeba, Lincoln met the leader of Guinea, Sékou Touré, who named her Aminata (which means trustworthy). In Zaire, Mobutu gave her the name Moseka.[134] Lincoln says that after that trip she discovered songs "coming out of [her] . . . It was the biggest surprise, I started writing them down when I was about 42. . . . In a way it's like catching the rain in your hand. It's everywhere."[135] While Lincoln has an Afrocentric personal style, unlike other artists such as pianist Randy Weston, she no longer stresses the relationship between jazz and Africa. "The Africans don't claim this music. The Africans do not send for this music."[136] Certainly, black South Africans such as Hugh Masekela (Makeba's former husband) and Abdullah Ibrahim (Dollar Brand) have claimed the music and contributed to its development. But here Lincoln sounds like many African Americans who have found themselves disowned by Africans as bastards. So much so that she says "I am not partial to Africans anymore. They are not my only ancestors. I claim the whole planet."[137] In a dialogue with Cassandra Wilson, Lincoln notes: "Our music is eclectic. It's European like I'm European. I have European relatives, yes. But my existence, my everything is African."[138]

Nonetheless, it was the experience in Africa that gave her a new name and opened her to the new music that would come through later on her albums. Unable to record in the United States, Lincoln found that the Japanese welcomed her and provided her the space to make her music. There, she recorded *People in Me,* her first recording since *Straight Ahead* and her first effort without Roach. She worked with a completely new lineup of musicians: David Liebman on soprano sax, tenor, flute, Kunimitsu Inaba on bass and Hiromasa Suzuki on piano. Miles Davis, who was touring in Japan at the time, stopped by the studio to lend his support and to share two musicians from his own band, James Mtume (congas) and Al Foster (drums). The album was released in the U.S. in 1979. *People in Me* introduces us to the mature, independent artist we know today. Like a phoenix, she is reborn from the ashes of her earlier lives.

When she returned to New York in the early eighties, Lincoln embarked full scale on what has become the most artistically productive period of her career. She did this by working with younger, innovative musicians such as Steve Coleman, choosing not only to be a lyricist but also a composer. She began to write and sing songs of enormous spiritual depth and generosity. As with Coleman Hawkins before her, and her contemporary Betty Carter, she is a singer who sees herself as an elder: "I see myself as an elder and a teacher. I share the information I got working with great musicians." She also considers herself a conduit of a tradition, part of a continuum: "I don't know what's going to happen to the music, but I'm part of a collection. I'm happy. My flower is in full bloom."[139]

During the last decade of the twentieth century, Lincoln has released approximately one album a year on Verve. She composed most of the songs on these albums. With Lincoln, lyrics matter. Many are affirmations, prayers and poems. As was the case with Holiday, Lincoln is an actress embodying her songs. She is a storyteller. Few of her songs are traditional love songs, songs of romance and sex. "There's more to life than just a relationship with another person. That gets boring. My songs go beyond that. There are other things to talk about. . . . This is a beautiful place we are in, but in terms of the culture we have made for ourselves, there's not enough in that culture for me. Why must everybody be hurt? Why must the children be disillusioned? We could do better. We could have better values than exist in this culture that we have made for ourselves. . . . Do you see why I don't think songs about the bedroom anymore?"[140] On *Wholly Earth* (Verve 1998) she offers "And It's Supposed to Be Love," a polyrhythmic duo with Maggie Brown, daughter of Oscar Brown, Jr. This is a song about domestic violence, a theme Lincoln first visited in the tune "Hey Lordy Mama," a song for which she wrote the lyrics and Nina Simone wrote the music.[141] The earlier song states the violence as a simple fact of a relationship gone bad. The more recent one questions the nature of a "love" in which brutality takes place. Both are departures from the lyrics of Holiday's songs: "I won't call no coppa if I'm beat up by my poppa," "He beats me too." So, although in her rendition of "Ain't Nobody's Business," Lincoln chose to sing the lyrics as they were written, in her own later lyrics she offers a critique of domestic abuse naturalized in the earlier songs.

In this phase of her career Lincoln also released three CDs in honor of Billie Holiday.[142] Having cited Billie Holiday's influence on her art from the earliest days of her career, she also expressed her desire to escape the perils that confronted Lady Day. At first Lincoln cited Holiday's courage in choosing to sing and record "Strange Fruit," but even at the time she sought to distinguish herself from Holiday's identification with songs of lost love and longing. During the sixties, Lincoln's recordings featured such songs as well as more political ones. With each recording since her three tribute CDs for Billie Holiday, Lincoln has moved away from the kinds of songs associated with the older artist, replacing them with songs of spiritual quests, love for life and social concern. She also moved most comfortably into her own voice. In fact, it is significant that the Lincoln of the two-volume tribute album sounds far less like Holiday than in her earlier jazz efforts.

The tribute recordings and her interviews reveal a great deal about Lincoln's own interpretation of Holiday's legacy. It is that interpretation with which I want to end this chapter. According to Lincoln, she first heard Holiday at the age of fourteen when her sister brought home from Chicago recordings by Holiday and Coleman Hawkins. By the time she was in her early twenties, Lincoln was working at Trade Winds in Honolulu. She heard Holiday performing at the Brown Derby, another club in Honolulu. Apparently Holiday twice came to hear Lincoln, but the two never spoke. Lincoln explains that she was both frightened and in awe of the legendary Billie Holiday.

When Lincoln speaks of Holiday, she speaks first of her artistry and her presence. "Billie was unadorned as far as her talent was concerned, the sound of her voice. She didn't try to sound good or anything, she didn't try to prove she was a great singer. She never made one sound that was insincere, for effect."[143] Interestingly, similar descriptions have been made about contemporary R&B queen Mary J. Blige, who has battled many of the demons that haunted Holiday and who is recognized by her generation as a singer of honesty and integrity, though lacking in the genuine artistry of Holiday: "Mary's voice—pretty, growly, sexy, sad, emotive, often perfect is life, too."[144] In addition, the description sounds much like Steve Coleman's description of Lincoln's own voice: "I appreciate her rhythm, the way she plays with time and space. The quality that I hear in her voice is the same that I hear in the voices of Louis Armstrong, James Brown or Billie Holiday. It's not a Eurocentric beauty. Even in jazz, vocalists are judged by the European classical tradition—whether they can sing high and how long they can carry a note. But Abbey has chosen an African-based esthetic that draws also from spirituals and work songs" (Jones, 28).

When speaking about Holiday's presence, Lincoln defends Holiday against crude depictions: "Billie Holiday was the first beautiful queen on stage. . . . She never came to the stage with a cigarette. . . . She was a queen without a court and she took stuff to dull her pain."[145] At another point she notes:

> Billie was this beautiful, delicate creature who didn't have her chariot waiting, or her footman and the maids and the people that were supposed to be around. She was disinherited, like we all are. She was a queen . . . a beautiful woman who was set up all her life to fail and [in] her death [she] was maligned. She suffered character assassination. That was one of the reasons I wanted to say to her "Thank you."

Lincoln portrays Holiday as unrecognized royalty; her description of the delicate, singing caged bird. Her Billie Holiday tributes are an offering to an honored ancestor in the tradition of Yoruba-based belief systems. On this shore, in the New World, we honor our ancestors because of the indignities they suffered, the challenge to their humanity, for their sacrifice and for their having created a culture and tradition of struggle for us. Lincoln's Holiday is disinherited royalty, like black Americans who were robbed of their birthright. In this instance it is especially important that we honor them, especially when they have been so maligned in death. Black artists have done this for other figures, such as Nat Turner and Malcolm X.

In honoring Holiday, Lincoln is also seeking a blessing: she does not want to be misinterpreted, maligned. In honoring Holiday, who is a part of her, she honors herself. "I seek to live a singular life, and I don't want anybody lying on me after I leave here. So this is my way of defending her and myself." Here we have Lincoln's contribution to the project I identified earlier as that of the black woman intellectual's responsibility to Holiday: to maintain a vigilant critique against efforts that assault her personhood and her intellect. In defending her, we defend ourselves.

This spiritual understanding of Holiday is not an effort to canonize her; she was not a saint. In New World embodiments of West African religions (Vodun, Condomble, Santeria) ancestors and orishas are not without their passions, their jealousies and their flaws. As I have discussed at length elsewhere, even in black Christian cultures informed by these belief systems, ancestors are central to an understanding of black art and history.

As elder and ancestor, Holiday has guided and steered Lincoln:

> She described the pitfalls, the holes that were there for me
> to fall into. She described the smell of things so I was able
> to defend myself when I got out in the world. I didn't fall
> prey to the pimps and the whores who lived in the corri-
> dors, who were all around everywhere the people came for
> the music.[146]

She uses Holiday's legacy as a map to help avoid the negative and, like Shange, as an inspiration to pursue her own creativity.

Holiday's fate as described by Lincoln is in many ways the fate of jazz music, misunderstood, exploited, disinherited from its own legacy but kept alive by the insistence and discipline of those who devote their own gifts to honoring it. As jazz becomes museum music, relegated to concert halls and the academy, it risks having little or no impact on the lives of far too many younger artists who will fail to honor the legacy. Unfortunately, too many contemporary artists (especially those who are commercially successful) have failed to study the lives of the ancestors, failed to heed the wise advice of the elders, and instead of constructing a new narrative for black artists, they have fallen prey to the traps that ensnared those who came before them.

Perhaps Lincoln's greatest creation has been herself. "My character is one that I design from the top of her head to the bottom of her feet; I am the one that decides. [The character I have designed] makes me independent. I don't have to depend upon somebody to interpret my life and make my clothes and maybe have me wearing something that doesn't really reflect the way I feel about myself. I am an ancient old soul from a long time ago."

For Lincoln, creativity and the arts are a way of life; she is a devout artist:

> The way I survived the turmoil and onslaught against my spirit was through practicing art at home. Sometimes I am a performing artist, but most of the time I am a Solitary Single Artist at home. Sometimes I paint. I've painted myself a few times and I write and search through dictionaries and old Encyclopedia Britannicas for a life that was privy to my ancestors that reinforces my life, a better understanding of where I am in the middle of nowhere. And I design and make my clothes. They are all disciplines and so I do this rather than be idle and find myself doing mischievous things that hurt me. (See endnote 146)

Her relationship to her art is deeply spiritual; because of this, her work has something to nourish any who take the time to really hear the story she tells. The music is a form of devotion. "For me this music is a holy experience and an experience that makes me feel whole. It is great music. It walks on water . . . It's revitalizing and it's about rhythm and life and energy."

Lincoln is a living artist who is self-consciously a bearer of the tradition. These days, I find I turn less to Holiday for solace. Instead I turn to Aminata:

> *Reaching for my hand, love walked away*
> *sighing to leave, but ready to stand,*
> *Love walked away, love walked away*
> *Love walked away and I*
> *walked away with love.*[147]

Abbey Lincoln stands at the crossroads as an important link between the tradition initiated and embodied by Billie Holiday and that which points to our future. Her work and interpretation of her life through that work can serve not as a model, but as an inspiration to all young people, especially young black women, regardless of their chosen paths. Hers is a life that offers much hope and promise. Interestingly, her model offers the possibility that young artists trying to find their own way with a sense of integrity might not need an encounter with a stronger, older man to do so. Lincoln did not have a model like the one she has become; however, her life allows us to imagine the possibilities of spiritual and artistic growth for Mary J. Blige, Lauryn Hill, Lil' Kim or any number of contemporary talented young black women. (As I watch the latter take off more clothes, become blonder and blonder and add blue contacts to her "look," I especially hope she will one day discover the possibilities offered by Abbey Lincoln's response to a culture that sought to use her in similar ways.) Even more important, though, Lincoln offers inspiration to women at any stage of life. As I leave the era of my youthful promise and look forward to a fully mature womanhood, I am so grateful to include the likes of Aminata Moseka (Abbey Lincoln) among my own models.

A circle of Ancestors and Elders:
Billie Holiday, Lester Young, Coleman Hawkins, Gerry Mulligan.
(Seven Lively Arts *show, December 8, 1957; CBS Worldwide, Inc.*)

CODA: A MORNING SONG

Life's a repetition, it's an action of repeat;
Act of doing, act of saying
something bitter, something sweet.
Acts of life that keep occurring,
ghosts appearing through the sound,
waving at us from the distance
'cause the whole wide world is round
and 'round, and round and round
Yes the whole wide world is round.

"WHOLLY EARTH," Abbey Lincoln

IN DECEMBER 1957, CBS broadcast "The Sound of Jazz" as part of its *Seven Lively Arts* series. Assembled by Nat Hentoff and Whitney Balliett at the request of CBS producer Robert Herridge, it was the first hour-long television program devoted to the art form. In this way, it remains unique. The program featured extraordinary artists such as Coleman Hawkins, Art Tatum, Count Basie, Thelonious Monk, Jimmy Rushing and Billie Holiday. Lady Day is part of a segment that features a group of distinguished musicians including Lester Young, Roy Eldridge and Coleman Hawkins. This show introduced legions of mainstream Americans to the music and its innovators. As such, the production mediates the presentation of jazz to the audience. Maybe the sponsors were just trying to sell soap. Maybe those viewers other than jazz fans wanted a glimpse of the legendary tragic queen of jazz. It doesn't matter, because what comes through is an insistence on the dignity, the beauty and the sheer brilliance of the Lady, her men and her music.

In the camera's gaze she is not objectified. Although other musicians join her, she is the subject of the short. She is not in isolation, observed by the males who inhabit the film with her. Although the film would position her as the inactive one—she sits, they stand, she is the only one who does not possess an instrument (other than her voice), especially not the phallic horn. It might seem she occupies the traditional role of women: the object of the gaze. However, she is not the flat, one-dimensional icon of this cinematic short. No, the film is about her as a singer in relation to other musicians, her responses to each of them, her dialogue and her encouragement. The spectator's gaze is her gaze. We don't watch the men watching her; we watch her watching them—especially Lester Young.[148]

SHE WALKS OUT, the only woman on a stage of dark-suited men. She is wearing a straight skirt, zipped on the side, and a pale sweater set—the epitome of fifties casual chic—trademark ponytail draped over her shoulder, hoop earrings that dangle from her lobes. With her, the cats. She sits on a stool, joining the circle of horns. The camera is situated behind the inner circle of Lady Day and a stellar lineup of hornsmen: Lester Young, Ben Webster and Coleman Hawkins on tenor sax; Gerry Mulligan on baritone sax; Vic Dickinson on trombone; Roy Eldridge and Rex Stewart on trumpet. Behind the sacred inner circle is an outer, almost protective semicircle of rhythm: Jim Hall on guitar, Milt Hinton on bass and Jo Jones on drums. The room is dark, the set stark. The camera provides us, the spectators, entrée to this mysterious ritual—the jam session.

The scene is constructed to look like an after-after-hours set, where only the serious are invited. The only thing missing is the audience: the voice of a people in love with the artists and their music—a people prepared to respond, to critique, to encourage, to affirm, to go along for the ride. We are invisible but present. Perhaps there shouldn't be an audience of the uninitiated. We are the voyeurs watching as they engage in a ritual of invoking some divine presence.

The horns open with the introduction as the camera closes in on her face—the riveting face. She begins one chorus of "My man don't love me/Treats me awful mean/My man, he don't love me, treats me awful mean/He is the lowest man that I have ever seen." Behind her the horns are like backup singers, all but the trumpet, which every once in a while will do a little response to her call, not necessarily an answer or an echo but a mild sound to fill in the spaces. Among the horns, the trumpet is a distinct voice. The horns sound like the human voice. Her voice resembles a horn. The boundary between the human instrument and the brass instrument blurs. Here, she is a member of the inner circle, another horn.

The drums, guitar and bass keep the rhythm, keep it steady as the voices soar, trickle, take flight, come back. The rhythm provides that safe place, the net that catches them should they fall, the place to which the voices return after the trip, somewhere out there.

Ben Webster follows her, his tone low, and then Lester Young comes in—higher, sweeter, mellow, he sounds like her. Her face follows him, sweetly anticipates his every move, nods approvingly, looks at him as if to say, "Aw Lester, what are you doing to me now?" It is a duet between the two of them, and she enters just when she should: "He wears high draped pants/stripes are really yellow/He wears high draped pants/stripes are really yellow/But when he starts in to love me/he is oh so fine and mel—low." Vic Dickinson on trombone followed by Gerry Mulligan on baritone sax sounding as if Robeson (maybe someone else, I am not sure, William Warfield or Brock Peters) turned into a blues-singing horn. Lady comes in for the third verse: "Love will make you drink and gamble, make you stay out all night long/Love will make you drink and gamble, make you stay out all night long/Love will make you do things, that you know is wrong."

Behind her that trumpet again. It's Rex Stewart followed by the legendary Coleman Hawkins. And then, Roy Eldridge takes us there with a trumpet solo that is filled with such intensity, such passion, such arrogant insistence, such flights of sheer absurdity that we know, were they not here before, the spirits of the ancestors have surely arrived and they are pleased.

Lady closes:

Treat me right baby
And I'll stay home every day.
Just treat me right baby
And I'll stay home night and day.
But you're so mean to me baby
I know you're gonna drive me away.

Love is just like a faucet
It turns off and on
Love is just like a faucet
It turns off and on.
Just when you think it's on, baby, it's turned off and gone.

Then she is gone.

I approach this performance as a lover of the music and as a listener who has a sustained, engaged emotional and spiritual relationship with it. For me, this sacred moment is church. The song is the sermon.

The circle has spiritual significance in many West African cultures and in the cultures of the descendants of enslaved Africans from these areas. Evident in the "ring shout," that sacred dance, it lives on in children's games, in the ring that forms around dancers who are especially good in house parties, block parties and clubs, and in the circle of performance. Sterling Stuckey writes: "The ring shout, prominent in Louisiana . . . helped form the context in which jazz music was created" (90). He goes on to note: "Wherever in Africa the counterclockwise dance ceremony was performed—it was called the ring shout in

North America—the dancing and singing were directed to the ancestors and gods, the tempo and revolution of the circle quickening during the course of movement" (12).

In the circle, the artists/priests acknowledge the dead and are visited by them. (Is the quotation of one soloist evidence of acknowledging the ancestor or of the ancestor's visitation upon the improvising one?) They call upon the spirits of the ancestor and/or of the Holy Ghost to visit, to bless, to ensure life and well-being of the living. Those who are about to leave this plane and become ancestors, Lady and Lester, are reconciled, voice and authority. The circle has no end. All that has come before is related to all that is and all that is to come. The circle indicates "the reciprocity between the living and the dead" (Stuckey, 87).

"Fine and Mellow" is one of the few formal blues Lady ever sang and, like "Billie's Blues," she penned this one herself. Significantly, as with "Billie's Blues" and "Now Baby or Never," this is not the sad blues of an abused woman, sitting, waiting for her man to abuse her further.[149] In this sermon, Lady is not preaching a doctrine of my man treats me so bad but I am going to stay. She is not singing a sermon of my man left and took my life and my love with him. No, in this sermon she asserts the problem: "My man is mean." Then she asserts the dilemma: "He is fine and he is a good lover." The consequences of not dealing appropriately with these contradictions are drinking, gambling, and staying out all night long. What to do? The text says if your man treats you badly but you want to stay, you should try to negotiate; let him know you will leave if things don't change. Be prepared to do so should they not. Give him a warning even. But if he doesn't get his act together, leave him.

Lady Day is the instructive elder here. As we gather together in the circle, not to bring closure but to learn what the past has to teach us, let us keep our eyes on this Lady: A woman who is no amateur, who loves her work, who respects and is respected by her peers. A woman who takes no shit. A woman of style, grace and dignity. A woman who, no matter how rough things are, gets it together and gives it her best. Let this be the gift of the ancestor, Lady Day.

The exquisite Dee Dee Bridgewater has heeded the call of Holiday as ancestor; she has honored Ella Fitzgerald's legacy as well. Bridgewater pays tribute to these ancestors, not by imitating them, but by keeping their memory alive and by honoring her own calling as bearer of the tradition. That's what Lady provides for us—a foundation upon which to build and then wind beneath our wings so that we too may fly with her musical heirs, from Miles Davis to Shirley Horn

Peggy Lee, Rosemary Clooney,

Carmen McRae, Anita O'Day,

Dianne Reeves, John Hicks,

Miki Howard, Etta James,

Terrence Blanchard, Erykah Badu, Mal Waldron;

From Frank Sinatra, to Tony Bennett, Madeleine Peyroux,

Betty Carter, Dinah Washington, Ruth Brown, Joni Mitchell,

Abbey Lincoln . . .

And, on the horizon,

There is a new moon rising,

I hear.

A lasting vision of Lady Day. All darkness and light—a softly singing siren . . . Listen. (*Chuck Stewart, circa 1955*)

Endnotes

1. In the groundbreaking anthologies *Representing Jazz* and *Jazz Among the Discourses,* Krin Gabbard argues that such artifacts "begin to constitute a history of their own." He notes that "even if we find these works to be flawed or even grossly inaccurate, can't we examine them critically to understand how American culture has actually received the music?" Krin Gabbard, *Jazz Among the Discourses* (Durham: Duke University Press, 1995). In my effort to provide a historical, theoretical and critical understanding of the emergence of these myths and artifacts, my work departs from that of Holiday biographers and joins the efforts of other scholars of the emerging field of jazz cultural studies. Among these I include Krin Gabbard, Jon Pannish, John Gennari, Guthrie Ramsey, William Lowe, Salim Washington, Hazel Carby, Robert O'Meally, Robin Kelley and Angela Davis. Also I hope that my work will be in dialogue with other critics and theorists of the iconization of creative and public figures. Mary Hamer on Cleopatra; Nell Painter on Sojourner Truth; S. Paige Baty on Marilyn Monroe; Celeste Goodridge on Michel Foucault, Robert Mapplethorpe and Elizabeth Bishop; J. M. Taylor on Eva Peron; Wayne Koestenbaum on Jacqueline Kennedy Onassis; and Michael Dyson on Martin Luther King, Jr. See J. M. Taylor, *Eva Peron: The Myths of a Woman* (Chicago: University of Chicago Press, 1979); Mary Hamer, *Signs of Cleopatra* (New York: Routledge, 1993); Nell Painter, *Sojourner Truth: A Life, a Symbol* (New York: W.W. Norton, 1996); S. Paige Baty, *American Monroe: The Making of a Body Politic* (Berkeley: University of California Press, 1995); Wayne Koestenbaum, *Jackie Under My Skin* (New York: Farrar, Straus & Giroux, 1995); Celeste Goodridge, *Consuming Lives: Biographers, Subjects and Readers* (work in progress).

2. Power can be confronted, but it is usually maintained by those who control the means of production and the apparatuses of the state. In Holiday's case this is evident even in her music. While she insists on her own voice and artistic vision, the distribution and reception of the music is nonetheless manipulated and controlled by powers beyond her control. Individuals can wage dissent

against and attempt to manipulate the powers that control, contain and survey them, but individual, personal effort is often powerless in these instances. That against which they wage dissent bears the full weight of the state and global capital. An examination of discrete instances where contests are waged over Holiday's image and icon, reveals instances where Holiday both complies with or resists dominant representations of her life. She is most sustained on a body of work—her recordings—yet the release, manipulation and sale of them is often in control of the very forces that she chose to resist.

3. http://www.kedar.com

4. http://www.kedar.com

5. hampton, dream. "All Woman." *Vibe* (April 1997): pp. 72–78.

6. Immanuel Kant offers one definition of genius that works for me here: "Genius is a talent for producing something for which no determinate rule can be given, not a predisposition consisting of a skill for something that can be learned by following some rule or other; hence the foremost property of genius must be originality. (2) Since nonsense, too, can be original, the products of genius must also be models, i.e. they must be exemplary; hence, though they do not themselves arise through imitation, still they must serve for this, i.e. as a standard or rule by which to judge." Immanuel Kant, *Critique of Judgment,* pp. 307–8. Lewis Gordon, though informed by Kant, offers a more succinct and less essentialist notion of genius: "Genius is one who can make creative use of the cultural realities available." Lewis Gordon, *Her Majesty's Other Children: Sketches of Racism from a Neo-Colonial Age* (Lantham, Md.: Rowman & Littlefield, 1997).

7. Bruce Crowther and Mike Pinfold, *Singing Jazz: The Singers and Their Styles* (San Francisco: Miller Freeman Books, 1986), p. 84.

8. *Ultimate Billie Holiday selected by Shirley Horn,* Liner notes, PolyGram Records, 1997. 314 539 0512.

9. Robert O'Meally, *Lady Day: The Many Faces of Billie Holiday* (New York: Arcade, 1991), p. 111.

10. Count Basie with Albert Murray, *Good Morning Blues* (New York: Random House, 1985), p. 200.

11. O'Meally, *Lady Day,* p. 48.

12. Ibid., p. 37.

13. Miles Davis and Quincy Troupe, *Miles: The Autobiography* (New York: Simon & Schuster, 1989), p. 236.

14. See Billie Holiday and William Dufty, *Lady Sings the Blues* (New York: Doubleday, 1956).

15. Charles Teagarden, Dick McDonough, and Artie Bernstein were also on this date.

16. Stuart Nicholson, *Billie Holiday* (Boston: Northeastern University Press, 1995), p. 121.

17. *Ultimate Billie Holiday selected by Shirley Horn,* Liner notes, PolyGram Records, 1997. 314 539 0512.

18. Author's correspondence with Lewis Gordon, November 2000.

19. John Hammond, *Melody Maker* (April 1933).

20. Evelyn Brooks Higginbotham, *Righteous Discontent: The Women's Movement in the Black Baptist Church* (Cambridge: Harvard University Press, 1993).

21. Salim Washington calls these "blues gestures" and explains them in the following way:

    "1. The clash of harmonies, in particular the major and minor thirds sounding simultaneously;

    2. The infusion of feeling to the point where the emotional content of a phrase supersedes the technical contours of the line. For instance, Aretha Franklin's melodies often ignore the harmonies underneath, but the strength and conviction of her delivery makes it perfect;

    3. The play of microtonal intervals, frowned upon in most Western contexts as 'out of tune' but favored in the blues and in blues gestures."

    Correspondence with the author, March 27, 2000.

22. *Lady Day: The Many Faces of Billie Holiday* (Long Branch, N.J.: Kultur International Films, 1991), documentary.

23. See Robert O'Meally.

24. Holiday's voice can be heard in films as diverse as *9 1/2 Weeks, La Femme Nikita* and *Schindler's List.*

25. S. Paige Baty argues, "The icon is reproduced on an object as a means of imprinting a history, person, ideology, etc. on the surface. This image then not only communicates explicit messages and histories, it also becomes an object of memory in and of itself." *American Monroe: The Making of a Body Politic* (Berkeley: University of California Press, 1995).

26. "I Cried for You" on *Billie Holiday's Blues,* recorded in Cologne, Germany, January 5, 1954. Jazz Heritage, Capitol Records, 1988. 512947X.

27. See Stephen Kandall, *Substance and Shadow: Women and Addiction in the United States* (Cambridge: Harvard University Press, 1996). Many of these images are available in Cynthia Palmer and Michael Horowitz, *Sisters of the Extreme: Women Writing on the Drug Experience* (Rochester, Vt.: Park Street Press, 1982, 2000).

28. O'Meally, *Lady Day,* p. 78.

29. See *United States* v. *Billie Holiday,* District Court of United States for the Eastern District of Pennsylvania, Philadelphia, Pennsylvania, May 27, 1947.

30. This clipping was in a file at the Institute of Jazz Studies at Rutgers University.

The date and name of the newspaper are not available. However, I surmise it was a New York newspaper because of the following reference (p. 16): "Miss Holiday, who last week started an engagement at the Club 18 at 131 W. 52nd St."

31. R. G. Peck, *Chicago Sunday Tribune,* July 15, 1956, p. 5.

32. *Library Journal,* August 1956.

33. Gilbert Millstein, *New York Times,* July 15, 1956, p. 10.

34. R. J. Gleason, *San Francisco Chronicle,* July 15, 1956, p. 23.

35. Saunders Redding,, Baltimore *Afro-American* magazine section, March 12, 1957, p. 2.

36. Whitney Balliett, *Saturday Review,* 39:32, July 14, 1956.

37. *Time,* 68:30, July 9, 1956.

38. Other chapter titles include: "Some Other Spring," "Good Morning, Heartache," "Travelin' Light," "Mother's Son-in-Law," "I Must Have That Man" and "God Bless the Child."

39. Feminist literary critics have taught us women's writing is filled with gaps, silences, ellipses that we must learn to read. Black feminist critics note that this is especially the case for black women's autobiography and fiction. See Evelyn Brooks Higginbotham, "Beyond the Sound of Silence: Afro-American Women in History," *Gender and History* I, no. 1 (1989), pp. 50–67. Farah Jasmine Griffin, "Beyond the Silence," in *Beloved Sisters and Loving Friends: Letters from Rebecca Primus of Royal Oak, Maryland, and Addie Brown of Hartford, Connecticut, 1854–1868* (New York: Alfred A. Knopf, 1999). Darlene Clark Hine, "Rape and the Inner Lives of Black Women in the Middle West: Preliminary Thoughts on the Culture of Dissemblance," *Signs* 14, no. 4 (1989). Deborah McDowell, Introduction to *Quicksand* and *Passing* (New Brunswick: Rutgers University Press, 1990); Valerie Smith, "Loopholes of Retreat: Architecture and Ideology in Harriet Jacobs' Incidents in the Life of a Slave Girl," in *Reading Black, Reading Feminist: A Critical Anthology,* ed. Henry Louis Gates, Jr. (New York: Meridian Books, 1990). Hortense Spillers, "Interstices," in *Pleasure and Danger: Exploring Female Sexuality,* ed. Carole S. Vance (Boston: Routledge, 1984). For exciting theories of reading the silences in women's work cross-culturally, check out Tillie Olsen's *Silences* (New York: Delacorte Press, 1978) as well as King Kok Cheung's valuable *Articulate Silences: Hisaye Yamamoto, Maxine Hong Kingston, Joy Kogawa* (Ithaca: Cornell University Press, 1993).

40. Nicholson, p. 42.

41. "Lady Day Story to Be Filmed." Baltimore *Afro-American,* September 21, 1957, p. 19.

42. See Donald Clarke, *Wishing on the Moon,* p. 400.

43. Among the films starring black actors and actresses in 1972: *Blacula, Buck and*

the Preacher, Come Back Charleston Blue, Hit Man, The Black Girl, The Legend of Nigger Charlie.

44. Donald Bogle, *Brown Sugar: Eighty Years of Black Female Superstars* (New York: Da Capo Press, 1990, ©1980), p. 127.

45. If the politics of respectability was a guiding principle in the political work of black leaders, it also informed the paradigms of the early days of African-American Studies as well. African-American Studies was born outside of the academy in the late nineteenth century with the goal of counteracting negative images and claims of genetic inferiority. In 1896 founders of the American Negro Academy declared that institution's goal: "To aid by publication the vindication of the race from vicious assaults in all lines of learning and truth." Consequently, African-American Studies was born in opposition to the racist onslaught that confronted and continues to confront black people. Today, after a century of practicing a politics of respectability, a century of being concerned with presenting "positive images" of black life, we have so policed our own intellectual efforts that often we find ourselves caught up with narrow representations that in no way allow for the full complexity and humanity of black people.

46. Writing on the ideological underpinnings of the Harlem Renaissance, Amiri Baraka writes: "There is still, for all the 'race pride' and 'race consciousness' that these spokesmen for the Negro Renaissance claimed, the smell of the dry rot of the middle class Negro Mind: The idea that somehow Negroes must deserve equality." Baraka, *Blues People* (New York: William Morrow, 1963), p. 134.

47. *Women in the Civil Rights Movement: Trailblazers and Torchbearers.* eds. Vicki Crawford, Jacqueline Anne Rouse and Barbara Woods (Bloomington: Indiana University Press, 1990).

48. In her pioneering book of 1993, *Righteous Discontent: The Women's Movement in the Black Baptist Church, 1880–1920,* Evelyn Brooks Higginbotham notes the scathing critiques against nonconformity that accompany the politics of respectability. She writes: "The politics of respectability equated non-conformity with the cause of racial inequality and injustice. The conservative and moralistic dimension tended to privatize racial discrimination, thus rendering it outside the authority of government regulation" (p. 187).

49. I am grateful to Robin Kelley for drawing this to my attention.

50. See O'Meally. "This woman who was decidedly not a member of the cult of true womanhood—that nineteenth-century mythic construct that posited the cardinal virtues for the 'true woman' as 'piety, purity, submissiveness and domesticity' did feel pressured to conform to 'true woman' rules" (O'Meally, p. 168).

51. Robert O'Meally, *Lady Day,* p.169.

52. Conversation with the author, October 1999.

53. James George Rowles was born in Spokane, Washington, on August 18, 1918. Rowles studied piano privately but began playing professionally at the urging of Ben Webster.

54. Rowles interview in book accompanying *The Complete Billie Holiday on Verve, 1945–1959,* pp. 181–3.

55. I am grateful to the members of the Couch Writing Collective—Daphne Brooks, Bill Lowe, Guthrie Ramsey and Salim Washington—for bringing this dynamic to my attention.

56. Rowles, interview in *The Complete Billie Holiday on Verve*.

57. Salim Washington, conversation with the author, April 10, 1997.

58. Washington, conversation with the author, June 22, 1997.

59. Bill Lowe, conversation with the author, June 14, 1997.

60. Guthrie Ramsey, conversation with the author, June 17, 1997.

61. I am deeply indebted to conversations with Bill Lowe and Salim Washington for helping me to understand this.

62. Donald Clarke, *Wishing on the Moon,* p. 459.

63. Some readers might question my decision to stress that Rowles is a white male musician rather than simply a male. I think my reasons for doing this should be obvious, but let me here explain the choice without making such assumptions. Given the tumultuous history of race/gender issues in our country, if black men speak in these terms, their statements would not carry the authority granted by whiteness in a racist society.

64. Scholars as diverse as Phyllis Rose, Tyler Stovall and Michel Fabre have documented the European myth of the black American entertainer and the African-American myth of Europe as a site of freedom from racial stigma.

65. Cesaria Evora in program notes for show at Berklee Music Center, 1996.

66. I am grateful to my colleagues Rita Barnard and Carol Mueller for providing information about Dolly Rathebe and Sathima Bea Benjamin, respectively.

67. Lisa Davenport, "Jazz and the Cold War: Black Culture as an Instrument of American Foreign Policy," in *Crossing Boundaries: Comparative History of Black People in Diaspora,* eds. Darlene Clark Hine and Jacqueline McLeod (Bloomington: Indiana University Press, 1999).

68. Hazel Scott, "What Paris Means to Me," *Negro Digest* (November 1961).

69. Jack Surridge, letter to author, October 3, 1998.

70. Jeremy himself has noted that the number of Brits who have written about Holiday include Alistair Cooke and Spike Hughes.

71. Stuart Nicholson, p. 153.

72. Inez Cavanaugh is one of the few black women to have written jazz criticism for major publications like *Metronome* as well as liner notes for artists such as

Duke Ellington. See Linda Dahl, *Morning Glory: A Biography of Mary Lou Williams* (New York: Pantheon, 1999), p. 169.

73. This list is not meant to be exhaustive.

74. Originally published in Nancy Cunard's *Negro Anthology*, reprinted in *Zora Neale Hurston: Folklore, Memoirs, and Other Writings*, ed. Cheryl Wall (New York: Library of America, 1995).

75. Aldon Lynn Nielsen, *Black Chant: Languages of African-American Postmodernism* (Cambridge: Cambridge University Press, 1997), p. 184.

76. Ibid., p. 183.

77. Ntozake Shange, *Sassafrass, Cypress and Indigo* (New York: St. Martin's Press, 1982).

78. Charles Keil is another writer who is influenced by *Blues People*. Keil's important *Urban Blues* shares and even exceeds Jones's sexism.

79. Chilton, *Billie's Blues*, pp. 68–69, 75, 160. Donald Clarke, *Wishing*, p. 163.

80. Forrest, "A Solo Long-Song: For Lady Day," in *The Furious Voice for Freedom: Essays on Life* (Wakefield, R.I.: Asphodel Press, 1994), p. 345.

81. See Michael Denning, *The Cultural Front: The Laboring of American Culture in the Twentieth Century* (London: Verso, 1996). Mark Naison, *Communists in Harlem During the Depression* (New York: Grove Press, 1984). David Margolick, *Strange Fruit: Billie Holiday, Café Society, and an Early Cry for Civil Rights* (Philadelphia: Running Press, 2000).

82. Denning, p. 343.

83. Ibid.

84. Nathaniel Mackey best articulates this when he writes: "To the extent that categories and the way things are defined . . . to the extent that those categories and definitions are rooted in social and political realities, anything one does that challenges them, that transgresses those boundaries and offers new definitions, is to some extent contributing to social change." *Callaloo* vol. 18, no. 4.

85. I am grateful to a young woman, Kionna Alycia Griffin, who attended one of my lectures at Duke University, for drawing the conversational nature to my attention.

86. Following Marx, Roland Barthes argued that cultural myths circulate in order to maintain the class interest of the economically privileged in a capitalist society. While Barthes and Marx have informed my exploration of the Holiday icon (especially in the chapter "Holiday Sales"), it is quite evident that the meaning of the icon is up for grabs and that at any given historical moment it is available to diverse segments of modern society.

87. See Wynton Marsalis, "What Jazz Is—and Isn't," *New York Times*, July 31, 1988, pp. 21–24.

88. I want to avoid conflating Murray, Crouch and Marsalis. While they have been engaged in the same project, there are important differences between them. For instance, Murray's analysis and theorizing are far more sophisticated than that of Crouch. Ironically, the older gentleman is much more fluid and open in terms of what he is willing to consider jazz and innovation than is the conservative Marsalis.

89. Murray, Crouch and Marsalis are deeply committed to the music, its tradition and history as well as perpetuating it well into the future. Neither Murray nor Crouch have become millionaires through their writing on the music, and while Marsalis probably is quite wealthy, his devotion to the music is not driven by material gain. But I speculate that the identification by corporate advertisers of jazz as a music that might sell high-priced items is in some way related to the changed image of the music and its practitioners set forth by Murray, Crouch and Marsalis.

90. See Wynton Marsalis, "What Jazz Is—and Isn't," *New York Times*, July 31, 1988, pp. 21–24.

91. See Scott De Veaux, "Who Listens to Jazz?" in *Keeping Time: Readings in Jazz History*, ed. Robert Walser (New York: Oxford University Press, 1999), p. 394.

92. For an astute summary and analysis of the findings of the SPPA, see Scott De Veaux, "Jazz in America: Who's Listening?" Research Division Report No. 31, National Endowment for the Arts (Carson, Calif.: Seven Locks Press, 1995), reprinted as "Who Listens to Jazz?" in *Keeping Time: Readings in Jazz History*, pp. 389–395.

93. Valerie, Gladstone, "Advertisers Play a New Tune: Jazz." *New York Times* on the Web. December 6, 1998.

94. Ibid.

95. For a more extensive discussion of poems about Holiday, see my "Dark Lady of the Sonnets" in *Brilliant Corners: A Journal of Jazz and Literature*, Winter 1997.

96. The following poets have written elegies: Frank O'Hara, Walt Delegall, Michael Harper. Poems that are specifically about her music: Quincy Troupe, Philip Levine. Poems that borrow from lyrics of songs she popularized: Gayl Jones. "Strange Fruit" poems: Cyrus Cassells, Joy Harjo. Poetic biographies: Nicholas Moore, Alexis De Veaux. Poems that construct an image of Holiday in order to trigger something else that the poem contemplates: Betsy Sholl, Al Young, Angela Jackson, Philip Levine, Lisel Mueller, Larry Levis, Jessica Hagedorn.

97. In addition to poetry, Billie Holiday also appears in novels: Alice Adams, *Listening to Billie* (New York: Alfred A. Knopf, 1977); Elizabeth Hardwick, *Sleepless Nights* (New York: Random House, 1979); Ntozake Shange, *Sassafrass,*

Cypress and Indigo (1982), to name a few; autobiographies (of the non-musicians, the autobiographies of Malcolm X and Maya Angelou are the best-known); plays (both *Lady Day at Emerson's Bar and Grill* and *Lady Day*); films (there is a Holiday character played by Lonette McKee in the film *'Round Midnight,* and McKee also played Holiday in *Lady Day* at *Emerson's Bar and Grill*) and essays (Leon Forrest's "A Solo Long-Song: For Lady Day"). But it is not my intention to provide an index of writings inspired by Billie Holiday.

98. Here I should distinguish between Abbey Lincoln the woman and Abbey Lincoln the public figure, the public persona she has created. While the two are clearly related, I cannot make any claims about Lincoln's life.

99. The "caged bird" certainly alludes to Paul Laurence Dunbar's poem "Sympathy." However, I am also reminded of Josephine Baker's Zou-Zou, who appears sitting in a large birdcage. Also, it is interesting that Maya Angelou and Abbey Lincoln, friends and contemporaries, both select the caged bird image for the titles of their works. (Maya Angelou, *I Know Why the Caged Bird Sings,* 1970).

100. In an interview with Lisa Jones, Abbey Lincoln notes that "I burned it in an incinerator to make sure I'd never wear it again." (*New York Times,* August 4, 1991, p. 28.)

101. Born Anna Marie Wooldridge; Lincoln's manager renamed her Gaby Lee and then Abbey Lincoln. Following a trip to Africa she was given the name Aminata Moseka. She goes by both names, performing as Abbey Lincoln and publishing her music under Aminata Moseka.

102. In the film, Mansfield's character cannot sing, but her gangster lover hires a man (played by Edmond O'Brien) to turn her into a star. As part of her training, Mansfield, epitomizing the sizzling dumb blond, goes to several nightclubs in order to cause a stir in the gossip press. In one of these nightclubs she sees Lincoln, who plays herself. In direct contrast to Mansfield, Lincoln can sing, and the filming is such that spectators are encouraged to compare the two. Lincoln is brown and beautiful in a tight red gown; Mansfield is porcelain-white, platinum-haired, in a tight white gown. Lincoln stands, sings and moves about the stage; Mansfield sits in a booth. Yet Lincoln's talent, sensuality and beauty are contained by the scene; as was the case with nineteenth-century European paintings, the brown Lincoln is here used to signify the sexuality of Mansfield. She is one in a montage of performers (one of whom is Little Richard), appears onscreen only for the brief time she is singing, and her performance is interrupted by the camera's return to Mansfield.

103. Francis Davis "Leading Lady," *High Fidelity* (May, 1986): p. 65.

104. Interview with Jazz Study Group, Columbia University, November 6, 1999.

105. For the persona of "Happiness Is a Thing Called Joe," personal contentment equals having a lover. This is a far cry from the Abbey Lincoln who, more than

twenty-five years later, wrote and recorded "I've Got Thunder and It Rings," not a song of romantic love: "I got love for climbing mountains, love for sailing over seas/I got love there is no stopping, love for sending like the breeze." Or better still, the Joan Griffin composition "I'm in Love": "I'm in love with life, you see."

106. Lincoln also has a collection of poetry titled *In a Circle Everything Is Up,* and a play, *A Pig in a Poke.*

107. *We Insist!* was the result of collaboration between Roach and Oscar Brown, Jr., that was to have been performed in 1963 on the centennial of the Emancipation Proclamation. Nat Hentoff, liner notes for *We Insist!*

108. Interviewed in documentary *Abbey Lincoln: You Gotta Pay the Band.*

109. Reference to slave woman's scream from author's conversation with William Lowe.

110. From an unidentified article in the Abbey Lincoln file at the Jazz Studies Institute, Rutgers University.

111. Jazz Study Group interview. November 5, 1999, New York, N.Y.

112. William Lowe, "Abbey Lincoln," in *Black Women in America: An Historical Encyclopedia* (Brooklyn: Carlson Publishers, 1993).

113. *Abbey Lincoln: You Gotta Pay the Band,* documentary.

114. Hentoff liner notes.

115. Schomburg Center Oral History Project.

116. In an interesting treatment of the relationship of black jazz musicians to the white club-owners, festival promoters, record producers and critics of the 1960s, "Black Nationalism in Jazz," Frank Kofsky writes: "Much in demand as a performer prior to 1962, when her infection with the malignancy of Black Nationalism at the hands of Max Roach, her husband, was mercilessly pilloried in the pages of *Down Beat,* Abbey Lincoln witnessed her career in music plummet into total obscurity. Almost two full decades would elapse before any recording company in the U.S. would again consent to release an album of her singing." Frank Kofsky, "Black Nationalism in Jazz: The Forerunners Resist Establishment Repression, 1958–1963," in *The Journal of Ethnic Studies* 10:2, p. 2.

117. Schomburg Center documentary.

118. A couple of scenes are pivotal in providing a sense of the roles played by black men and women and their courtship in a racist society. Early scenes show Duff working the open road—laying track in the company of other black men. In one crucial scene, immediately following the beginning of his courtship, Duff watches as his fellow workers chase a rabbit into the tall grass, grab the animal with their bare hands and cook him over an open fire. The men gather around the fire to eat the rabbit. Immediately following this scene, the narrative shifts to Josie in her classroom, teaching young elementary-school black children. When they begin to prematurely pack up their bags, she reminds them that

they are not free to go until she dismisses them. Then, looking outside the window and seeing Duff, she lets the students go. Just as he and the other men find themselves in open spaces laying tracks for the railroad (which has enormous significance in the black musical and folk tradition) the children relish being outdoors. The railroad signifies mobility, the primary trait of Duff's life before he meets Josie. As a colored schoolteacher, it is her job to train and educate the young students for their place in an apartheid society. The implication is that she seeks to do the same with Duff.

119. Hilton, Als, "Body and Soul: Betty Carter, Abbey Lincoln," in *Village Voice* (March 23, 1993): pp. 65–66.

120. This is a tradition reaching back to abolitionists Frances Ellen Watkins Harper and Harriet Jacobs, and including race men and women Alexandar Crummell and Anna Julia Cooper, and twentieth-century figures such as W. E. B. Du Bois, Malcolm X and Elijah Muhammad. Elsewhere, I have described this as a "politics of protection." See Griffin, "Ironies of the Saint: Malcolm X, Black Women, and the Politics of Protection"; "W. E. B. Du Bois, Respectability, Protection and Beyond," forthcoming in untitled volume edited by V. P. Franklin and Bettye Collier Thomas, New York University Press, 2000; and "Chorus and Conflict: Reconsidering Toni Cade Bambara's *The Black Woman*," forthcoming in Eddie Glaude, ed., *It's Nation Time: Reconsidering Black Nationalism* (Chicago: University of Chicago Press).

121. Elsewhere, Lincoln says the separation and disdain between black men and women is one of the legacies of slavery. "Billie [Holiday] said 'My man don't love me,' which is really a terrible thing to have to say. But that is a part of what we inherited from slavery. . . . The greatest thing in the world is a man and woman, and if you can manage to pull them asunder, you have gone a long ways in conquering a people." Schomburg Oral History interview.

122. Moynihan got much of his thesis from black sociologist E. Franklin Frazier, but unlike Frazier he emphasized black matriarchy over white supremacy and the state. Moynihan's report would give birth to two decades of critique from creative and critical black women intellectuals. Lincoln's is one of the first. This is important because Lincoln, an important intellectual, is one of the first to articulate a critique of the Moynihan Report.

123. Valerie Wilmer, *As Serious as Your Life: the Story of the New Jazz* (Westport, Conn.: L. Hill, 1977), p. 197.

124. Me'Shell Ndegeocello, "Soul on Ice," in *Plantation Lullabies*. Maverick Records, 1993.

125. Griffin, "Ironies of the Saint: Malcolm X, Black Women, and the Politics of Protection." in *Sisters in Struggle: Black Women in the Civil Rights and Black Power Movements* (NYU Press, 2001).

126. Lisa Jones, "Late Bloomer in Her Prime." *New York Times,* August 4, 1991, p. 28.

127. *Abbey Lincoln: You Gotta Pay the Band*, documentary.

128. Schomburg Center Oral History Project.

129. It was during this period that Lincoln began to paint, a practice she has continued since then. Jazz Study Group interview.

130. Francis Davis "Leading Lady," *High Fidelity* (May 1986): p. 65.

131. *Abbey Lincoln: You Gotta Pay the Band,* documentary.

132. Davis, "Leading Lady."

133. Jones, "Late Bloomer in Her Prime."

134. Lincoln notes the irony in this, as Mobutu was the man responsible (with the assistance of the CIA) for the assassination of Patrice Lumumba.

135. Lincoln Verve biography. Verve Records, New York, N.Y.

136. Schomburg.

137. Schomburg.

138. "A Sisterhood of Spirit," in *Jazziz,* vol. 16, no. 16 (June, 1999): p. 50.

139. Verve biography.

140. Interview on liner notes *You Gotta Pay the Band*, Gitanes, 1991. So few traditional love songs appear on Lincoln's later albums that she released *Where There Is Love* in 1992. Of this work she said: "It's true that I do have a somber outlook and assessment of the world in which we live, but I also have love, love for the beautiful man that makes life bearable in an otherwise unbearable world. So this is my offering on the altar of conjugal love."

141. "Hey Lordy Mama," words by Abbey Lincoln and music by Nina Simone. On Abbey Lincoln's *A Turtle's Dream*, Verve, 1995. 314 527 382 2.

142. For the liner notes on the CDs, she was extensively interviewed by Adger Cowans.

143. Interview with Abbey Lincoln by Adger Cowans. Liner Notes from *Abbey Sings Billie,* vol.2.

144. Ibid.

145. Danyel Smith, *Vibe* (September 1999): p. 163.

146. Schomburg interview.

147. "Love Walked Away."

148. She is not like the conventional woman of film described by Laura Mulvey in her classic essay "Visual Pleasure and Narrative Cinema."

149. Lyrics taken from *The Norton Anthology of African American Literature,* eds. Henry Louis Gates, Jr., and Nellie Y. McKay (New York: W.W. Norton, 1996), p. 34. "Though the song uses traditional blues progressions and lyrics, Holiday is credited as its composer and lyricist (1939)."

My man don't love me
Treats me oh so mean
My man he don't love me
Treats me awful mean
He's the lowest man
That I've ever seen

He wears high draped pants
Stripes are really yellow
He wears high draped pants
Stripes are really yellow
But when he starts in to love me
He is so fine and mellow

Love will make you drink and gamble
Make you stay out all night long
Love will make you drink and gamble
Make you stay out all night long
Love will make you do things
That you know is wrong

But if you treat me right baby
I'll stay home every day
Just treat me right baby
I'll stay home night and day
But you are so mean to me baby
I know you're gonna drive me away

Love is just like a faucet
It turns off and on
Love is just like a faucet
It turns off and on
Sometimes when you think it's on baby
It has turned off and gone

Further Reading and Listening

ANYONE INTERESTED IN learning more about Billie Holiday's life and work should start with the following list of books and recordings, which provides a fairly comprehensive overview.

Stuart Nicholson's *Billie Holiday.* Boston: Northeastern University Press, 1995. This is the most comprehensive and well-rounded of Holiday biographies. Nicholson does an extraordinary job of providing details about Holiday's life. His discussion and analysis of her music and historical context of the times that produced her and that she helped to shape is especially valuable. The book includes several appendices that provide more information about her music, the most important of which is the thorough discography by Phil Schaap. Schaap's discography opens with a brief essay narrating the stages of Holiday's career, followed by a listing of all of her recordings, complete with dates and personnel.

The most beautiful Holiday book is Robert O'Meally's *Lady Day: The Many Faces of Billie Holiday.* New York: Arcade, 1991. O'Meally's is an eloquently argued extended essay focusing on Holiday's artistry and her contributions to American music. The book is filled with extraordinary black-and-white photographs from every stage of Holiday's life.

The Billie Holiday Companion: Seven Decades of Commentary, edited by Leslie Gourse (New York: Schirmer Books, 1997), provides an invaluable collection of essays and reminiscences on Billie Holiday by major critics and writers such as Nat Hentoff, John Hammond, Amiri Baraka and others.

Ken Vail's *Lady Day's Diary: The Life of Billie Holiday* (Chessington, Surrey, UK: Castle Communications, 1996) provides a detailed listing of events in Holiday's life from 1937 to 1959. The diary is also filled with photographs, newspaper clippings, personal correspondence and reviews of Holiday's recordings and performances.

Fortunately, most of Holiday's music is in print. There are numerous compilations that claim to gather the "best" of Lady Day for the true beginning listener. Of these I especially recommend *Priceless Jazz Collection: Billie Holiday* (GRD9871, 1997) because it has versions of well-known torch songs such as "My Man" as well as upbeat favorites such as "Now Baby or Never" and "My Sweet Hunk O' Trash," a wonderful duet with Louis Armstrong. Another collection, *Tutti Legends: Billie Holiday* (Sony Music, A 26850, 1996) draws from Holiday recordings from 1937 to 1956.

Much of Holiday's work is available on a number of boxed sets. Booklets filled with information and photographs accompany each one:

Billie Holiday: The Legacy (1933–1958), Sony Music Entertainment, 1991. A set of three discs primarily from the early part of Holiday's career recorded for Columbia, though two of the selections are recordings from 1958. This set includes Holiday's first recording, "Your Mother's Son-in-Law" with Benny Goodman and his Orchestra, and "Saddest Tale," with Duke Ellington and his orchestra. A number of Holiday's recordings with Teddy Wilson are available on this set, and there are a number of songs where Lady is accompanied by Buck Clayton and Lester Young. For many critics, this set represents Holiday at her best, though several have expressed disappointment in the sound quality. Includes a 60-page book.

Billie Holiday: The Complete Commodore Recordings, GRP Records, 1997. This set of two CDs is taken from recordings originally produced by Milt Gabler; the reissue is produced by Orrin Keepnews and Joel Dorn. It includes several recordings of Holiday's most famous songs, including "Strange Fruit," "I Cover the Waterfront" and "Billie's Blues." Commodore was an independent label founded in 1938 by Milt

Gabler, who worked as a producer for Decca as well. This collection provides an intensive vision of three sessions, on April 20, 1939; March 25, 1944, and April 8, 1944. Includes a 41-page book.

Billie Holiday: The Complete Decca Recordings, GRP Records, 1991. A two-disc set covering Holiday's recordings from 1944 to 1950, also produced by Milt Gabler. While Commodore focused on jazz, the Decca recordings were pop tunes—though in the case of Holiday the boundaries are always blurred. This set includes "Lover Man," which became a major hit for her. The Decca recordings are the torch songs for which Holiday is best known, including "My Man" and "Don't Explain." Includes a 39-page book.

Billie Holiday: The Complete Billie Holiday on Verve 1945–1959, Polygram Records, 1992. Produced by Phil Schaap, this is the most extensive of the boxed sets and my favorite. It includes rehearsals and studio dialogue as well as several takes. In addition there are live recordings from the Carnegie Hall concert in 1946 and Newport in 1947. One disc has several selections from Holiday's Jazz Club USA concert in Cologne, Germany, in 1954. The accompanying book includes interviews with musicians who performed with Holiday, including Harry "Sweets" Edison, Jimmy Rowles, Oscar Peterson and Barney Kessel. In addition there is a virtual archive of photographs and transcriptions of discussion between musicians, as well as reproductions of Holiday's Verve album covers. This is an extraordinary record of Holiday's performances for the Verve label, owned by Norman Granz.

Bibliography

Adams, Alice. *Listening to Billie*. New York: Knopf, 1978.

Als, Hilton. "Body and Soul: Betty Carter, Abbey Lincoln." *Village Voice,* March 23, 1993: 65–67.

Appadurai, Arjun. "Commodities and the Politics of Value." In *The Social Life of Things: Commodities in Cultural Perspective,* pp. 3–63. Cambridge: Cambridge University Press, 1986.

Armstrong, George M. "The Reification of Celebrity: Persona as Property." *Louisiana Law Review,* 5 (1991): 443–68.

Attali, Jacques. *Noise: The Political Economy of Music*. Minneapolis: University of Minnesota Press, 1985.

Baraka, Amiri (LeRoi Jones). *Blues People*. New York: William Morrow, 1963.

———. *Black Music*. New York: Da Capo Press, 1998 (1967).

——— and Amina Baraka. *The Music: Reflections on Jazz and Blues*. New York: William Morrow, 1987.

———. *Home: Social Essays*. Hopewell, N.J.: Ecco Press, 1998 (1966).

Barthes, Roland. *Camera Lucida: Reflections on Photography,* translated by Richard Howard. New York: Hill & Wang, 1981.

———. *Mythologies*. New York: Hill & Wang, 1972 (1957).

———. *The Responsibility of Forms*. Berkeley: University of California Press, 1991.

Basie, Count. *Good Morning Blues: The Autobiography of Count Basie as told to Albert Murray*. New York: Random House, 1985.

Baty, S. Paige. *American Monroe: The Making of a Body Politic*. Berkeley: University of California Press, 1995.

Berliner, Paul F. *Thinking in Jazz: The Infinite Art of Improvisation*. Chicago: University of Chicago Press, 1994.

Blumenfeld, Larry. "A Sisterhood of Spirit." *Jazziz,* June 1999: 45–50.

Brackett, David. "Family Values in Music? Billie Holiday's and Bing Crosby's 'I'll Be Seeing You.'" In *Interpreting Popular Music,* pp. 34–74. Cambridge: Cambridge University Press, 1995.

Chilton, John. *Billie's Blues: The Billie Holiday Story 1933–1959*. New York: Da Capo, 1989 (c. 1975).

Clarke, Donald. *Wishing on the Moon: The Life and Times of Billie Holiday.* New York: Viking Press, 1995.

Clement, Catherine. *Opera: Or the Undoing of Women.* Minneapolis: University of Minnesota Press, 1988.

Cogan, Robert. *New Images of Musical Sound.* Cambridge: Harvard University Press, 1985.

Crawford, Vicki, Jacqueline Anne Rouse, and Barbara Woods, eds. *Women in the Civil Rights Movement: Trailblazers and Torchbearers.* Bloomington: Indiana University Press, 1990.

Crowther, Bruce. *Singing Jazz: the Singers and their Styles.* London: Blandford, 1997.

Dahl, Linda. *Morning Glory: A Biography of Mary Lou Williams.* New York: Pantheon Books, 1999.

Davenport, Lisa E. "Jazz and the Cold War: Black Culture as an Instrument of American Foreign Policy." In *Crossing Boundaries: Comparative History of Black People in Diaspora,* edited by Darlene Clarke Hine and Jacqueline McLeod, pp. 282–315. Bloomington: Indiana University Press, 1999.

Davis, Angela. *Blues Legacies and Black Feminism.* New York: Pantheon Press, 1998.

Davis, Miles, and Quincy Troupe. *Miles: The Autobiography.* New York: Simon & Schuster, 1989.

De Veaux, Alexis. *Don't Explain: A Song of Billie Holiday.* New York: Harper & Row, 1980.

De Veaux, Scott. "Constructing the Jazz Tradition: Jazz Historiography." In *Black American Literature Forum* 25.3 (1991): 525–60.

Dyson, Michael. *I May Not Get There With You: The True Martin Luther King.* New York: Free Press, 2000.

———. *Making Malcolm: The Myth and Meaning of Malcolm X.* New York: Oxford University Press, 1995.

Ellison, Ralph. *Shadow and Act.* New York: Vintage, 1972 (1964).

Feinstein, Sascha. *Jazz Poetry from the 1920's to the Present.* Westport, Conn.: Praeger, 1997.

Floyd, Samuel A., Jr. *The Power of Black Music: Interpreting Its History from Africa to the United States.* New York: Oxford University Press, 1995.

Forrest, Leon. "A Solo Long-Song: For Lady Day." In *The Furious Voice for Freedom: Essays on Life.* Wakefield, R.I.: Asphodel Press, 1994.

Gabbard, Krin. *Jazz Among the Discourses.* Durham, N.C.: Duke University Press, 1995.

———. *Jammin at the Maryins: Jazz and the American Cinema.* Chicago: University of Chcago Press, 1996.

———. *Representing Jazz.* Durham, N.C.: Duke University Press, 1995.

Gaines, Jane. *Contested Culture: The Image, the Voice, and the Law.* Chapel Hill: University of North Carolina Press, 1991.

Gordy, Berry. *To Be Loved: The Music, the Magic, the Memories of Motown: An Autobiography*. New York: Warner Books, 1994.

Gourse, Leslie. *The Billie Holiday Companion: Seven Decades of Commentary*. New York: Schirmer Books, 1997.

———. *Billie Holiday: The Tragedy and Triumph of Lady Day*. New York: Franklin Watts, 1995.

Hall, Kim. "Fair Texts/Dark Ladies: Renaissance Lyric and the Poetics of Color." In *Things of Darkness: Economies of Race and Gender in Early Modern England*, pp. 62–122. Ithaca: Cornell University Press, 1995.

Hamer, Mary. *Signs of Cleopatra: History, Politics, Representation*. New York: Routledge, 1993.

Hardwick, Elizabeth. "Billie Holiday." In *New York Review of Books*, March 4, 1976.

———. *Sleepless Nights*. New York: Random House, 1979.

Hartman, Charles O. *Jazz Text: Voice and Improvisation in Poetry, Jazz, and Song*. Princeton: Princeton University Press, 1991.

Hentoff, Nat. *Jazz Is*. New York: Limelight, 1992.

Hobsbawm, Eric. *Uncommon People: Resistance, Rebellion and Jazz*. New York: New Press, 1998.

Holiday, Billie, and William Dufty. *Lady Sings the Blues*. New York: Doubleday, 1956.

James, Burnett. *Billie Holiday*. Kent, England: Tunbridge Wells, 1984.

James, William H., and Stephen L. Johnson. *Doin' Drugs: Patterns of African American Addiction*. Austin: University of Texas Press, 1996.

Jones, Lisa. "Late Bloomer in Her Prime." *New York Times*, August 4, 1991, pp. 22, 28.

Jones, Max. *Talking Jazz*. New York: W. W. Norton, 1988.

Kandall, Stephen. *Substance and Shadow: Women and Addiction in the United States*. Cambridge: Harvard University Press, 1996.

Kernfeld, Barry. *What to Listen For in Jazz*. New Haven: Yale University Press, 1995.

Kliment, Bud. *Billie Holiday, Singer*. Los Angeles: Chelsea House, 1990.

Koeninger, Anthony Shawn. *Poems for Billie Holiday*. Santa Barbara: Glen Annie Press, 1993.

Kofsky, Frank. "Black Nationalism in Jazz: The Forerunners Resist Establishment Repression, 1958–1963." *The Journal of Ethnic Studies* (Bellingham, Wash.),10:2: 1–27.

Lincoln, Abbey. "Who Will Revere the Black Woman?" In *Black Woman*, edited by Toni Cade. New York: New American Library, 1970.

Lubiano, Wahneemah. "Black Ladies, Welfare Queens and State Minstrels: Ideological War by Narrative Means." In *Racing Justice, Engendering Power*, edited by Toni Morrison. New York: Pantheon Books, 1992.

Macine, Jim. "Abbey Lincoln:'My Songs are Scripts.'" *Down Beat,* July 1997: 26–29.

Mackey, Nathaniel. *Discrepant Engagements: Dissonance, Cross-Culturality and Experimental Writing.* Cambridge: Cambridge University Press, 1993.

———— and Art Lange, eds. *Moment's Notice: Jazz in Poetry & Prose.* Minneapolis: Coffee House Press, 1993.

Margolick, David. *Strange Fruit: Billie Holiday, Café Society and an Early Cry for Civil Rights.* Philadelphia: Running Press, 2000.

Meltzer, David, ed. *Reading Jazz.* San Francisco: Mercury House, 1993.

Monson, Ingrid. *Saying Something: Jazz Improvisation and Interaction.* Chicago: University of Chicago Press, 1996.

Morgan, H. Wayne. *Drugs in America: A Social History 1900–1980.* Syracuse: Syracuse University Press, 1981.

Moten, Fred. "Stanza, Record, Frame: Temporality, Technics and Artifact in Shakespeare/Baraka/Eisenstein." *Semiotics* vol. 21–24, October 1993: 268–78.

Murray, Albert. *Stomping the Blues.* New York: Da Capo Press, 1976.

Nicholson, Stuart. *Billie Holiday.* Boston: Northeastern University Press, 1995.

Nielsen, Aldon Lynn. *Black Chant: Languages of African-American Postmodernism.* New York: Cambridge University Press, 1997.

O'Meally, Robert. *Lady Day: The Many Faces of Billie Holiday.* New York: Arcade Publishing, 1991.

Painter, Nell. *Sojourner Truth: A Life, A Symbol.* New York: W. W. Norton, 1996.

Palmer, Cynthia, and Michael Horowitz. *Sisters of the Extreme: Women Writing on the Drug Experience.* Rochester, Vt.: Park Street Press, 2000 (1982).

Panish, Jon. *The Color of Jazz: Race and Representation in Postwar American Culture.* Oxford: University of Mississippi Press, 1997.

Porter, Lewis. *A Lester Young Reader.* Washington: Smithsonian Institution Press, 1991.

Ramazani, Jahan. *Poetry of Mourning: The Modern Elegy from Hardy to Heaney.* Chicago: University of Chicago Press, 1994.

Ross, Diana. *Secrets of the Sparrow.* New York: Villard Books, 1993.

Shange, Ntozake. *Sassafrass, Cypress and Indigo.* New York: St. Martin's Press, 1982.

Small, Christopher. *Music of the Common Tongue: Survival and Celebration in Afro-American Music.* New York: Riverrun Press, 1987.

Sontag, Susan. *On Photography.* New York: Farrar, Straus & Giroux, 1977.

Stewart, Susan. *On Longing: Narratives of the Miniature, the Gigantic, the Souvenir, the Collection.* Durham, N.C.: Duke University Press, 1987.

Stuckey, Sterling. *Slave Culture: Nationalist Theory and the Foundations of Black America.* New York: Oxford University Press, 1987.

Taraborrelli, J. Randy. *Call Her Miss Ross: The Unauthorized Biography.* New York: Ballantine, 1989.

Vail, Ken. *Lady Day's Diary: The Life of Billie Holiday 1937–1959.* Chessington, Surrey, U.K.: Castle Communications, 1996.

Von Eschen, Penny M. *Race Against Empire: Black Americans and Anticolonialism 1937–1957.* Ithaca: Cornell University Press, 1997.

Watts, Jerry Gafio. *Heroism and the Black Intellectual: Ralph Ellison, Politics, and Afro-American Intellectual Life.* Chapel Hill: University of North Carolina Press, 1994.

Wicke, Jennifer. *Advertising Fictions; Literature, Advertisement, and Social Reading.* New York: Columbia University Press, 1988.

Williams, Martin. *The Jazz Tradition.* New York: Oxford University Press, 1970.

Wilmer, Valerie. *As Serious as Your Life: The Story of the New Jazz.* Westport, Conn.: Lawrence Hill & Co., 1981.

Wilson, Teddy. *Teddy Wilson Talks Jazz.* London: Cassell, 1996.

Wyatt, Gail Elizabeth. *Stolen Women: Reclaiming Our Sexuality, Taking Back Our Lives.* New York: John Wiley, 1997.

X, Malcolm (with Alex Haley). *The Autobiography of Malcolm X.* New York: Ballantine Books, 1992.

Chronology

April 7, 1915	Born in the Philadelphia General Hospital in Philadelphia, Pennsylvania.
January 1925	Sent to the House of Good Shepherd for Colored Girls.
March 1925	Baptized at House of Good Shepherd.
December 1926	Raped by Wilbert Rich and sent back to House of Good Shepherd.
1927	Begins to work in Baltimore brothel owned by Alice Dean.
1928	Migrates to Harlem.
May 1929	Holiday and mother arrested in raid on brothel. Holiday sentenced to 100 days in workhouse.
1930	Begins to sing at various Harlem after-hours spots.
1932	Meets John Hammond.
November 27, 1933	First recording, "Your Mother's Son-in-Law," with the Benny Goodman orchestra.
November 1934	Appears at the Apollo Theatre.
July 1935	Begins recording with Teddy Wilson orchestra.
March 1937	Joins Count Basie orchestra.
March 1938	Joins the Artie Shaw orchestra.
December 1938	Leaves Artie Shaw; opens at Café Society.
April 20, 1939	Records "Strange Fruit."
May 1941	Sings "Strange Fruit" at May Day celebration in Union Square, New York City.

August 25, 1941	Marries Jimmie Monroe.
August 1944	Signs with Decca.
April 1945	Claims to marry Joe Guy. Friends say they never married.
September 1946	Begins filming *New Orleans*.
October 6, 1946	Mother, Sadie, dies.
March 22, 1947	Begins three-week "cure" from her drug habit at Park West Hospital in Manhattan.
May 19, 1947	Arrested in New York.
May 28, 1947	Enters the Federal Reformatory for Women at Alderson, West Virginia.
March 16, 1948	Released from Alderson.
March 27, 1948	Appears at Carnegie Hall to standing-room-only crowd.
May 1948	Begins to see John Levy, a nightclub owner.
January 1949	Holiday and Levy arrested in San Francisco for possession of narcotics; she beats the rap.
December 1951	Marries Louis McKay.
1952	Begins to record with Norman Granz's Verve label.
January 1954	Holiday travels to Europe, where she gives concerts in Sweden, Norway, Denmark, Germany, France and England.
February 23, 1956	Arrested with Louis McKay in Philadelphia.
July 1956	*Lady Sings the Blues* is published.
December 8, 1957	*The Sound of Jazz* premieres on CBS.
February 1958	Records *Lady in Satin*.
December 1958	Performs in Europe to mixed reviews. Forced to perform at the Mars Club in Paris for a percentage of the gate.
May 31, 1959	Admitted to Metropolitan Hospital in Manhattan.
June 12, 1959	Arrested on her hospital bed.
July 17, 1959	Dies in New York City.

Acknowledgments

To my ancestors, especially my father, Emerson Maxwell Griffin, and Billie Holiday—Lady Day. Both of you have given me so much, and through this project you each have helped lead me back to my own voice. Thank you. Sylvia Ardyn Boone and my late aunt, Eunice Cogdell, two courageous and independent women whose legacies continue to teach me.

My mother, Wilhelmena Griffin, my alpha and my omega. Thank you for allowing me to come into this world through you, for loving me unconditionally and for keeping me supplied with gardenia plants.

The Couch, my beloved writing group: Daphne Brooks, William Lowe, Guthrie Ramsey and Salim Washington. Daphne, you inspire me. Bill, fellow Piscean, thank you for the music lessons. Guy, what a blessing it has been to have you as a friend and colleague. Salim, thank you for so much but particularly for helping me to have a more complex relationship to the music, for teaching me about chords, teaching me to play "Naima," asking me to provide lyrics to your music, and in so doing letting me participate in the making of this extraordinary form.

Edjohnetta Miller—my "big sister," an artist of vision who supports me in all of my efforts; Imani Perry—my "little sister," for the beauty of her spirit, her brilliance, her generosity. I thank God for putting her in my life. "Heaven must be missing an angel."

Richard Yarborough for reading early drafts, forwarding articles, and keeping me supplied with the hippest music in the world. Jim Miller for indulging my passion for the music and for Lady with books, boxed sets and for talking to me about everything, always.

Robert O'Meally and the Jazz Study Group, especially Fred Moten, Krin Gabbard, Robin Kelley and Brent Edwards. Robin read the entire manuscript carefully, offered advice, support, insight and encouragement. I feel like we are involved in a collective project and am grateful to have him as a travel companion on the journey. I am also grateful to Diedra and Elleza for graciously allowing me to share his time.

My colleagues and friends Barbara Savage, Michael Awkward, Houston Baker, Lewis Gordon, and George Lipsitz, all of whom read drafts of this book at various stages and offered much valued advice. Michael and Houston, I am especially grateful for the time and care you provided for the manuscript. Barbara, on more than one occasion you have helped to pull me through with laughter and love.

Florence Ladd and my Bunting Sisters, especially Celeste Goodridge, Barbara Smith, Jane Kamensky, Alex Chasin, Barbara Holechek, Elizabeth King, Fran Peavy, Julia Scher, Jane Palatini Bowers and A. J. Verdelle. Aje, I am so inspired by you, your work, your words and your friendship.

Each of the following individuals have offered words of support and encouragement and models of intellectual and cultural work: Tukufu Zuberi, the late Thom Harris, Alexa Birdsong, Hazel Carby, Nicole Brittingham-Furlonge, Ian Strachan, Lisa Sullivan, Susan Pennybacker, Tony Montiero, Mary Hamer, Quincy Troupe, Errol Louis, Cornel West, Jerry Watts, Tricia Rose and Michael Dyson. I read Dyson's *Making Malcolm* as I was starting this book and *I May Not Get There With You* as I was finishing it. His influence is apparent in these pages. Similarly, I also read Quincy's *Miles and Me* as I put the finishing touches on this manuscript. His words of encouragement helped me to finally bring it to an end. Thank you.

I am blessed to have had Saidiya Hartman and Julia Turner Lowe provide countless hours of conversation and counsel. Shaun Biggers, Cheryl Dorsey, Lynelle Granady, Nina Henderson, Karen O'Neal—just because. Cheryl is my ideal reader. My sister, Myra Lindsay, for always being in my corner and sensing the unspoken fears, concerns and confusions. I have always been amazed by the psychic nature of our bond.

N'jeri Yasin of the Federal Bureau of Investigation, Freedom of Information section, for her efforts in tracking down Holiday's FBI files. Hilary Mac Austin for the lead on a Holiday photograph in the NAACP archives. Darlene Clark Hine for her support and encouragement throughout this project. Julie Chiang for providing me with a number of poems about Billie Holiday. Maurice Black, proofreader; Hayley Thomas, Regine Jean-Charles, Kira Wells, Nicole Childers—all fabulous research assistants for supplying the bare necessities. Ms. Childers deserves a special thanks, as she continued to provide important research long after she left my employ. Valerie Savage Pugh for keeping my budget and finding little-known Holiday treasures. Mr. Jack Surridge for sharing his love of Billie Holiday and for maintaining a valued and wonderful correspondence with me.

Maxine Gordon for tales of Lady and Dexter Gordon, for her support and encouragement. Phil Schaap for his incredible generosity. Carol Mueller and Rita Barnard for sharing information on Billie Holiday and South African artists. Mary Ellen Ray for searching high and low for evidence of an "African Lady." W. S. Tkweme for inspiring me to give a second listen to Linda Sharock and introducing me to her "Black Woman" (with Sonny Sharock) and "Angel Eyes" (with Joe Bonner), and for his incredible knowledge about all kinds of music ever produced, anywhere.

My editor, Elizabeth Maguire, for her patience, her vision, her attention to my work and her belief in me. Bruce Nichols, who inherited this project after Liz left the Press, has been a model of generosity, patience and professionalism. The same is true of Dan Freedberg at The Free Press. I also wish to thank David Frost of The Free Press. My agent, Loretta Barrett, for caring about me as much as she cares about my books. Deborah Chasman, friend and fellow traveler, for your kindness and wisdom. Dee Dee Bridgewater for giving me more in a five-minute conversation about Lady than most books about her have given me in a lifetime. Abbey Lincoln for the generosity of her spirit and her work and for the most memorable afternoon of the Jazz Study Group Meeting. Oliver Lake for his beautiful spirit-filled music and for agreeing to read my rantings on Lady Day and a number of other subjects. Chuck Stewart for the photograph and more.

A number of institutions that provided money, time and other resources along the way: Billie Holiday Circle, Kent, England; the Bunting Institute of Radcliffe College; University of Pennsylvania Research Foundation; University of Michigan; Columbia University; University of Illinois, Champaign/Urbana; Schomburg Center; The Africana Studies Faculty Seminar at New York University; especially Robin, Fred, Tricia Rose, Phil Harper, Troy Duster, Paulette Caldwell, and Derrick Bell. Students in graduate seminars 1996–1999 at Columbia University and the University of Pennsylvania.

I am especially grateful to artists whom I don't know but love nonetheless: Nina Simone, Cassandra Wilson, Roy Hargrove and Me'Shell Ndegeocello. Thank you for daring to take risks, to follow where spirit and love lead you and especially for sharing what you discover along the way. Twice in the course of writing this book, your music has helped to heal and sustain me, perhaps even helped to save my life. As this book goes to press, Abbey Lincoln has released another CD, *Over the Years*, proving once again the power and beauty of her vision and voice. Now as always, her work and example remind me of the limitless possibility of life. Finally, to all of the musicians of this extraordinary tradition—thank you, thank you, thank you.

Index